DEEP-ROOTED THINGS

DEEP-ROOTED THINGS

Empire and Nation
in the Poetry and Drama of
WILLIAM BUTLER YEATS

ROB DOGGETT

UNIVERSITY OF NOTRE DAME PRESS
NOTRE DAME, INDIANA

Manufactured in the United States of America

Excerpt from "Exposure" in *Opened Ground: Selected Poems, 1966–1996* by Seamus Heaney. Copyright © 1998 by Seamus Heaney. Reprinted by permission of Farrar, Straus and Giroux, LLC.

Yeats excerpts reprinted with the permission of Scribner, an imprint of Simon & Schuster Adult Publishing Group, from:

The Collected Works of W. B. Yeats. Vol. 3. *Autobiographies*, edited by William H. O'Donnell and Douglas N. Archibald. Copyright © 1916, 1936 by The Macmillan Company; copyright renewed © 1944, 1964 by Anne Yeats; *The Collected Works of W. B. Yeats*. Vol. 5. *Later Essays*, edited by William H. O'Donnell. Copyright © 1994 by Michael Yeats; *The Collected Works of W. B. Yeats*. Vol. 8. *The Irish Dramatic Movement*, edited by Mary Fitzgerald and Richard Finneran. Copyright © 2003 by Anne Yeats; *The Collected Works of W. B. Yeats*. Vol. 10. *Later Articles and Reviews*, edited by Colton Johnson. Copyright © 2000 by Anne and Michael Yeats; *Essays and Introductions* by William Butler Yeats. Copyright © 1961 by Mrs. W. B. Yeats; *Explorations* by William Butler Yeats. Copyright © 1962 by Mrs. W. B. Yeats; *Memoirs*, edited by Denis Donoghue. Copyright © 1972 by Michael Butler Yeats and Anne Yeats; *Mythologies*. Copyright © 1959 by Mrs. W. B. Yeats; *The Variorum Edition of the Plays of W. B. Yeats*, edited by Russel K. Alspach and Catherine C. Alspach Copyright © 1965 by The Macmillan Publishing Company. Copyright © 1966 by Russell K. Alspach and Bertha Georgie Yeats; *A Vision* by William Butler Yeats. Copyright © 1937 by W. B. Yeats; copyright renewed © 1965 by Bertha Georgie Yeats and Anne Butler Yeats.

(excerpts of poems):

"Easter, 1916"; "A Prayer for my Daughter" in *The Variorum Edition of the Poems of W. B. Yeats*, edited by Peter Allt and Russell K. Alspach. Copyright © 1924 by The Macmillan Company; copyright renewed © 1952 by Bertha Georgie Yeats.

"A Dialogue of Self and Soul"; "All Souls' Night"; "Among School Children"; "From 'Oedipus at Colonus' "; "Leda and the Swan"; "Meditations in Time of Civil War"; "Nineteen Hundred and Nineteen"; "On a Picture of a Black Centaur by Edmund Dulac"; "Sailing to Byzantium"; "The New Faces"; "The Three Monuments"; "The Tower"; "Youth and Age" in *The Variorum Edition of the Poems of W. B. Yeats*, edited by Peter Allt and Russell K. Alspach. Copyright © 1928 by The Macmillan Company; copyright renewed © 1956 by Bertha Georgie Yeats.

"A Dialogue of Self and Soul"; "Fragments"; "Vacillation" in *The Variorum Edition of the Poems of W. B. Yeats*, edited by Peter Allt and Russell K. Alspach. Copyright © 1933 by The Macmillan Company; copyright renewed © 1961 by Bertha Georgie Yeats.

"Meru"; "Parnell's Funeral" in *The Variorum Edition of the Poems of W. B. Yeats*, edited by Peter Allt and Russell K. Alspach. Copyright © 1934 by The Macmillan Company; copyright renewed © 1962 by Bertha Georgie Yeats.

"Cuchulain Comforted"; "Lapis Lazuli"; "Reprisals"; "The Black Tower"; "The Circus Animals' Desertion"; "The Man and the Echo"; "The Municipal Gallery Revisited"; "The Statutes"; "Three Marching Songs"; "Under Ben Bulben," in *The Variorum Edition of the Poems of W. B. Yeats*, edited by Peter Allt and Russell K. Alspach. Copyright © 1940 by Georgie Yeats; copyright renewed © 1968 by Bertha Georgie Yeats, Michael Butler Yeats, and Anne Yeats.

"A Coat"; "Adam's Curse"; "Fergus and the Druid"; "Red Hanrahan's Song about Ireland"; "The Hosting of the Sidhe"; "The Old Men Admiring Themselves in the Water"; "The Phases of the Moon"; "The Sad Shepherd"; "The Song of the Happy Shepherd"; "To Ireland in the Coming Times"; "To the Rose upon the Rood of Time"; "Who goes with Fergus?" in *The Variorum Edition of the Poems of W. B. Yeats*, edited by Peter Allt and Russell K. Alspach (New York: Macmillan, 1957).

Library of Congress Cataloging-in-Publication Data
Doggett, Rob, 1969–
    Deep rooted things : empire and nation in the poetry and drama of William Butler Yeats / Rob Doggett.
       p.   cm.
    Includes bibliographical references and index.
    ISBN-13: 978-0-268-02583-0 (pbk : alk. paper)
    ISBN-10: 0-268-02583-5 (pbk : alk. paper)
    1. Yeats, W. B. (William Butler), 1865–1939—Criticism and interpretation.   2. Nationalism in literature.
3. Yeats, W. B. (William Butler), 1865–1939—Political and social views.   4. Politics and literature—Ireland—
History—20th century. I. Title.
    PR5908.N28D64   2006
    821'.8—dc22

2006000838

∞*This book is printed on acid-free paper.*

for
Megan

CONTENTS

ACKNOWLEDGMENTS

I am deeply grateful to the people whose intellectual, professional, and personal support helped to make this book possible. My thanks go to my professors at Gettysburg College: Mary Baskerville, who first sparked my interest in literature; James Myers, who inspired my passion for Irish literature in general and Yeats in particular; and Peter Stitt, who taught me how to analyze poetry. My thanks also to my colleagues at the University of Maryland who read and commented on early drafts: Elizabeth Driver, Matthew Elliott, and, especially, Nels Pearson, whose conversations always push my thinking and inspire my writing.

Marjorie Howes, Helen Vendler, David Latham, Christopher Ivic, and Jahan Ramazani offered informed suggestions on certain chapters and on the shape of the book as a whole. I am also grateful to Amanda Lagoe, my student intern at SUNY, Potsdam, who provided valuable research assistance and to Maureen Cahill, my student intern at SUNY, Geneseo, who helped with proofreading and indexing. I wish to thank especially my editor at Notre Dame, Barbara Hanrahan, for her encouragement and thoughtful guidance during the process of readying the manuscript for publication.

My deepest intellectual debt goes to the professors at the University of Maryland who provided extensive advice from the outset of this project. My thanks to Jackson Bryer and Brian Richardson, who have offered tireless support throughout my academic career, and, in particular, to Sangeeta Ray, whose knowledge of and suggestions about postcolonial theory had a deep, lasting impact on the direction of this book. And, of course, my thanks to Elizabeth Loizeaux, whose astute comments, pointed observations, and unwavering belief in my work truly made this book possible.

A version of chapter 1 appeared as "Mixing Everything at the Beginning: Telling Stories about Empire in Yeats's *On Baile's Strand*," in *Modern Drama* 45, no. 4 (Winter 2002): 545–566; and a version of chapter 3 appeared as "Writing Out (Of) Chaos: Constructions of History in Yeats's 'Nineteen Hundred and Nineteen' and 'Meditations in Time of Civil War,'" in *Twentieth Century Literature* 47, no. 2 (Summer 2001): 137–168. My thanks to both journals for permission to reprint and to Simon & Schuster for permission to use quotations from Yeats's *Collected Works*.

My deepest personal debt goes to my family, whose positive, lasting influence simply cannot be measured in words, and to Megan, without whose love and support I could not have written this book.

ABBREVIATIONS

The following abbreviations have been adopted for frequently recurring references to works by W. B. Yeats. Full citation information is provided in the Bibliography at Yeats, William Butler.

Au	*Autobiographies*
CL3	*The Collected Letters of W. B. Yeats,* vol. 3
EI	*Essays and Introductions*
Ex	*Explorations*
IDM	*The Irish Dramatic Movement*
L	*The Letters of W. B. Yeats*
LAR	*Later Articles and Reviews*
LDW	*Letters on Poetry from W. B. Yeats to Dorothy Wellesley*
LE	*Later Essays*
LSM	*W. B. Yeats and T. Sturge Moore: Their Correspondence, 1901–1937*
M	*Mythologies*
Mem	*Memoirs*
SS	*The Senate Speeches of W. B. Yeats*
UP1	*Uncollected Prose by W. B. Yeats,* vol. 1
UP2	*Uncollected Prose by W. B. Yeats,* vol. 2
V1	*A Critical Edition of Yeats's A Vision* (1925)
V2	*A Vision* (1937)
VP	*The Variorum Edition of the Poems of W. B. Yeats*
VPl	*The Variorum Edition of the Plays of W. B. Yeats*

INTRODUCTION

I thought 'my children may find here
Deep-Rooted things,' but never foresaw its end
        —W. B. Yeats, "The Municipal Gallery Re-visited"

One cannot sum up a nation intellectually.
        —W. B. Yeats, *Memoirs*

Deep-Rooted Things examines Yeats's shifting relationship with the discourses of British cultural imperialism and Irish nationalism during Ireland's transition from colony to (partially) independent nation in order to provide new, historically grounded readings of his poetry and drama. It demonstrates how Yeats's writings represent a thoroughgoing and often conflicted response to the multiple and competing formulations of identity, nationhood, and history central to these discourses and to the broader pressures, ambiguities, and paradoxes of (post)-coloniality. Focused on the key historical events that he witnessed and on the nationalist movements that he both embraced and resisted, *Deep-Rooted Things* reads the core features of Yeats's aesthetic program, his tendency to reinvent himself as an artist and to privilege contradiction over resolution, as repeated attempts to provide in art a foundation for national unity throughout this period of transition or national crisis. Exactly how Yeats responds to the events and movements that he witnessed—from the expansion of cultural and militant nationalism during the late 1800s and the Abbey Theatre conflicts of the early 1900s, to the Easter Rising (1916), Anglo-Irish War (1919–1921), Irish Civil War (1922–1923), and consolidation of the Irish Free State—varies widely, as he never remained content for long with one specific political or aesthetic position. Yet, it is precisely this willingness to change, this tendency toward fluidity and even internal contradiction, that makes Yeats such a compelling figure. And it is this multifaceted Yeats, this poet and dramatist whose art gives voice to a violent, divided, tragic, and, at times, heroic (post)colonial Ireland, that *Deep-Rooted Things* seeks to reveal.

By emphasizing a multidimensional and conflicted Yeats, my work follows the lead of some recent scholarship, most notably that of Marjorie Howes, whose important and insightful book, *Yeats's Nations,* demonstrates the extent to which the poet's conceptions of "nationality" and "Irishness" are contingent upon "specific configurations of gender and class."[1] While my own study touches upon similar questions of class and, in particular, gender, it differs from Howes's by reading the divergent nationalist stances that emerge in Yeats's poetry and drama as rooted directly in his continued attempts to negotiate the political, economic, and cultural conditions of Irish (post)coloniality. At the same time, *Deep-Rooted Things* departs substantially from the majority of current works devoted to the "postcolonial Yeats." Although I incorporate postcolonial theory with an eye toward the unique features of the Irish context, I have sought to move beyond the usual question of how or why Yeats can be properly considered a postcolonial writer. In part, this is because other critics, such as Jahan Ramazani, have skillfully responded to the question; and, in part, because the question, most recently addressed in the collection *W. B. Yeats and Postcolonialism,* often produces strained readings designed either to adopt Yeats into the now fashionable club of Third World writers or to attack him (once again) for his sometimes conservative political stances.[2] Resisting the prevailing desire to hang a positive or negative label on Yeats's political and nationalist commitments, I have aimed to tease out the diverse features of those commitments as they emerge in his art by privileging complexity over political value, internal instability and contradiction over consistency.

I have also sought to break new ground by challenging and reconfiguring the postcolonial theoretical paradigms that have informed much of the recent scholarship, particularly the almost ubiquitous reliance upon Frantz Fanon. His cogent remarks on the pitfalls of nationalism and his distinction between a regressive "national consciousness" and a progressive "political and social consciousness" are certainly applicable to the Irish context.[3] We need only recall the Irish Free State's censorship of film and literature, bans on divorce and contraception, and at times brutal suppression of dissension to recognize the dangers of an insular national consciousness that persists in the aftermath of colonial rule. Yet his theories, when applied broadly to Yeats, have the tendency to limit our perspective. While Fanon himself, as I discuss in chapter 4, is careful to distinguish among different forms of nationalist resistance, the Fanon lens tends to inscribe a form of binary thinking. As a teleological narrative of decolonization that posits, in the words of Edward Said, a progression from "nativism" to "liberation"—from a nationalist stance that remains fixated on "local identity" and communal "essences" to an alternative stance that embraces "a more generous and pluralistic vision of the world"—the Fanon model appears to suggest a clear division between these two stages, promoting the belief that all types of nationalism are identical and equally problematic.[4] My point is not to defend nationalism, nor is it to reject wholesale the findings of those critics who have examined Yeats by way of Fanon, such as Said, or who have outlined the politically suspect features of Yeatsian nationalism, such as Richard Kearney, Seamus Deane, Terry Eagleton, and others.[5] Rather, my intent is to shift the terms of the debate in order to recognize that where imperialism "succeeds" as a form of political, social, and economic domination precisely because it is fluid and adaptable, nationalism is equally fluid and adaptable, equally multifaceted. Just as the nation cannot, for Yeats, be apprehended "intellectually" (*Mem*, 143), or cannot be reduced to one knowable, quantifiable thing, nationalism in Yeats's works is never one discrete position or mode of writing.

Deep-Rooted Things thus attends to those ambivalent moments in Yeats's verse and drama that, because they exceed ready-made political labels, prompt us to reexamine and to reformulate our understanding of the complex and pervasive relationships among literature, colonialism, and nationalism. The chapters introduce, combine, and reconfigure elements from more broad-based discussions of postcoloniality (psychological co-dependency, nationalist constructions of history, metaphoric exile, Fanon's conception of "nationalitarianism") and from other theoretical paradigms (feminist performance theory, Marxist approaches to modernism), to offer fresh readings of central poems and plays in the Yeats canon. The specific goal is to expand the scope of Yeats scholarship by presenting his work as part of an ongoing and often troubled dialogue with the multiple discourses of British colonialism and Irish nationalism. Because Yeats's writings also engage with the overarching and uneven development of Ireland as a modern nation, the larger goal is to place Yeats—canonical "British" high modernist and conflicted Irish nationalist—at the center of groundbreaking debates concerning the development of literary modernism in light of postcolonial theory.[6]

Yeats is a particularly important figure for extending the parameters of postcolonial theory and for exploring questions of modernist aesthetics in relation to questions of empire and nationhood because he writes from an interstitial position, a space between imperial center and colonial periphery. Like the character Lois in Elizabeth Bowen's *The Last September* (1929), an Anglo-Irish woman who experiences a sense of disconnect from both her aristocratic British relations and from the peasant Irish who work her family's land, Yeats the Protestant nationalist and nationalist critic remained estranged from the British-cum-Anglo-Irish culture that represented his familial and literary heritage and from the Irish culture that fundamentally informed his politics and inspired his art. Indeed, it is no coincidence that *Reveries over Childhood and Youth* (1916), the first volume of his *Autobiographies*, opens with two "fragmentary" and "contemporaneous" memories that evoke feelings of cultural isolation, as the child Yeats recalls "looking out of an Irish window" and "looking out of a window in London" (*Au*, 41). Yeats's anxious attempt in later years to identify with an enlightened Protestant tradition, founded upon fantasies of a mythic Ireland where landlord and peasant exist in harmony, is symptomatic of this uncomfortable, interstitial position, as is his tendency, during his early *Celtic Twilight* (1893) period, to adopt a celebratory nativist view of the Irish peasantry. His outsider status also accounts, in part, for his consistent willingness to challenge the dominant positions of the Protestant and Catholic leadership. Although he steadfastly rejected any form of extreme unionism, he was equally ready, when the Catholic majority came to power, to voice the concerns of the Protestant minority, famously arguing against specific measures, such as the ban on divorce, and against the Free State's broader isolationist policies.

Yeats's interstitial position is, however, most significant as a shaping force in the development of the core assumptions that underpin his various political and nationalist stances. Although Yeats, as a nationalist, owes a clear debt to the Young Ireland movement of the mid-1800s, which posited cultural revival as the first step toward national unity, his underlying beliefs are unique with respect to the Irish context, sharing elements with a number of later nationalist movements that emerged in Africa and Asia. As the theorist Partha Chatterjee has argued, Indian nationalism responds to the pervasive influence of colonization "by dividing the world of social institutions and practices into two domains — the material and the spiritual": an "external" realm of science and commerce in which the West reigns supreme, and an "internal" realm of the spirit in which the traditions of native culture and the "essential" features of the East are preserved. Crucially, the aim is not simply to maintain this division but also to create a new independent nation in which the spiritual realm becomes a living presence in all facets of the modern community. This, writes Chatterjee, is nationalism's "most powerful, creative, and historically significant project: to fashion a 'modern' national culture that is nevertheless not Western."[7] Yeats's own vision relies upon a similar, though not identical, set of assumptions.

For Yeats, who associates Western modernity not only with the apotheosis of British imperial culture, industrial capitalism, and bourgeois society but also with the emergence of empirical, rational, scientific, and utilitarian modes of thought, the West is less a geographic space and more a form of consciousness. Described variously in his writings as "abstract," "mechanical," "objective," or, with some qualifications, "modern," this type of thought pervades contemporary society, creating and maintaining nations in which individual creativity is supplanted by mass consciousness, as spirituality hardens into religious orthodoxy, an awareness of the past as a living force gives way to a deadening sense of duty to tradition, and all things, including art, are judged according to their economic, political, or moral use value. As Yeats writes of phase twenty-four in *A Vision* (1924, 1937), the phase of Queen Victoria, "a code of personal conduct, . . . formed from social and historical tradition, remains always concrete in the mind. All is sacrificed to this code" (*V2*, 169–170). In such nations, this "code" operates on an ideological level—"its subconscious purpose," explains Yeats, "is to compel surrender of every personal ambition" (*V2*, 170)—by prompting individuals to embrace passively the will of the collective, promoting what an early theorist of nationalism, Ernest Renan, describes as "the individual's abdication for the good of the community."[8]

Anticipating Ashis Nandy's contention that "colonialism colonises minds in addition to bodies,"[9] Yeats came to associate this ideology of passive abdication, this mindset in which the individual "is flooded with the joy of self-surrender" (*V2*, 170), with both the imperial center and the colonial periphery, frequently arguing that popular nationalism—with its emphasis on moral purity, duty to tradition, and the political importance of art—functions not as an alternative to but as an extension of Western consciousness. "English provincialism," notes Yeats, "shouts through the lips of Irish patriots who have no knowledge of other countries to give them a standard of comparison, and they, with the confidence of all who speak the opinions of others, labour to thwart everybody who would dig a well for Irish water to bubble in" (*IDM*, 116).

Yeatsian nationalism is thus based on a fundamental desire to create an Ireland that is modern, in the sense that it can take an active role in the global community, without being a mirror image of England, an Ireland that shapes and is shaped by its interaction with other nations without losing its cultural autonomy—"It is, I think, an insult to the country," explains Senator Yeats, "to suggest that it is to be kept up by law and artificial barriers" (*SS*, 47). Specifically, he imagined a nation in which all people, "artist and poet, craftsman and day-labourer . . . accept a common design" (*Au*, 167), but he did not mean that the people should be compelled to embrace one specific vision of the community. As he wrote in 1905, "Nobody can force a movement of any kind to take any pre-arranged pattern to any very great extent" (*IDM*, 89). Rather, for Yeats—who believed that communities, like the occult societies he frequented, are bound by spiritual, nonrational connections—true national unity only emerges organically. That is, each individual, by deliberately seeking to actualize his or her own creative self in all facets of life, will unconsciously partake in the collective labor of shaping the nation, this "common design."[10]

In promoting this vision, Yeats sought to fulfill the ultimate goal of nationalism: the creation of a nation that is predicated not upon Western modes of thought, whether they are in the service of imperial assimilation or colonial resistance, but upon an alternative form of consciousness that preserves creative individuality and allows the nation to take shape out of the untapped imagination of the people. That Yeats's ardent desire to actualize this ideal vision led him to flirt with fascism and to slip into a reactionary mindset is not surprising, and, depending on our political leanings, we can applaud the attempt or criticize the result. In this book, however, I want to focus on how these core assumptions impact the drama and poetry, as Yeats raises and engages with a series of issues that, in part because of his own literary and cultural legacy, have remained central to Irish and postcolonial studies to this day: identity and nationhood, historiography and epistemology, tradition and modernity.

In order to explore Yeats's engagement with these issues and to highlight the connections between his art and the historical contexts within which it is produced, I have confined the opening four chapters of my study to two discrete periods: the first decade of the twentieth century, when Yeats was involved in the creation and promotion of an Irish National Theatre Society; and the years from 1919 to 1928, when Yeats the artist and senator struggled to reinvent himself as a cultural nationalist against the backdrop of the Anglo-Irish War, the Irish Civil War, and the consolidation of the Free State. As a dramatist writing in the years after the death of Charles Stewart Parnell and the subsequent emergence of competing nationalist movements, from Gaelic revival, to land policy reform, to militant resistance, Yeats was particularly concerned with questions of identity and nationhood. Convinced that, as he would later write, "nations, races, and individual men are unified by an image, or bundle of related images" (*Au*, 167), he sought to present in plays such as *Cathleen ni Houlihan* (1902) an image of heroic Irish identity, of noble self-sacrifice, that expresses and harmoniously balances individual consciousness and communal consciousness: the image of a young man who, in asserting his own will by choosing to embrace a glorious death over a mundane life, paradoxically asserts the deeper will of the collective, the desire for national autonomy. Yet the almost cult-like following that *Cathleen ni Houlihan* generated helped Yeats to recognize the inherent dangers of an aesthetic program rooted in a metonymic relationship between individual identity and national identity. Instead of achieving a harmonious balance, communal consciousness entirely supplants individual consciousness, thereby perpetuating a reactionary nationalist climate in which the negative stereotypes of British cultural imperialism are simply replaced by positive images, with the whiskey-drinking "stage Irishman" giving way to the hard-working peasant farmer, the chaste wife, and the noble martyr.

Because of his outsider status and thoroughgoing attachment to personal artistic sincerity, Yeats was, perhaps to a greater extent than other cultural nationalists, acutely aware that artists who confine themselves to promoting such models of Irish identity are doomed not simply to produce bad art but also to reinforce an insular, provincial outlook that is ultimately detrimental to the national cause. Intuiting what subsequent postcolonial authors and theorists would describe as nationalism's Manichean logic, Yeats explains that "a nation is injured by the picking out of a single type and setting that into print or upon the stage as a type of the whole nation. . . . If Ireland were at this moment, through a misunderstood terror of the stage Irishman, to deprive her writers of freedom . . . she would lower her dignity in her own eyes and in the eyes of every intellectual nation" (*IDM*, 87). The controversies over the plays of John Millington Synge—in which hard-line nationalists rejected Synge's subversive models of peasant identity as "calumny gone raving mad" and a "gross and wanton insult to the Irish people"—served only to reinforce Yeats's skeptical position.[11]

Unlike other writers who chose cosmopolitan exile as a liberating answer to Irish provincialism, such as George Moore, James Joyce, and, later, Samuel Beckett, Yeats remained committed at this point in his life to a decidedly nationalistic program that, by preserving artistic individuality, would simultaneously provide a foundation for Irish national unity. As he writes in 1901, the artist who remains true to personal expression—who does not "try to make his work popular" and who instead "make[s] his work a part of his own journey towards beauty and truth"—will enable "Ireland to re-create the ancient arts . . . as they were understood when they moved a whole people and not a few people who have grown up in a leisured class" (*EI*, 206–207). As an artist struggling to actualize this vision at a time when cultural and militant nationalists increasingly demanded explicitly political art, the Yeats of this period offers plays that raise and respond to a series of questions that underscore the possibilities and limitations of his own ambiguously nationalistic program: Is there a form of nationalist drama that can evoke a sense of homogeneous communal identity, while simultaneously remaining true to the heterogeneous voice of the individual? Can such nationalist art register and resist the constructions of Irish identity found in the discourses of cultural imperialism without reinscribing another form of essentialist logic, the replacement of one stereotype with another? Is it possible, in short, to create a truly national theater that rejects both sublation, the promulgation of "universal" works that ignore questions of cultural difference, and sublimation, the production of works that fetishize cultural difference by merely celebrating positive images of native identity?

These questions, which speak to the uneasy connections between Yeats's art and the identity-based rhetoric of colonialism and nationalism, form the basis of chapters 1 and 2. In the first, I examine Yeats's important early play, *On Baile's Strand* (1904, 1906), in relation to the discourses of mid- and late-nineteenth-century cultural imperialism, focusing in particular on how the play responds to the racial theories of Matthew Arnold and to the legacy of colonization in the Ireland of Yeats's day. Since questions of identity are invariably bound up with questions of gender, in chapter 2 I address performances of gender and nationhood in two key works from this period: *Cathleen ni Houlihan* and *Deirdre* (1907). For most feminist scholars, focusing on Yeats's gendered formulations of nationhood means focusing on representation, the degree to which his female characters reinscribe or challenge conventional notions of femininity popularized in the discourses of patriarchal nationalism. In so doing, they tend to ascribe to Yeats's work a developmental narrative in which the patriarchal or nationalist representations of female identity in his early plays, the woman as nation and the woman as guardian of the domestic sphere, give way to the protofeminist or antinationalist representations of his "mature" plays, the woman as desiring subject and complex, willful heroine.[12]

Without entirely rejecting this reading, I have, in keeping with my broader desire to tease out the ambiguities and multiple stances of Yeatsian nationalism, incorporated performance as both an alternative theoretical vantage and focal point for engagement. As a theoretical vantage, performance, which calls attention to the unstable nature of representation itself, shifts the focus to the conflicts and uncertainties of Yeats's nationalist project that manifest themselves in his dramatic constructions of femininity, masculinity, and the nation. As a focal point for engagement, performance highlights the degree to which gender and nationhood are not abstract issues in Yeats's work but are bound up with his attempts, during this transitional period in his life, to condition audience reception in a theater that seeks to fulfill the larger drive of nationalist art, the realization of communal unity, without adopting the conventions of "popular" nationalist drama.

Like the first decade of the twentieth century, the years from 1919 to 1928 represent a time of national crisis for Ireland and of personal crisis for Yeats. Always quick to see his own work in the realm of culture as the driving force behind Ireland's independence movement (a position that revisionist historians have since called into question),[13] Yeats felt responsible, in every sense of the word, for the supposed transformation in the Irish mind that had sparked not simply the revolution itself but also the internal divisions that erupted in the Civil War and that continued to haunt the Free State. Although Yeats viewed his dramatic movement as a popular success, he describes it, in his 1919 essay "A People's Theatre," as "to me a discouragement and a defeat," for it had achieved not the organically unified nation he had imagined, but an Ireland dominated by the mechanical Western consciousness he so reviled: "the objectivity of the office and the workshop, of the newspaper and the street, of mechanism and of politics" (*IDM*, 128). Ireland had indeed become a mirror image of England, a nation shaped by a rigid understanding of nationalism that fixes the gaze of the people not upon the complexities of the present but upon the sacrifices of the past, a nation where art and thought are judged according to political use value and all individual "actions" are submitted to "the most unflinching [self-] examination . . . 'Have I done my duty as well as So-and-so?' 'Am I as unflinching as my fathers before me?'" (*V2*, 171).

Yeats confronted this modern Ireland by exploring in art questions of historiography and epistemology, ways of writing and knowing the past and present. As I argue in chapter 3, which focuses on his two seminal war poems, "Nineteen Hundred and Nineteen" and "Meditations in Time of Civil War," Yeats responds directly to the evolutionary narratives of history central to the discourses of imperialism and nationalism: narratives of colonization, which point to Britain's "civilizing" role in Ireland in order to justify military intervention; and narratives of nationalism, which laud the sacrifices of previous generations in order to legitimate further acts of violence. The poems foreground what I term "historiographic desire"—the desire to use history as a means of giving order to the present—by repeatedly frustrating that desire, as Yeats prompts his reader to view the unfolding violence as violence and to recognize that the old progressive modes of understanding history must be cast aside before new, alternative visions of a truly independent Ireland can be imagined.

In chapter 4, I expand upon this notion of alternative vision by examining, as a whole, Yeats's finest volume of poetry, *The Tower* (1928). I argue that the collection charts a cycle of imaginative disengagement followed by reengagement on the part of the poet, as Yeats struggles to discover an external vantage— a position of "imagined exile"—from which the recent past may be meditated upon and new forms of communal unity, always presented in his verse as possibilities, not certainties, might be envisioned. My aim in both chapters, again, is not to judge his work on political grounds but to demonstrate how his poetry, through its engagement with the varied discourses of empire and nationhood, testifies powerfully and ably to the chaos, uncertainty, and incoherence of Ireland's violent emergence from centuries of colonial rule.

The final chapter extends the scope of my analysis by addressing directly the relationship between Yeats the nationalist and Yeats the modernist. Traditionally, scholars have tended to present his commitment to nationalism and to modernist aesthetics as two discrete and conflicting impulses in his work, juxtaposing the politically engaged artist who, in the words of David Young, sought "to write for and about Ireland" with the "symbolist-turned-modernist" who, in meditating upon such universal themes as the ephemeral nature of love, the decay of the body, and the winding gyres of history, strove "to create radically new forms and ways of perceiving the world in the service of art."[14] Other scholars, particularly those Marxist and postcolonial critics who focus specifically on Yeats's aesthetics in relation to British colonization and Irish colonial resistance, frequently emphasize the degree to which Yeatsian modernism represents not an alternative to nationalism but an extension of that project.[15] Both Yeats the nationalist and Yeats the modernist respond to the pressures of modernity, a bourgeois Ireland dominated by materialism and a blind attachment to patriotic idealism, by embracing the aesthetic and the mythic as means of giving order to and retreating from the chaos of the present. Such readings underscore a key assumption at the heart of most current postcolonial and Marxist readings of literary modernism: the belief that any aesthetic project that deploys the autonomous art object in response to the material realities of history necessarily represents a form of false consciousness, a retreat from the real into an abstract, ahistorical realm of myth and universal "truths."

Recent criticism aimed at rescuing Yeats from the modernist abyss has tended to do so by placing him in alternative theoretical camps, viewing him either through a postmodern lens that stresses chance and linguistic play or from a postcolonial vantage that, by linking Yeats with writers such as Derek Walcott and Salman Rushdie, emphasizes a relentlessly deconstructive or hybrid aesthetics.[16] My own approach is to begin with the assumption that Yeats does indeed embrace the aesthetic in response to the pressures of modernity—but by this I mean a certain kind of response and a certain form of modernity. In contrast with T. S. Eliot and Ezra Pound, the two high modernist poets with whom he is usually associated, Yeats adopts a poetics that is relentlessly dialectical, continually shuttling between unity and disunity, never remaining content for long with the type of "objective" closure that Eliot realized in *Four Quartets* or that Pound sought to achieve in the overarching narrative of the *Cantos*. This dialectical feature of his art, often stressed in more traditional approaches,[17] emerges out of Yeats's encounter with Irish modernity, a space in which the "grand narratives" of colonialism and popular national resistance are always revealed as fundamentally contingent, modes of seeing that, while promising to extricate the subject from the decay of modern life and the tide of meaningless history, only serve to enforce a deadening adherence to a pragmatic form of Western consciousness in which the individual is sacrificed to the abstract dictates of the state. Yeats was also sensitive to a key paradox facing the Irish writer: the fact that the English language itself, the basis of art and thought, continually reminds the native subject of his or her own alienated position within the "civilizing" narratives of imperial conquest. Although Yeats never advocated a return to Gaelic, a move that he saw as promoting isolation from the global community, he remained cognizant of the link between the dispossession of the Irish language and the growing influence of Western consciousness in Ireland, forms of apprehension that operate, on the level of language, to reduce art to some utilitarian purpose.

In chapter 5, I also argue that Yeats responds to this encounter with Irish modernity by adopting a form of negative dialectics, offering the autonomous art object as a means of registering and resisting the pressures of a (post)colonial Ireland in which art, language, and thought are always judged, whether from the vantage of colonial assimilation or nationalist resistance, according to their use value—an Ireland, that is, in which the poet is compelled to produce committed art. Yeats's turn to the autonomous art object functions not only as a retreat from the chaos of an Ireland in transition but also as an alternative means of engaging with and responding to the material pressures of that period of flux, of national crisis. As is the case with all five chapters in this book, my aim, in rejecting compartmentalized political readings of his art, is to allow the complex and multifaceted nature of Yeats to emerge, to demonstrate how his poetry and drama, in engaging with the contested discourses of British imperialism and Irish nationalism, offer powerful and sophisticated responses to the incoherence of a (post)colonial Ireland that, as W. H. Auden has famously written, "hurt [Yeats] into poetry."[18]

Because *Deep-Rooted Things* focuses on specific moments during which Yeats engages with the uncertainties and tensions of an Ireland in transition, it is not intended as a chronological or exhaustive account of his extensive body of work. Rather, the movement of the chapters—from his early work in the theater, to the war poems and *The Tower* as a whole, to the symbolist and more recognizably modernist verse of his early and middle phases—is intended to mirror the uneven or "mixed" course of Irish history, as questions concerning identity, historiography, and the impact of modernity continually resurface in new forms. Because this book stresses the relationship between Yeats's work and issues of colonization and colonial resistance, it confines itself to Yeats the conflicted nationalist and nationalist critic. There are, of course, other Yeatses, including the figure who first attracted my own passionate interest: the poet whose verse encompasses larger themes such as the bitterness of desire, love and memory, the longing for permanence in art, the relationship between self and soul or body and mind, and the ultimate attempt on the part of one man to go "Proud, open-eyed and laughing to the tomb" ("Vacillation").[19] My own representation of Yeats the politically attuned artist is not designed to replace this celebrated poet but to uncover new possibilities for reading his verse and drama. By using different theoretical approaches—never as ends in themselves but as means to present fresh perspectives on the literature—I hope to enhance our understanding of one discrete yet important aspect of Yeats: the extent to which his art, in its engagement with questions of nationhood and the broader impact of British colonization, remains deeply rooted in his conflicted attitude toward the land of his birth—an Ireland where, as Yeats wrote late in life, "No people hate as we do in whom that past is always alive" (*LE,* 210).

CHAPTER
ONE

Mixing Everything Up at the Beginning

Telling Stories about Colonization in *On Baile's Strand*

There is no longer beauty or consolation except in the gaze falling on horror, withstanding it, and in unalleviated consciousness of negativity holding fast to the possibility of what is better.

—Theodor Adorno, *Minima Moralia*

What a mix-up you make of everything, Blind Man! You were telling me one story, and now you are telling me another story. . . . How can I get the hang of it at the end if you mix everything at the beginning?

—The Fool, in *On Baile's Strand*

The words of a fool spoken to a blind man—a fool and a blind man bound together by necessity and mutual distrust. One needs wisdom, the other sight. One lacks guidance, the other passion. A story to be understood, mixed from the beginning, mingled in the telling, uncertain in the closing. In this play written for Ireland's fledgling National Theatre, drawn from Ireland's mythic past, and centering on the self-defeating passion of a legendary Irish hero, it is perhaps more than fitting that the Fool, with the insight of his Shakespearean namesake, should ask his eternal companion about beginnings and endings, narrating past and present, finally getting the hang of the story. For these are the questions of a colonized people whose sense of identity is inextricably bound with empire and whose history is not one tale but a tangle of multiple stories, silences, erasures, buried myths of heroism and tragic defeat. Although Yeats wrote late in life that he felt "enchanted" by "the dream itself" of *On Baile's Strand*—the image of Cuchulain, "Character isolated by a deed," turning his sword upon "the ungovernable sea" ("The Circus Animals' Desertion")—the play has other stories to tell. These are stories of colonization and colonial memory, of two cultures bound together in mutual fascination and animosity, and of an artist and a people who, in the words of Seamus Heaney, "keep striking / Inwards and downwards" into the past only to find that "Every layer they strip / Seems camped on before."[1]

Yet these are not the stories found in scholarly readings of *On Baile's Strand*. In part, this is due to the fact that the play—first performed in 1904 at the opening of the Abbey Theatre and staged again, after substantial revising, in 1906—is generally considered a transitional text that marks a departure, both aesthetically and politically, from the type of romantic and, in the case of *Cathleen ni Houlihan*, more directly anti-imperial nationalism expressed in Yeats's early verse and drama.[2] As Yeats himself explains in a 1904 letter to George Russell, much of his work from the 1890s suffered from "an exaggeration [*sic*] of sentiment & sentimental beauty" (*L*, 434), and in his notes for *In the Seven Woods* (1904) he characterizes *On Baile's Strand* as "foreshadowing . . . a change that may bring a less dream-burdened will into my verses" (*VP*, 814). Yeats was equally clear regarding his political attachments, describing the first years of the twentieth century as a period when, as he would later write in "J. M. Synge and the Ireland of his Time" (1910), he experienced "the dissolution of a school of patriotism that held sway over my youth," a school of patriotism devoted to the idealization of all things Irish, to the denigration of all things British, and to an uncompromising, revolutionary agenda as it might be "understood by a child in a National School" (*EI*, 312, 313). Cultural nationalism had, by privileging the political over the aesthetic, failed to produce the type of lasting art that truly "define[s] races," and, in keeping with his critique of his own work, Yeats suggests that such art had, from the time of Thomas Davis to the present, remained "rhetorical, conventional, [and] sentimental" (*EI*, 341, 313). Accordingly, those critics who examine *On Baile's Strand* in political terms (a relatively small number given the amount of scholarship that the play has generated) frequently target Yeats's complex and progressively critical attitude toward both militant nationalism and his own cultural nationalism, arguing, in the manner of Susan C. Harris, that the play functions to undercut "a petrified nationalism that . . . has lost the ability to adapt to new challenges and precludes any innovative approach to the problem of Ireland's political or cultural liberation."[3]

From a postcolonial perspective, particularly one that would find affinities between Yeats and other more recognizably postcolonial writers, this type of nationalist focus offers a useful point of entry. Yeats's rejection of a nationalist project founded exclusively on Irish culture, suspicious of all outside, particularly British cosmopolitan influences, and bent upon the subjugation of art to directly political ends, marks him as one of the earliest colonial artists to confront fully the limitations of anti-imperial nationalism. To be sure, his antipathy is motivated in part, as Conor Cruise O'Brien and others have suggested, by hostility toward Ireland's emerging Catholic middle class—the primary advocates, according to Yeats, of "popular," unabashedly patriotic drama—and in part by an increasing sense of disconnection from the political and militant vanguard of the nationalist movement.[4] Yet, in both these respects, as C. L. Innes notes, Yeats shares much in common with other colonial and postcolonial writers and intellectuals from Africa, India, Australia, and elsewhere.[5] Yeats came to realize, implicitly if not expressly, the essentially derivative nature of anti-imperial nationalism: its uncritical adoption of imperial models of nationhood and freedom "organized around," as Gerry Smyth neatly summarizes, "notions such as tradition, authenticity and sovereignty"; its necessary yet fundamentally limiting desire to reverse empire's binary logic, to celebrate that which had marked the colony as Other, and thus to replicate rather than challenge the very value system by which empire legitimates itself; and its dangerous insistence upon national purity, a call for hegemony that, like imperialism's ideological imperatives, serves to silence dissenting voices.[6] When Yeats, in 1903, castigates the Irish politician who "is more concerned with the honour and discipline of his squad than with the most beautiful or the most profound thought" and the Irish nationalist who "refuses to use, even in the service of one's own cause, knowledge acquired by years of labour, when that knowledge is an Englishman's" (*LAR*, 100), he may be accused of (perhaps reactionary) idealism, yet his desire to challenge an inflexible nationalist program represents an important intervention that, as Edward Said has argued, necessarily prefigures "a more openly liberationist" movement.[7]

To read *On Baile's Strand* in this manner is thus to appreciate Yeats's willingness to address directly the limitations of nationalism as an essentially derivative discourse. But it is also to confine our own analysis to the terms established by Yeats himself. As a writer who, in the words of R. F. Foster, always maintained a "powerful sense of his own history,"[8] Yeats often stressed, in later years, a clear division between his youthful attachment to cultural nationalism and his rejection, in the aftermath of *Cathleen ni Houlihan* and the controversies surrounding Synge's plays, of a nationalist mindset "full of abstractions and images created not for their own sake but for the sake of party" (*EI*, 316). This developmental narrative is central to Yeats's autobiographical self-fashioning as an aloof artist for whom cultural nationalism was simply the product of youthful enthusiasm, "a coat / Covered with embroideries / Out of old mythologies" that he quickly discarded ("A Coat").

At the time when Yeats began writing *On Baile's Strand*, however, his position with respect to nationalism was considerably less certain. Though his essays repeatedly stress his growing dissatisfaction with the *Celtic Twilight* school of his youth, they also record his continual struggle to articulate the contours of a truly national theater, one that will provide the foundation for popular unity precisely because it remains true to artistic sincerity, a "theatre where the capricious spirit that bloweth as it listeth has for a moment found a dwelling-place" (*IDM*, 35). If he rejects propaganda art, he also views literature as "the great teaching power of the world, the ultimate creator of values" (*IDM*, 34). If he cautions dramatists against focusing exclusively on Irish subjects in order "to change or strengthen opinion," he concedes that "if, in the sincere working-out of the plot, they alight on a moral that is obviously and directly serviceable to the National cause, so much the better" (*IDM*, 33). In this respect, Yeats's national theater occupies a position between the pedagogical narratives of popular cultural nationalism and the relentlessly skeptical discourses of explicitly antinational art. Although his later pronouncements suggest a clear progression from the former to the latter, his vision of the theater from the 1900s reminds us that nationalism is not a coat that can be easily cast aside but a complex series of stances containing possibilities that the Yeats of this period struggles to exhaust. If, as Said has argued, "nativisim is *not* the only alternative" to the essentialist logic of cultural imperialism, Yeats demonstrates that a rejection of nativism does not necessarily amount to a wholesale rejection of anti-imperial nationalism.[9]

Where *On Baile's Strand* is concerned, our emphasis on the complexities of Yeatsian nationalism enables us to view the play not simply as a negative response to the ideological imperatives of popular cultural nationalism but also as a work that engages fundamentally with the discourses of cultural imperialism. While the play certainly does signal a departure from *Cathleen ni Houlihan* and even more so from the conventions of popular nationalist melodrama,[10] *On Baile's Strand* remains true in spirit to the revolutionary impulse driving these earlier works: the desire to expose the influence of colonization and to transform an imperial narrative of Ireland's past, which records only the failures of a people bent upon but incapable of governing themselves, "into," in the words of D. E. S. Maxwell, "a history of artistic triumph."[11] Whereas Yeats sought in *Cathleen ni Houlihan* to do so by adopting preexisting nationalist codes, presenting imperialism as an exclusively material-level phenomenon, an immediately recognizable evil against which Ireland's heroic martyrs have tirelessly struggled, in *On Baile's Strand* he rejects those codes to offer a more complex engagement with Ireland's colonial past and present.

Though the play is set in Ireland's heroic age, a mythical time preceding British colonization, *On Baile's Strand* responds directly to British imperialism in three specific ways: by laying bare the power dynamics of cultural imperialism, by exposing the psychological impact of colonization, and, ultimately, by transforming Ireland's tragic past into art, a move which, as I will argue at the close of this chapter, should not necessarily be dismissed as a politically regressive retreat from the material into the realm of the aesthetic. In terms of cultural imperialism, *On Baile's Strand* can be productively read within the context of Matthew Arnold's "racial" theories as they are outlined in his influential work "On the Study of Celtic Literature" (1867), specifically Arnold's juxtaposition of the emotional Celt against the practical-minded Anglo-Saxon and his vision of a British nation saved from "Philistinism" by the harmonious incorporation of Celtic "sensibility."[12] While the play's Arnoldian affinities, as several critics have noted, are readily apparent—Yeats himself evoked Arnold's racial distinctions when he described Cuchulain as "wandering passion" and Conchubar as "reason" (*CL*3, 527)—scholars have failed to appreciate the extent to which *On Baile's Strand* represents a subversive response to Arnold's relatively "liberal" form of cultural imperialism, an imperial project that, from the perspective of the colonized, demands submission even as it offers a seemingly benign form of incorporation.

Matthew Arnold's dialectical understanding of race relations and his belief in the essential superiority of British culture over Irish culture—"The more intensely the Irish desire a separate Parliament, the more it proves that they ought not to have one,"[13] was his response to William Gladstone's 1886 Home Rule Bill—accorded with the racial theories promulgated by his contemporaries, though he differed slightly in placing a limited "value" on certain Celtic traits. In this respect, he was similar to the French linguist Ernest Renan, whose essay "The Poetry of the Celtic Races" (1854) establishes the racial tropes later adopted by Arnold. Just as Renan describes the Celtic race as lacking "any aptitude for political life" but capable of an "infinite delicacy of feeling," Arnold, while criticizing the Celt's fundamental lack of "steadiness, patience, [and] sanity," suggests that "the sensibility of the Celt, if everything else were not sacrificed to it, is a beautiful and admirable force."[14] Like Renan, Arnold subscribed to the general belief that "superior" races must naturally supplant "inferior" ones, and he was content to see the eradication of Gaelic as a living language—witness his commitment as Inspector of Schools to English over Welsh—and of Celtic culture as a living culture.[15] But with one qualification: Arnold called for the incorporation of the Celtic "spirit," those "admirable qualities" of the Celt that should be preserved, into an Anglo-Saxon culture that, in England, had degenerated into Philistinism. According to Arnold, the laws of racial history pointed to this inevitable and, from his perspective, positive submergence of Celtic culture into Anglo-Saxon culture: "The fusion of all the inhabitants of these islands into one homogeneous, English-speaking whole, the breaking down of barriers between us, the swallowing up of separate provincial nationalities, is a consummation to which the natural course of things irresistibly trends; it is a necessity of what is called modern civilisation, and modern civilisation is a real, legitimate force; the change must come, and its accomplishment is a mere affair of time."[16]

Arnold's incorporative vision presents the Irish as a people whose culture had been and might again be harvested for the betterment of the colonizer. As Robert Young persuasively argues, Arnold's call for the establishment of a "Chair of Celtic" at Oxford speaks directly to the cultural imperialist basis of this vision: "Never was the colonial relation to other cultures in the nineteenth century more clearly stated: the force of 'modern civilization' destroys the last vestiges of a vanquished culture to turn it into an object of academic study. . . . The function of the chair is to reactivate the traces of the colonized so as to transform the moribund culture of the colonizer, and even 'to send a message of peace to Ireland.'"[17] Not surprisingly, this "message of peace" held considerable appeal for "English liberals," to quote Declan Kiberd, "who agreed that Celtic spirituality and poetry might repair many gaps in the English personality."[18] Arnold's views were, of course, less palatable to the Irish—Yeats devotes much of his 1897 essay, "The Celtic Element in Literature," to debunking many of Arnold's claims—but his basic assumptions, re-presented so as to idealize those Celtic traits that Arnold denigrates, fundamentally influenced the revivalists, including Yeats. Notes Kiberd:

> It is remarkable, in retrospect, how durable such thinking proved, even among those Irish who fancied that they had exploded it. Many embraced the more insulting clichés of Anglo-Saxonist theory on condition that they could reinterpret each in a more positive light. The modern English, seeing themselves as secular, progressive and rational, had deemed the neighbouring islanders to be superstitious, backward and irrational. The strategy of the revivalists thus became clear: for bad words substitute good, for *superstitious* use *religious*, for *backward* say *traditional*, for *irrational* suggest *emotional*.[19]

Yeats's 1901 essay, "At Stratford-on-Avon," offers one example of this type of reversal, and before turning to *On Baile's Strand*, I will briefly examine that essay, in part because its anti-imperial elements have not been entirely appreciated and in part because the essay, which ultimately replicates many of Arnold's basic assumptions, provides a clear contrast to the more radical strategy undertaken in the play.

In "At Stratford-on-Avon," Yeats responds to the Shakespeare scholarship of his day, concentrating primarily on the work of his father's close friend,

Edward Dowden, Irish-born professor of English literature at Trinity College, unionist sympathizer, and author of *Shakspere* [sic]: *A Critical Study of His Mind and Art* (1875). According to Dowden, a model for Shakespeare's ideal state administrator can be found in *Henry V*: "It is clear and unquestionable that King Henry V is Shakspere's ideal of the *practical* heroic character. He is the king who will not fail. He will not fail as the saintly Henry VI failed, nor as Richard II failed, a hectic, self-indulgent nature, a mockery king of pageantry and sentiment and rhetoric."[20] Replace "Richard" with "the Celt" and we have nearly a direct paraphrase of Arnold's characterization of the "sentimental" Celtic race, a people "undisciplinable, anarchical, and turbulent by nature," who, like Richard, are easily captivated by the outward finery of military displays: "The Gauls had a rule inflicting a fine on every warrior who, when he appeared on parade, was found to stick out too much in front. . . . Such a rule is surely the maddest article of war ever framed."[21] But unlike Arnold—who was accused by Yeats's younger contemporary, Wyndham Lewis, of emphasizing Shakespeare's Celtic qualities[22]—Dowden constructs a distinctly Anglo-Saxon Bard. Relying on Arnold's basic assumptions yet eschewing his critique of current British culture, Dowden offers a Shakespeare whose ideal leader, Henry, embodies a set of Anglo-Saxon traits at once abstract and essentially British: "With his glorious practical virtues, his courage, his integrity, his unfaltering justice, his hearty English warmth, his modesty, his love of plainness rather than of pageantry, his joyous temper, his business-like English piety, Henry is indeed the ideal of the [successful] king."[23]

What is interesting about Dowden, however, is that he does not read Shakespeare, in the manner of most of his contemporaries, exclusively as a transparent example of Victorian pragmatism. For Dowden, Shakespeare, as an artist and a businessman, is a composite of two temperaments, the emotional and the reasonable, and Shakespeare's success is the result of his ability to harmoniously balance this internal division by exhibiting "self-control," a type of "serene self-possession which he had sought with . . . persistent effort."[24] Though the Bard may give voice to the passionate broodings of a Hamlet or to the deluded idealism of a Falstaff, he always remains grounded in the rational, policing his own emotions so that he does not ultimately succumb to the irrational or sentimental. This emphasis on internal control speaks to the cultural imperialist function of Dowden's biographical reading of Shakespeare. Writing at a time when Irish land-league groups had begun to agitate for a militant uprising, Dowden's Shakespeare provides a universal model for how the colonial subject might police himself, continually repressing his passionate or violent emotions by turning to reason and sanity. Thus, in the following passage that summarizes Dowden's position, the term "rebel" takes on an added and directly political resonance: "[Shakespeare] is inexorable in his plays to all rebels against . . .

fact; because he was conscious of the strongest temptation to become himself a rebel."[25]

Yeats neatly reverses the racial dialectic upon which Dowden's reading is based, adopting Shakespeare as, in the words of Philip Edwards, "an honorary Celt."[26] Indeed, just as Wole Soyinka has stated that Shakespeare "may turn out to be an Arab after all,"[27] Yeats's Shakespeare turns out to be Celtic after all. If Dowden's Shakespeare views Richard with contempt, Yeats's Shakespeare views him with "sympathetic eyes" (*EI*, 105). If Dowden and his fellow critics characterize Richard as "sentimental, weak, selfish, insincere," Yeats, presenting Richard's emotional temperament in a positive light, describes him as "lovable and full of capricious fancy" (*EI*, 103–105). More important, Yeats lays bare the cultural bias implied in Dowden's celebration of Henry, arguing that Dowden and his successors, who "grew up in a century of utilitarianism" (*EI*, 102), discovered in Shakespeare, in high culture itself, a set of decidedly Anglo-Saxon values that they immediately present as universal, the essential qualities of the true heroic statesman. Yeats astutely links this desire with cultural imperialism, offering a type of postcolonial critique, echoed later by Said and others,[28] in which the universal and essential are revealed as fundamentally contingent, a set of Western constructions used to legitimate the supremacy of imperial culture and to justify its colonizing mission: "In Professor Dowden's successors this apotheosis went further; and it reached its height at a moment of imperialistic enthusiasm, of ever-deepening conviction that the commonplace shall inherit the earth, when somebody of reputation, whose name I cannot remember, wrote that Shakespeare admired this one character alone out of all his characters" (*EI*, 104–105).

The person whose name Yeats cannot remember was likely Sidney Lee,[29] a British scholar who describes Shakespeare's Henry V as "evok[ing] a joyous sense of satisfaction in the high potentialities of human character and a feeling of pride among Englishmen that one of his mettle is of English race."[30] For individuals such as Lee who, writes Yeats, assume "that Shakespeare judged men with the eyes of a Municipal Councillor weighing the merits of a Town Clerk" (*EI*, 105), Shakespeare's Henry functions as a source of racial pride that validates their own rational, Enlightenment-based, Anglo-Saxon values. For the Irish-born Dowden the case is more complicated. His valorization of Henry and "distaste" for Richard, Yeats provocatively argues, are the result of a colonial mindset whereby the colonized finds only shame in his own country and admiration for the imperial country: "He lived in Ireland, where everything has failed, and he meditated frequently upon the perfection of character which had, he thought, made England successful. . . . [He] thought that Henry V . . . was not only the typical Anglo-Saxon, but the model Shakespeare held up before England" (*EI*, 104).

"At Stratford-on-Avon," by stressing the cultural biases of Dowden and his successors, serves as an important anti-imperial critique, a work that, as Kiberd briefly notes, "restore[s] to Shakespeare's texts an openness which they had once had, but long since lost under the distortions of an imperial interpretative psychology."[31] At the same time, the essay, because it relies upon Arnold's basic racial assumptions, represents a fundamentally derivative exercise that reverses but does not, in the end, radically undermine empire's binary logic. Indeed, Yeats's essay, written from the perspective of an Irishman touring in England, serves as a fascinating example of the colonized unconsciously mimicking the travel writings of the colonizer.

Arnold begins his essay by recalling a holiday on Britain's Welsh coast, a device that he uses to foreshadow the contrast between the dark, hard world of the Saxon and the light, soft world of the Celt.[32] Gazing across a bay, eastward toward Liverpool, "that Saxon hive," Arnold finds the view decidedly lacking in charm: "The horizon wants mystery, the sea wants beauty, the coast . . . has a too bare austereness and aridity." Gazing westward toward Wales, "Everything is changed." The landscape is bathed in "the eternal softness and mild light of the west," and the hills fade away "in an aerial haze."[33] Yeats employs the same strategy. London, the imperial center, is described as a place where "the first man you meet puts any high dream out of your head," while the quaint, exotic landscape of Stratford is a place ripe for dreams and filled with "an unearthly energy" that Yeats immediately links with Ireland: "I have felt as I have sometimes felt on grey days on the Galway shore, when a faint mist has hung over the grey sea and the grey stones, as if the world might suddenly vanish and leave nothing behind, not even a little dust under one's feet" (*EI*, 97). Both men—Arnold in a Welsh landscape "where the past still lives"[34] and Yeats in the "quiet streets" of Stratford "where gabled and red-tiled houses remember the Middle Ages" (*EI*, 96)—discover in their travels a world connected with the past, a Celtic world in which art remains alive, the very antithesis of Arnold's Saxon east and Yeats's materialistic London. However, while Yeats, in the manner of the colonial pioneer, would encourage others to follow in his stead— "adventures like this of Stratford-on-Avon show that people are ready to journey from all parts of England and Scotland and Ireland . . . to live with their favorite art" (*EI*, 98)—Arnold, in the manner of the cultural imperialist, calls upon the British nation to recognize the intellectual and artistic use value of Celtic culture, to reawaken and reincorporate that Celtic spirit that has been the wellspring of Britain's greatest poetry.

"At Stratford-on-Avon" thus demonstrates Yeats's debt to Arnold's racial theories and the extent to which Yeats, even as he critiques Dowden, remains bound in empire's dialectical logic. The case is different with *On Baile's Strand*. While

Yeats again relies upon Arnold's racial tropes, he fundamentally challenges Arnold's notion of cultural incorporation by giving voice to the underlying power dynamics, submission masked as productive incorporation, that remain silent in Arnold. The play opens with an apparent vision of racial harmony, as the emotional Fool—a decidedly Celtic figure in touch with Ireland's spiritual world—praises the reasonable Blind Man, his "clever" Saxon counterpart:

> What a clever man you are though you are blind! There's nobody with two eyes in his head that is as clever as you are. Who but you could have thought that the henwife sleeps every day a little at noon? I would never be able to steal anything if you didn't tell me where to look for it. And what a good cook you are! You take the fowl out of my hands after I have stolen it and plucked it, and you put it into the big pot at the fire there, and I can go out and run races with the witches at the edge of the waves and get an appetite.[35]

The two—dependent upon each other for the most basic of needs, the acquisition of food—would seem to embody a productively hybrid relationship, the Blind Man serving as intellect and the Fool as body, or, to use Arnold's terms, Saxon "steadiness" blended with Celtic "sensibility,"[36] or, at the risk of reading the play as political allegory, imperial planning coupled with colonial manpower, the mind of the colonizer benevolently guiding the hand of the colonized.

Yet, to tease out the political ramifications of this relationship, we need not turn to the allegorical. The issue of power immediately surfaces as the Fool and the Blind Man discuss the High King's desire to bind the intractable Cuchulain to an oath of fidelity whereby, as the Blind Man plainly states, Conchubar will become "Cuchulain's master in earnest from this day out" (*VPl*, 463). During this initial discussion, what begins as a comic exchange, with the Blind Man voicing the opinions of Conchubar and the Fool of Cuchulain, quickly becomes a not entirely veiled debate over racial superiority, as the Blind Man asserts the primacy of Saxon reason over Celtic passion. When the Fool, with characteristic naïveté and insight, exclaims, "Cuchulain's master! I thought Cuchulain could do anything he liked," the Blind Man responds with cold logic: "So he did, so he did. But he ran too wild, and Conchubar is coming to-day to put an oath upon him that will stop his rambling and make him as biddable as a housedog and keep him always at his hand" (*VPl*, 463). The Blind Man's characterization, applicable both to Cuchulain and to the Fool, draws upon notions of racial hierarchy present in Arnold and common in late nineteenth-century British popular culture. Just as Arnold emphasized the Celt's penchant for anarchy[37] and just as the Irish Celt was represented in myriad political cartoons, especially during periods of revolutionary agitation, as an unruly beast that must be tamed, an aggressive animal that responds only to the firm hand of a stronger ruler, Cuchulain is described as "too wild," a "rambling" figure whom Conchubar will make "as biddable as a house-dog."[38]

In the voice of the Blind Man, in this curt summation of Conchubar's later arguments, we also hear the authoritative voice of Arnold's brand of cultural imperialism, addressed this time not to the colonizer but to the colonized: "Take the oath, Cuchulain. I bid you take the oath. Do as I tell you. What are your wits compared with mine, and what are your riches compared with mine? And what sons have you to pay your debts and to put a stone over you when you die? Take the oath, I tell you. Take a strong oath" (*VPl*, 463–465). These are the questions that Arnold implicitly asks of the Celt who, "in spite of his admirable gifts of quick perception and warm emotion," in spite of his achievement in "the comparatively petty art of ornamentation, in rings, brooches, crosiers, [and] relic-cases," has "in material civilization . . . been ineffectual."[39] The Fool's response—"(*crumpling himself up and whining*): 'I will not. I'll take no oath. I want my dinner'" (*VPl*, 465)—is at once comic and subversive, arising out of a downward shift in the level of discourse from the national to the individual. By highlighting a basic need (particularly, given the haunting presence of the Famine in Irish culture, the need for food), the Fool's reply marks a disruptive gap in what Homi Bhabha terms the "performative" narratives of nationhood,[40] between, in this case, the desires of imperial nationalism, the interpolation of the racially Other colonial subject into a cohesive narrative of Enlightenment progress, and the actual, heterogeneous desires of that subject. The Blind Man's command, which calls upon the Celtic Fool to assume the role of silent colonial citizen, is belied by the Fool's unconsciously subversive response, as a vision of harmonious hierarchy gives way to comic difference, a narrative of national progress juxtaposed with a basic human want, the desire for food. Indeed, the fact that a fowl is stolen suggests that this is a (colonial) realm where individuals compete over limited resources, a subtle reminder of the material inequalities that cultural imperialist narratives of productive hybridity continue to conceal.

This early dialogue neatly foreshadows the debate between Conchubar and Cuchulain, serving to cast Conchubar's seemingly adroit arguments in an ironic light, but a second level of irony is introduced when we consider the oath discussion within the particular context of Arnold's racial theories and the broader context of cultural imperialism. Initially, Conchubar plays upon Cuchulain's secret longing for a child—"I have heard you cry, aye, in your very sleep, / 'I have no son'"—suggesting that the oath will prevent Cuchulain's "house and lands" from "pass[ing] into a stranger's keeping" (*VPl*, 483).[41] Because Cuchulain appears frequently in Irish popular culture as the embodiment of Ireland itself,[42] what is at stake here is not simply Cuchulain's individual legacy but that of the Irish nation and, by extension, the Celtic race. According to Arnold, the Celt, once "the Titan of the early world, who in primitive times fills so large a place on earth's scene," has, for "want of sanity and steadfastness," failed to evolve. He "dwindles and dwindles as history goes on, and at last is shrunk to what we now see him. For ages and ages the world has been constantly slipping, ever more and more out of the Celt's grasp."[43] Just as Arnold notes that "the Celt [has been] ineffectual in politics,"[44] Conchubar reminds Cuchulain that he is "but a little king and weigh[s] but light / In anything that touches government" (*VPl*, 481). And, where Arnold points to the Celt's steadfast idealism as a weakness, his readiness "to [react] against the despotism of fact"[45] as a fundamental flaw that prevents him from developing, Conchubar cries in exasperation: "Now as ever / You mock at every reasonable hope, / And would have nothing, or impossible things" (*VPl*, 485). Conchubar assumes that national (and thus cultural) evolution will only take place through adaptive incorporation, a blending of Celtic passion with Saxon reason:

> Will you be bound into obedience
> And so make this land safe for [your followers]?
> You are but half a king and I but half;
> I need your might of hand and burning heart,
> And you my wisdom. (*VPl*, 491)

However, as with the previous argument between the Fool and the Blind Man, a certain degree of what we might term ideological slippage occurs. "For Enlightenment itself, to assert its sovereignty as the universal ideal, needs its Other."[46] Thus writes Partha Chatterjee, and, while his comments are directed toward colonial nationalism's desire "to represent itself in the image of the Enlightenment,"[47] the image of imperial progress, they speak also to the hegemonic desire of cultural imperialism and to the place of the colonized Other within that desire circuit. Throughout the oath debate, Cuchulain's responses serve to expose the contradiction between an imperial narrative of progress—one that calls upon the colonized to reject his primitive (Celtic) past and embrace a modern future, to "leave," in Conchubar's words, "a strong and," tellingly, "settled country" (*VPl*, 479)—and the colonized's actual position within that narrative. Unlike the Fool's comic response, Cuchulain's words indicate an awareness of the role that he is called upon to assume, an awareness that Conchubar's gift of stability contains only the chains of "obedience":

> And I must be obedient in all things;
> Give up my will to yours; go where you please;
> Come when you call; sit at the council-board

Among the unshapely bodies of old men;
I whose mere name has kept this country safe. . . .
Must I, that held you on the throne when all
Had pulled you from it, swear obedience
As if I were some cattle-raising King?
                         . . . Am I
So slack and idle that I need a whip
Before I serve you? (*VPl*, 479)

The passage bluntly counters the High King's talk of harmonious incorporation. For Cuchulain, the oath calls him to renounce his autonomy, which has
kept his kingdom safe, and to play the role of "some cattle-raising King" who
cringes before the whip of progress and Saxon reason.

Moreover, Cuchulain's arguments, which echo Yeats's comments on the cultural biases of Dowden and his followers, reveal the extent to which Conchubar's
seemingly universal and essential notions of progress are, in fact, contingent, dependent upon the assumption that the listener embraces the same value system as
the speaker. "For you thought," notes Cuchulain, "That I should be as biddable
as others / Had I their reason for it; but that's not true" (*VPl*, 463). Cuchulain's
use of the word "reason" is provocatively ambiguous. Viewed from one angle,
Cuchulain is simply noting that Conchubar's appeals, his claims about children,
are not applicable to Cuchulain, the Irish hero who, at this point in the play, mistakenly believes that he has no child. Viewed from a second angle, Cuchulain is
referring to a type or mode of reasoning. In other words, Conchubar's pragmatic
arguments do not apply to Cuchulain because he does not reason in the manner
of Conchubar or Conchubar's followers. Indeed, Cuchulain's reply works nicely
as a counter to Arnold's (and, for that matter, Dowden's) claim that "balance,
measure, and patience" represent "the eternal conditions . . . of high success."[48] It
is not the case that Cuchulain, as a Celtic figure, lacks the ability to reason; rather,
he perceives that reason is itself a construct, that what Conchubar views as a reasonable course of action is, from Cuchulain's position, entirely unreasonable.
Power is again at the root of this disagreement, a fact made clear when Cuchulain
notes: "For I would need a weightier argument / Than one that marred me in the
copying" (*VPl*, 483–485). The printing metaphor is subtle, for the implications
of Conchubar's argument are not abstract but immediate. The imposition of
a Saxon/imperial worldview writes Cuchulain into a new narrative of cultural
progress that "mars" him "in the copying" because it interpolates him as bondsman, as the Celtic subject who must renounce his will to the pragmatic demands
of the state's true leader, the eminently rational Conchubar.

Despite his awareness of what is at stake, Cuchulain does eventually agree
to accept the oath. His decision to do so is abrupt, based not upon Conchubar's

appeals but upon the desires of Cuchulain's own followers. Given that Yeats himself showed scant interest in conventional realism, particularly the type of drama that explores the psychological motives of individual characters, it is not surprising that critical discussions of *On Baile's Strand* rarely focus on this moment of transition. "A search for a motive," writes Rupin Desai, "would be in vain, for there is no motive. . . . Cuchulain's about-face . . . is intended to remain slightly inexplicable and nonrealistic."[49] While true up to a point, the question of motive is, in fact, of central importance. When Cuchulain's men suggest that he should embrace Conchubar's proposal, the High King remarks: "There is not one but dreads this turbulence / Now that they're settled men" (*VPl*, 493). The adjective "settled" perhaps hints of colonization, though the primary reference is to a change in popular attitude, as if the passionate heart of Celtic society had already been displaced by the practical mind of Saxon culture. Cuchulain's words bear this out:

> I understand it all.
> It's you [his men] that have changed. You've wives and children now,
> And for that reason cannot follow one
> That lives like a bird's flight from tree to tree. —
> It's time the years put water in my blood
> And drowned the wildness of it, for all's changed. (*VPl*, 493)

All has changed. What seemed possible during the oath debate, the rejection of Conchubar's values and a new blossoming of Celtic society, had been foreclosed from the start. It is Cuchulain alone who has remained true to his Celtic roots, existing, like Arnold's defeated Celtic titan, in a fundamentally altered world that he no longer controls. The absence of motive indicates an absence of viable options, the absence, from Cuchulain's perspective, of any real choice. As the Blind Man states early on, "Cuchulain *is* going to take an oath to Conchubar who *is* High King" (*VPl*, 471, emphasis added). The past has determined the present. Irish culture has changed, and Cuchulain must change with it. Viewed from this angle, the play speaks to an Irish present that is truly mixed from the beginning, a present in which cultural incorporation has already occurred, a present in which the fact of colonization, even when the focus is Ireland's heroic age, remains a palpable force. Indeed, *On Baile's Strand*, as I will argue in the next section, is as much about the process of colonization as it is about the legacy of colonization, the psychological impact of Ireland's mingled past as experienced by both Saxon and Celt, colonizer and colonized, master and bondsman.

As several postcolonial theorists—from Frantz Fanon, to Albert Memmi, to Abdul JanMohamed—have argued, the psychology of colonizer and colonized is shaped by the fact of empire, with each viewing the other with a mixture of disdain and desire.[50] For the colonizer, the colonial subject represents both the uncivilized and the primitive exotic whose backward ways, numerous character flaws, and supposed connection to humanity at its most basic—that which has been lost in modern, industrial society—justify, on the level of culture, empire's economic project, its incorporation of the unenlightened into the civilized imperial state. For the colonized, the imperial subject represents an oppressive force, the ruler bent on exploitation, but he also embodies that which the colonized would become, the modern cosmopolitan subject. Thus, argues Memmi, both imperial subject and colonial subject acquire their senses of identity in relation to the projected Other: "The colonial relationship . . . chain[s] the colonizer and the colonized into an implacable dependence, mold[ing] their respective characters and dictat[ing] their conduct."[51] This "implacable dependence," this co-dependency, is mediated by power, as each subject conceives of himself or herself in a hierarchical relationship with that projected Other, the slave to be ruled or the master to be served, the primitive to be idealized (and thus granted symbolic but not actual power) or the cosmopolitan to be emulated.

On Baile's Strand anticipates a type of later postcolonial drama perhaps best exemplified by the Caribbean writer Aimé Césaire's *A Tempest* (1969), in which co-dependency operates as a pervasive force, defining, in Césaire's case, the relationship between Prospero (imperial master) and Caliban (colonial slave). In Yeats, co-dependency functions as a partially conscious subtext that haunts, particularly if we attend to the 1906 revisions, the relationship between the Fool and the Blind Man and between Cuchulain and Conchubar. In the 1904 version, the Fool and the Blind Man, named respectively Barach and Fintain, are relatively realistic characters who interact with other characters on stage, including several young Irish kings. Barach clearly represents a Celtic figure whose outward appearance, "a tall thin man with long ragged hair, dressed in skins," and opening lines, "I will shut the door, for this wind out of the sea gets into my bones" (*VPl*, 456), suggest an organic connection with primitive Ireland. He speaks in a lyrical manner, and his words are colored by a Celtic landscape inhabited by spirits, witches, and "the Riders of the Sidhe," his description of an encounter with a changeling reminiscent of numerous characters from Yeats's early verse: "Yesterday when I put out my lips to kiss her, there was nothing there but the wind" (*VPl*, 458).[52] Fintain, is, by contrast, "somewhat older," a "fat blind man" whose clipped speech—as he feels about the room asking, "What's this and this?" (*VPl*, 458)—indicates a concern with practical matters. In the 1906 version, Yeats again emphasizes the division between the emotional Fool and the pragmatic Blind Man, but here the co-dependent nature of their relationship is brought to the fore. They are given generic names, are dressed in an equally "ragged" manner, speak only to each other and, significantly, to

Cuchulain alone, and in later performances wear masks.[53] Always appearing together on stage, they represent two halves of a complete individual, relying upon each other for the basic acquisition of food, as Yeats highlights by moving the discussion of the stolen fowl, which appears at a later point in the first version, to the opening.

The interplay of opposites, the clash between the emotional and the rational, is nothing new in Yeats. Nearly all of his early plays dramatize this theme. The use of the subplot, however, represents a significant departure that Yeats, as he writes in 1903, adopted from Shakespeare: "The Shakespearian drama gets the emotion of the multitude out of the sub-plot which copies the main plot, much as a shadow upon the wall copies one's body in the firelight. We think of *King Lear* less as the history of one man and his sorrows than as the history of a whole evil time" (*EI*, 215). And it is by attending to the power dynamics evident in the subplot that we begin to view *On Baile's Strand* less as an abstract exploration of dialectical opposition and more as a direct investigation of an Irish present infected by its colonial past, the "history of a whole evil time" expressed in the eternal co-dependency of Fool and Blind Man, slave and master.

The Blind Man has, throughout the play, contrived to keep the stolen fowl all to himself by, appropriately enough, distracting the Fool with words. Left with nothing, the Fool, in a speech that gives voice to the frustrations of the slave, rails against his master, responding to the Blind Man's question—"If I did not take care of you, what would you do for food and warmth?" (*VPl*, 516)—with abject hatred: "You take care of me? You stay safe, and send me into every kind of danger. You sent me down the cliff for gulls' eggs while you warmed your blind eyes in the sun; and then you ate all that were good for food. You left me the eggs that were neither egg nor bird" (*VPl*, 516). Compare the Fool's comments with those of Césaire's Caliban: "You [Prospero] haven't taught me anything at all! Except of course to jabber away in your language so as to understand your orders: chop the wood, wash up, fish, plant vegetables; all because you're far too idle to do it yourself."[54] Significantly, the Blind Man's treachery has occurred before, suggesting that their "hybrid" relationship predates the action of the play. In addition, if we again bear in mind the specter of the Famine in Irish culture—British ships laden with food departing in full view of starving Irish peasants—the Fool's words take on a new, tragic poignancy, expressing the rage of the (colonial) bondsman who has yielded the material resources of the land to the languishing (imperial) master and has received scant compensation for his labors, "eggs that were neither egg nor bird," potatoes unfit for consumption.

Despite the Fool's awareness of his partner's betrayal, their relationship, as the play's conclusion reveals, will continue, in fact must continue, for they cannot, as both companions instinctively understand, exist apart from each other.

When Cuchulain, having realized that he has killed his own son at Conchubar's behest, attacks the waves, the Fool is briefly possessed with an almost revolutionary zeal, reading Cuchulain's battle against the ocean (which occurs off stage and is reported to the audience through the Fool) as a nationalist might read a tale of failed independence, with every blow a strike against empire: "There, he has struck a big one! He has struck the crown off it; he has made the foam fly. There again, another big one! . . . There is a big wave. It has gone over him. I cannot see him now. He has killed kings and giants, but the waves have mastered him, the waves have mastered him!" (*VPl*, 524). The Fool's words are at once comic and tragic, but they are also, considered within the context of nationalist melodrama, decidedly parodic and play upon a nationalist tradition that, in the manner of *Cathleen ni Houlihan*, glorifies the tragic death of the Irish hero. Cuchulain falls before the indomitable sea, yet, because his death is rendered from the perspective of the Fool, whose naïve enthusiasm prevents him from grasping the fundamentally tragic nature of Cuchulain's actions, the audience cannot read the play (from a nationalist vantage) simply as another example of heroic martyrdom or (from a liberal, cultural imperialist vantage) as an instance of the Celt's tragic nobility. Each wave has been divested of its crown, but the sea itself cannot be destroyed. Whether conceived as martyrdom, a sacrifice that will fire the blood of future revolutionaries, or as an example of the tragic failures of Celtic culture, a confirmation of Arnold's belief that the Celts "went forth to war . . . *but they always fell*,"[55] Cuchulain's death is, in the end, merely the tale of a fool told to a blind man.

What remains is eternal co-dependency, as the Fool, though temporarily inspired by a call for change that he seemingly cannot grasp, returns to the Blind Man:

Blind Man: Come here, I say.

Fool (coming towards him, but looking backwards towards the door): What is it?

Blind Man: There will be nobody in the houses. Come this way; come quickly! The ovens will be full. We will put our hands into the ovens. (*They go out.*) (*VPl*, 525)

Unlike Césaire's play, in which Caliban ultimately exposes and rejects empire's binary logic, revealing the extent to which Prospero's sense of self is conditioned by the presence of the disempowered Other, the subplot of *On Baile's Strand* does not reach this moment of postcolonial revelation-revolution. Instead, the cycle of desire and disdain, of hierarchy masked as hybridity, will continue, as the two companions again go in search of food and experience the pleasure and pain of thrusting their hands into ovens for sustenance, the pleasure and pain of colonial co-dependency.

The subplot establishes the relationship between the two characters as a frame, seemingly affirming empire's binary logic as an inescapable trap that Cuchulain, like the Fool, is forced to confront. As Reg Skene insightfully argues, the Fool and the Blind Man, because they appear only to Cuchulain, "may be taken . . . as symbolizing principles operating in the mind of Cuchulain, the Fool symbolizing Cuchulain's intuition and imagination, the Blind Man his critical and prudential intelligence."[56] We have already suggested how these dual principles speak to Arnold's racial theories, and here we can usefully politicize Skene's analysis by positioning the Fool and the Blind Man as two poles of an ambivalent colonial psyche, the colonized Celt whose sense of self oscillates between these two conflicting, yet inextricably linked, subject positions.[57]

Prior to the oath, Cuchulain castigates his followers for embracing a pragmatic worldview—"I had thought you were of those that praised / Whatever life could make the pulse run quickly"—and he mocks the legalistic formality of the oath, asking with ironic defiance: "If the wild horse should break the chariot-pole, / It would be punished. Should that be in the oath?" (*VPl*, 497–499). Following the oath, his outlook abruptly changes, marking a transition whereby the Celt temporarily adopts the "reasonable" mindset of the Saxon. When the Young Man arrives at the instant the oath ritual has concluded, Cuchulain senses a kinship with his unrevealed son, and, having completed one oath of allegiance, immediately attempts another, spreading out a cloak and invoking the "Nine queens out of the Country-under-Wave / [who] Have woven it" (*VPl*, 511). In the manner of the newly colonized who finds himself operating in a world structured by a fundamentally different political and cultural system, Cuchulain, in attempting to establish a second, parallel oath, simply follows the example of Conchubar, the metaphoric colonizer. In essence, Cuchulain would play the role of Conchubar; the Celt would mimic the Anglo-Saxon, the bondsman the master. Though Cuchulain's actions are labeled by the other kings of Ireland as the product of delusional thinking, of "witchcraft,"[58] they are entirely consistent with the outward trappings of Conchubar's pragmatic worldview. Yet Cuchulain, entirely at sea as a practical statesman, is deluded in assuming that the rules of the game are the same for slave and master, that the Celt can simply become the Anglo-Saxon—that Saxon logic applies to all subjects, that incorporation means equality. This assumption blinds Cuchulain to the fact that, just as the water ritual is incompatible with the previously enacted fire ritual, this second oath violates the dictates of the first. From the perspective of Conchubar, the Young Man, the representative of an enemy nation, must be expelled, and the sovereignty of the nation must be privileged above the will of the individual.

As Conchubar's champion, Cuchulain cannot establish a personal alliance with the enemy. Thus, Conchubar quickly halts the ritual—"No more of this. I will not have this friendship. / Cuchulain is my man, and I forbid it" (*VPl*, 511)—and Cuchulain, in a flight of confused passion, turns upon his son and kills the child whom he had secretly longed to embrace.

Cuchulain's sudden reversal, his seemingly inexplicable attack upon the Young Man, has been the source of considerable scholarly consternation, but our reading of the play in terms of colonial relations offers one possible explanation. In a present structured by empire's co-dependent logic, formalized in the High King's oath, the Celt, the once autonomous Irish hero, is defined as bondsman ("Cuchulain is my man"), an individual whose own will is given over to that of his Saxon master. The death of Cuchulain's son represents the inevitable outcome of the oath, the ultimate fulfillment of the bondsman's role, the sacrifice of the Celt's own child at the bidding of his Saxon master. Indeed, as C. L. Innes argues, the conflict between father and son, while a common literary theme, "takes on a number of additional weightings" in nationalist literatures, with the son's challenge to the father indicative of a challenge on the part of the colonized "to the patriarchal authority of the colonizer."[59] *On Baile's Strand* gives an ironic twist to this standard nationalist theme by presenting a Celtic figure who, having renounced his own desires to that of the Saxon, unintentionally slays his own son, the very individual who might have carried on Cuchulain's legacy.

Main plot and subplot merge when Cuchulain returns from the strand to find the Fool and the Blind Man locked in physical confrontation, and in this moment, in Cuchulain's attempt to comprehend the "story" of the Fool and the Blind Man—the story of a stolen fowl, the story of his son's arrival, the story of a relationship rooted in betrayal, mutual disdain, and desire—Yeats offers an Irish hero suddenly realizing his own position bound within empire's binary logic. The Blind Man and the Fool speak simultaneously, the former again employing the rhetoric of the supposedly benevolent imperial guardian who "must be always thinking," and the latter sounding the triumphant cry of the colonized in revolt, the Celt who speaks in verse:

> When you were an acorn on the tree-top,
> Then was I an eagle-cock;
> Now that you are a withered old block,
> Still am I an eagle-cock. (*VPl*, 518–519)

The Fool plays the part of eagle to Cuchulain's hawk, imagining, in the manner of the romantic nationalist, that his master has been overcome, that freedom is at hand, that the spirit of the Celt has outlived the now "withered old block" of

Saxon might. But for Cuchulain, the tale yields not triumphant hope but tragic despair, as the Blind Man finally reveals the identity of the Young Man.

Like the Fool, Cuchulain recognizes that he has been betrayed. The hero who had been governed only by his individualistic impulses has now been reduced to the status of slave, a man who has killed his own son at the behest of his imperial ruler, and, like the Fool, Cuchulain temporarily revolts. In a second act of passionate violence, he turns upon Conchubar's throne, figuratively killing the master:

> Now I remember all.
> (*Comes before Conchubar's chair, and strikes out with his sword, as if Conchubar was sitting upon it.*)
> 'Twas you who did it—you who sat up there
> With your old rod of kinship, like a magpie
> Nursing a stolen spoon.[60] No, not a magpie,
> A maggot that is eating up the earth!
> Yes, but a magpie, for he's flown away.
> Where did he fly to? (*VPl*, 522–523)

Cuchulain's words neatly capture the despair of the colonized Celt, the Irishman who, "remember[ing] all," recognizes his now fundamentally disempowered position. Conchubar is likened to a maggot that, in a reference to imperial expansion, "is eating up the earth," and to a magpie, a creature of the air that is not confined to any one geographic space. Both metaphors—indeed, the fact that Cuchulain vacillates between metaphors—serve to mark Conchubar as all-encompassing, a ruler of land and air who cannot be expelled any more than the sky can be rid of birds or the earth of maggots. Cuchulain thus departs ready to avenge his son, calling, "Conchubar, Conchubar! The sword into your heart!" (*VPl*, 523), but it is clear that the master cannot be destroyed. Pausing before Conchubar, Cuchulain, as if recognizing the futility of his revolutionary desire, turns upon the waves to fight a battle that he cannot win. In contrast with Césaire's *A Tempest*, written during a period when former Caribbean colonies had begun to achieve independence, *On Baile's Strand*, written during a period, after the fall of Parnell, in which British colonial rule remained firmly in place, does not conclude with the hope of colonialism's demise. Despite Cuchulain's awareness of his disempowered position, despite the tragic nobility of his final act, empire's co-dependent logic will, as the reuniting of the Fool and the Blind Man indicate, continue into the future.

If co-dependency remains in place and if the Celt's dream of killing his Saxon master merely yields the Celt's ultimate destruction, is it nevertheless possible to read *On Baile's Strand* as a revolutionary anti-imperial work? At first glance, the answer would seem to be "no." Indeed, what Yeats offers as a response to imperialism—the Irish hero tragically hurling himself against the sea—would appear to represent, from a critical postcolonial perspective, an example of nativism, a retreat from history into the realm of essences. In a particularly revealing moment recorded in Joseph Holloway's journals, Yeats claims to have "had Charles Stewart Parnell in his mind when he wrote *On Baile's Strand*. 'People who do aught for Ireland,' he said, 'ever and always have to fight with the waves in the end.'"[61] Playing the role of political hero to that of Synge, the artistic hero, Yeats's Parnell embodied an uncompromising Irish individualism, what Yeats, writing in 1904, terms "the permanent character of the race": "If one remembers the men who have dominated Ireland for the last hundred and fifty years, one understands that it is strength of personality, the individualising quality in a man, that stirs Irish imagination most deeply in the end. There is scarcely a man who has led the Irish people, at any time, who may not give some day to a great writer precisely that symbol he may require for the expression of himself" (*Ex*, 147–148). If Yeats had Parnell in mind, it is likely because both Parnell and Cuchulain perfectly express, not in triumph but in failure, the "strength of personality" that "stirs [the] Irish imagination," a distinctly Irish form of heroism, "a gay struggle without hope," as Yeats would write later in life (*LSM*, 154). Where "contemporary English literature takes delight in praising England and her Empire," Irish art dwells "on ideas living in the perfection of hope, on visions of unfulfilled desire, and not on the sordid compromise of success. The popular poetry of England celebrates her victories, but the popular poetry of Ireland remembers only defeats and defeated persons" (*UP2*, 187, 196).

Viewed from this perspective, *On Baile's Strand* would seem to fulfill the dictates of "popular" Irish art, thereby affirming rather than challenging empire's binary logic. Caught in an irrevocably altered world that calls him to play the role of Celtic slave, Cuchulain remains true to his individualistic Irish heart, embracing, like so many Irish "martyrs" before and after him, his tragic fate. What remains for the nationalist artist is to transform that moment of self-destruction into art: to express, in the death of the Irish hero, the pure soul of an Irish nation ever beautiful in defeat. As a reading based upon the work of G. C. Spivak would suggest, in *On Baile's Strand* the subaltern—the "native"—"speaks" through Cuchulain's suicide, yet in that act of speaking we do not hear the voice of the colonized Irish but the voice of Yeats, the nationalist artist who offers, in precisely the manner of Arnold, tragic failure as the defining characteristic of the Irish hero and an essential quality of the Celtic race. Considered from this vantage, Yeats occupies the position of the elite colonial artist who, while avoiding the Scylla of imperial modernization, the temptation (in the manner of Dowden) to embrace a British model of Enlightenment progress, runs afoul of the Charybdis of colonial nativisim, the temptation to speak the authentic voice of the primitive Irish Celt.

Without entirely dismissing this reading, I will close by offering an alternative based upon a model of counterhegemonic art and theory formulated by the postcolonial critic Asha Varadharajan. In *Exotic Parodies*, Varadharajan employs Theodor Adorno, particularly his emphasis on negative dialectics, to complicate a now standard postcolonial framework that "shifts the interest from [as Spivak writes] 'rendering vocal the individual' to 'rendering visible the mechanism' of silencing,"[62] a framework in which the subaltern "object . . . continues to function as a dark continent of sorts, a species of otherness whose point of reference remains the Eurocentric and masculine self."[63] If postcolonial theory repeatedly calls attention to the production of the object by the subject, a form of "identity thinking" whereby the elite intellectual (Western critic or, in Yeats's case, Protestant nationalist) reproduces the colonial subject in his or her own image, negative dialectics, by insisting upon the "recalcitrance" of the object, its critical resistance to this subsuming project, provides a different critical mode. Focused on "the estranged appearance of reality" that "harbors . . . the truth of reification and thus can be unriddled to elicit something besides its deceptive appearance," negative dialectics conceptualizes the subaltern "object as containing both its history and its denied possibilities," a form of subaltern conscious that is more than, in Spivak's words, "the displaced figuration of the 'third-world woman' caught between tradition and modernization."[64] For our purposes, Varadharajan's model is important because it allows us to perceive in *On Baile's Strand*, in a work that seemingly retreats from the material fact of colonization into essential notions of Irish identity, a form of strategic negation, a manifestation of subaltern consciousness that registers empire's co-dependent logic but that does not fetishize the subaltern as heroic victim.

On Baile's Strand anticipates a type of revolutionary drama that lays bare empire's crippling co-dependent legacy but that does not simply adopt a nativist or explicitly nationalist position precisely because Yeats, despite Cuchulain's final, seemingly heroic resolution to thrust his sword into Conchubar's heart, remains true to the original Cuchulain myth by having him suddenly turn his sword upon the waves and not the High King. To attack Conchubar, regardless of whether or not Cuchulain succeeds, would readily affirm the dictates of overtly political nationalist art by reenacting symbolic revolution (the death of Conchubar) or by reenacting symbolic revolutionary failure (the death of Cuchulain at the hands of the High King's men). Cuchulain, caught within empire's dialectical logic and cognizant of the role he has embraced, chooses a different alternative. Where Césaire's Caliban rejects his position as primitive by renouncing the name Prospero has given him—"Call me X. . . . Like a man without a name. Or, to be more precise, a man whose name has been stolen"—Cuchulain renounces his position as Celtic bondsman by a more radical act, destroying himself.[65] Conchubar's position as master and his vision of a "settled" Ireland governed by Saxon reason and protected by Celtic strength are contingent upon Cuchulain silently assuming his role within that co-dependent relationship: to be the Saxon master, Conchubar requires his Celtic slave. By refusing to accept that role, Cuchulain opts out of the equation, thus achieving, in an act that refuses both sublation and sublimation, a negative affirmation of his own autonomy. Adorno's words from *Minima Moralia* are certainly applicable here: "There is no longer beauty or consolation except in the gaze falling on horror, withstanding it, and in unalleviated consciousness of negativity holding fast to the possibility of what is better."[66] *On Baile's Strand* does not offer the quiet comfort of nationalist melodrama, nor does it affirm the Celt's tragic nobility; rather, it tells the story of colonization and its legacy, fixing its audience's gaze upon the death of an Irish hero who, by refusing to play the role of tragic or heroic revolutionary bondsman, reminds us of "the possibility of what is better," a new story of Ireland.

CHAPTER

TWO

Setting Ireland's House in Order

Performances of Gender and Nationhood in
Cathleen ni Houlihan and *Deirdre*

Terms of cultural engagement, whether antagonistic or affiliative, are produced performatively.

—Homi Bhabha, *The Location of Culture*

There was a time when every young man in Ireland asked himself if he were not willing to die for his country. Ireland was his sweetheart, his mistress, the love of his life, for whom he faced death triumphantly. That is the theme of my "Kathleen ni Houlihan." And it is not over-drawn, as those who know Ireland may attest. But Ireland has changed. The patriotism of the Irish is the same, but the expression is different. . . . Ireland is no longer a sweetheart but a house to be set in order.

—W. B. Yeats, interview in *Chicago Journal*

Sweetheart and mistress, courtly love object and Aisling muse,[1] homeland and home: when Yeats conjured up these iconic representations of Irish femininity during a 1914 reading tour of the United States, his primary focus was not the gendered discourses of cultural nationalism[2] but the uncertain political climate of the Ireland from which he had recently departed. Determined to advance a constitutional reform position at a time when the British Parliament was debating a new Home Rule Bill, he deftly praises the revolutionary sentiments commonly expressed by Irish-American emigrant groups while asserting that moderate and not militant nationalism has now become the driving force in Irish politics. What is noteworthy about the interview, however, is not his rhetorical skill or his (perhaps wishful) assessment of Ireland's political climate, but the extent to which gender—the nation as "sweetheart" and as "house to be set in order"—remains a site of tension in Yeats's discursive formulations of nation-hood. The logic of his argument rests upon the assumption that young men in Ireland once imagined the nation as a beautiful maiden worthy of self-sacrifice, as if "my" (actually his and Augusta Gregory's) *Cathleen ni Houlihan* merely re-produces a gendered image consistent with that preexisting mindset—"as those who know Ireland may attest."[3]

The very fact that Yeats must qualify his (nativist) assertion with this quasi-legalistic statement, an epistemological claim that, in rhetorical terms, cannot be disputed, calls attention to the absence of any essential link between communal ethos and gendered image. It also calls attention to the internal contradictions of nationalism with respect to gender, for the "real" Irish woman—the indi-vidual whose role is neither revolutionary male martyr nor abstract symbol of the imagined community—is necessarily removed from the discussion. The un-spoken assumption is that Irish women should serve as spiritual guardians of the home,[4] an assumption that Yeats's "new" image of the nation as domestic space to be set in order implicitly affirms. Thus, his words (re)enact rather than reflect a vision of the nation organized around decidedly patriarchal conceptions of female identity, at once concealing and revealing the disjunction between that homogeneous vision and the heterogeneous desires of individual subjects—which is another way of saying that Yeats's gendered representations of nation-hood are produced performatively.

This is not to suggest that Yeats—who often noted the confining fea-tures of Irish domesticity and who, in the *Chicago Journal* interview, goes on to mention "clerical opposition" as a key problem facing the suffrage cause[5]—conceptualized the nation in a manner identical to that of conventional, patriar-chal Irish nationalism, but merely to highlight the extent to which all representa-tional discourses of nationhood are articulated in a gendered and a performative manner.[6] As theorists including Homi Bhabha and Judith Butler have argued, performance indicates the process during which supposedly natural categories such as "the people" and "sex" are being constructed as essential categories, a "temporal process" that exposes the "power of discourse to produce the phe-nomena that it regulates and constrains."[7] For our purposes, the important point is that, during this process, "gaps and fissures are opened up as the constitutive instabilities in such constructions, as that which escapes or exceeds the norm, as that which cannot be wholly defined or fixed by the repetitive labor of the norm."[8] In other words, discourses that purport to represent "femininity," "mas-culinity," or "the people" always attempt to reach a moment of closure—the instant when the representational image is identical with its object—that never occurs, as the very act of representing these categories reveals the fundamental inability of the linguistic or visual signifier to be that which it signifies: the "true" woman, man, or nation. As Bhabha argues, "the people" (like "sex") remains as a performed category bound in "the inexorable *movement of signification* that both constitutes the exorbitant image of power and deprives it of the certainty and stability of centre or closure."[9]

For most feminist scholars who examine the gendered images of nationhood found in Yeats's drama, the emphasis is not on performance but on representation—the degree to which his female characters embody, or strategically fail to embody, the standard categories of femininity found in the patriarchal discourses of romantic art and cultural nationalism. In reading Yeats's drama in this manner, such critics tend to assert that his plays follow a clear, developmental trajectory: from the stock, woman-as-nation figure of *Cathleen ni Houlihan*, to the more complex, willful heroines of *Deirdre*, *The Only Jealousy of Emer* (1919), and *The Player Queen* (1919)—from the "false" women of nationalist discourse to the "true" women of Ireland's present.[10] While the former play offers the woman as object of nationalist desire, the latter three present women as desiring subjects, strong female characters who are not transparently identifiable with the land and who do not silently embrace the confines of domesticity. Although there is some validity to this teleological reading—particularly when we note that this protofeminist impulse emerges in conjunction with Yeats's growing dissatisfaction with popular nationalism as a decidedly patriarchal discourse—critics who embrace this model run the risk of perpetuating the logic of the very system that a (postcolonial) feminist reading seeks to dismantle, that is, the logic of patriarchal nationalism in which gender and nationhood are "fixed," essential categories, in which representation is reproduction.

As a framework in which representation is conceptualized as a performative process, performance theory offers a new and useful vantage for exploring the two plays most often discussed in feminist readings of Yeats's drama, *Cathleen ni Houlihan* and *Deirdre*. Specifically, it prompts us to shift our attention from the "truth content" of his representations, the presence or absence of patriarchal nationalism, to that which his constructions of femininity, masculinity, and Irishness can never fully contain: forms of (female) identity and Irishness that "exceed" dramatic (re)productions of those categories. Thus, this chapter does not confine itself to the types of questions found in most current studies: Are Yeats's gendered representations consistent with or at odds with Irish cultural nationalism? Do they affirm a conservative, patriarchal, or nationalist outlook with respect to female identity, or do they help to advance a progressive, feminist, or antinationalist agenda? Instead, it asks: What gender-based tensions, ambiguities, and contradictions emerge as Yeats's drama (re)produces femininity, masculinity, and the people? What "cannot be wholly defined or fixed" in Yeats's performances of gender and nationhood? What "escapes or exceeds the norm" in plays that, often simultaneously, seek to affirm, challenge, or transcend the gendered imperatives of Irish cultural nationalism?[11]

On a practical level, performance theory also reminds us that Yeats's plays were designed specifically for the stage, thus shifting our focus from abstract notions of representation to the different ways in which his nationalist theater conditions, or attempts to condition, the relationship between audience and representation. Broadly speaking, there are, according to Peggy Phelan, two "representational econom[ies]" that structure this relationship in theater. In the first, "representation reproduces the Other as the Same," as the dramatic conventions facilitate the audience's belief that the image is an essential reproduction of a preexisting category: the "real" female, male, nation. In the second, "the reproduction of the Other *as* the Same is not assured," as the dramatic conventions undermine the audience's belief in and desire for reproduction by exposing representation as explicitly performance, as construction.[12] The former, as Elin Diamond argues, is typically evident in bourgeois realism, which, because it "depends on, insists on a *stability* of reference, an objective world that is the source and guarantor of knowledge," works to fulfill the spectator's desire for unified subjectivity, to naturalize traditional gender roles, and to assuage, as Bertolt Brecht first argued, the anxieties produced by the material contradictions of lived reality.[13] It is also, we can add, typical of nationalist theater, for nationalism—while devoted to revealing the contradictions of imperialism— must provide a stable ontological and epistemological base upon which to advance its revolutionary program and cannot allow the deeper, often gender-based contradictions of indigenous society to fracture its larger, hegemonic drive. In contrast, performance, the latter representational economy, is usually associated with postmodern art and theater, feminist and postcolonial drama, avantgarde modernism, and Brecht's "epic theater." While the specific political ends of these forms of drama differ widely, they generally seek to destabilize the passive satisfaction of repetition, to undermine the notion of the "ahistorical referent," and to expose, as Phelan writes of feminist performance theater, "how thoroughly bodies inhabit signifying systems *and* how signifying systems are always organized as bodies."[14]

The crucial point for Yeats is that his theater participates simultaneously in both representational economies. *Cathleen ni Houlihan* and, to a greater extent, *Deirdre* explicitly work to challenge the conventions of bourgeois realism and popular nationalist drama, as Yeats dismisses those types of drama that "reflect the surface of life" (*IDM*, 89) and embraces an antimimetic form, incorporating the symbolic into both works, and, in *Deirdre*, the chorus and a group of "dark-faced men" whose features anticipate his later use of the mask. In so doing, he creates a theatrical experience in which the process of representation itself is brought to the fore, thereby disrupting the "pleasure of resemblance and repetition [that] produces," in the theatrical space of bourgeois realism and traditional nationalist drama, "both psychic assurance and political fetishization."[15] To put it another way, Yeats employs a form that expressly reveals that which popular drama, particularly popular nationalist drama, always seeks to conceal: the "constructedness" of nationhood, masculinity, and femininity.

Yet, this aesthetic is dual-edged, for Yeats's goal during this transitional period in his career remains ultimately nationalistic, the establishment of a theater in which a heterogeneous nation—contemplating what he often called "the speech of the soul itself" (*EI*, 333), a deeper "vision of reality" free from "all that is exaggerated, lifeless, frozen in the attitudes of party" (*IDM*, 121)—becomes a homogeneous nation. As he would later write in *The Trembling of the Veil* (1922), Yeats had intended to "set before Irishmen for special manual an Irish literature which, though made by many minds, would seem the work of a single mind" (*Au*, 204–205), a truly national literature that combines individuality with continuity. For Yeats, "All creation requires one mind to make and one mind for enjoyment; the theatre can at rare moments create this one mind for an hour or so, but this grows always more difficult" (*Mem*, 215). The problem for Yeats—the reason that "this grows always more difficult"—is that he chose, in rejecting the representational economy of bourgeois realism and conventional nationalism, exactly the wrong theatrical form, the wrong "special manual" to achieve that particular nationalist end. By producing drama in which representation is consistently revealed as performance, Yeats creates a theatrical situation in which his own attempts to represent the "true" Irish woman, the "true" Irish nation, are themselves revealed as performances. Hence, his plays are marked by ambivalence and internal contradiction not simply because, as Butler and Bhabha assert, the process of representation, reiteration, and normalization always reveals that which cannot be contained, but also precisely because his theater aims to be nationalist without adopting the conventions of nationalist theater. These points of ambivalence and internal contradiction manifest themselves in the plays' representations of gender and nationhood, as Yeats attempts to condition audience reception, to reveal the performative function of gender in the discourses of conventional nationalism, and, at the same time, to conceal the performative function of gender within his own nationalist dramatic project.

When Frank Fay, theater reviewer for Arthur Griffith's nationalist paper *The United Irishman* and later a principal actor in the Irish National Theatre Society, challenged Yeats in 1901 to "give us a play in verse or prose that will rouse this sleeping land" and that will "in no uncertain words point out . . . the road to success in the future,"[16] he could hardly have expected a better response than

Yeats and Augusta Gregory's collaborative effort, *Cathleen ni Houlihan*. A dramatization of a young hero's decision to forsake the comforts of marriage and to participate in the ultimately doomed 1798 Rising, *Cathleen ni Houlihan*, staged in Dublin on April 2, 1902, with the celebrated beauty and nationalist activist Maud Gonne in the title role, quickly became, in the words of P. S. O'Hegarty, a "sort of sacrament" for revolutionary nationalists, managing, as C. L. Innes has observed, "to bring and hold together, for the moment, a number of strands in what were actually diverse, and sometimes conflicting, nationalist movements."[17] This was accomplished, in large measure, by integrating Catholic myths of blood sacrifice into a powerful, revolutionary allegory of geographical reclamation, thereby imbuing the 1798 Irish "martyrs" with Christ-like significance.

It was also accomplished by tapping into a set of gendered tropes shared by these diverse movements. As a number of critics have argued, the play, like other nationalist allegories,[18] employs what Joseph Valente calls "the strategy of the double woman," the "bifurcat[ion] of the mythic personification of Irish society"[19] into two representations of female identity: the ultimately passive woman of the private sphere, represented by the character Michael Gillane's fiancée, Delia, and his mother, Bridget, and the mythical woman/nation of the public sphere, represented by the Old Woman, who is transformed, through Michael's decision to follow her, from an aged hag into "a young girl [with] the walk of a queen" (*VPl*, 231). On this reading, *Cathleen ni Houlihan* grants the Irish woman metaphorical significance as the embodiment of the nation even as it calls upon the female audience member to identify with the "ordinary" peasant woman whose proper place within Ireland's revolutionary struggle remains the home— a viewpoint that is entirely consistent with turn-of-the-century nationalist discourse concerning domesticity and female identity. "The spark struck on the hearthstone will fire the soul of the nation," explains Mary E. Butler in a Gaelic League pamphlet, while a *Sinn Féin* women's advice column reminds its readers: "No Irishwoman can afford to claim a part in the public duties of patriotism until she has fully satisfied the claims her 'home' makes on her."[20]

That *Cathleen ni Houlihan* ultimately works to fulfill the gendered imperatives of patriarchal nationalism is thus readily apparent, and, given the extent to which conventional revivalist notions of femininity shaped and, in some respects, continue to shape Ireland's cultural landscape, critics have rightfully called attention to the play's pedagogical function, its deployment of the woman as symbol of the nation and its valorization of the woman as silent guardian of the domestic sphere. Substantially less attention, however, has been paid to the play as performance, as a work that reveals both the process during which female identity is being constructed and the extent to which Yeats's theater attempts to condition the relationship between audience and representation as this process occurs. While this shift in perspective may appear slight, it is significant, for *Cathleen ni Houlihan*, considered from the latter vantage, is fraught with gender-based tensions that, despite its immediate and lasting popularity among Republicans, are never fully reconciled. The play's (re)production of the woman, during the opening section and, in particular, during Yeats's later symbolic section, is marked by points of rupture and of excess meaning that expose the fundamental inability of nationalist drama to erase difference, to represent the gendered Other as Same, and to account for the possibility of female self-will and desire.

The first of these tensions begins to emerge during the opening, "peasant realism" section that, as James Pethica has convincingly argued, was written almost entirely by Lady Gregory.[21] The curtain parts to reveal a scene of domestic stability, as a married peasant couple proudly discuss the upcoming marriage of their eldest son:

> *Bridget:* Come over here, Peter, and look at Michael's wedding clothes.
>
> *Peter (shifts his chair to table):* Those are grand clothes, indeed.
>
> *Bridget:* You hadn't clothes like that when you married me, and no coat to put on of a Sunday more than any other day.
>
> *Peter:* That is true, indeed. We never thought a son of our own would be wearing a suit of that sort for his wedding, or have so good a place to bring a wife to. (*VPl*, 215)

A conventional dramatic device, the planned marriage establishes the necessary tone of optimism soon to be undone by the arrival of the Old Woman, but the specific emphasis on clothes serves an additional function. Throughout the later portions of the nineteenth century, British stereotypes of the effeminate or lecherous Irish male were often conjoined with negative representations of the Irish home: travel writings, newspapers, and other popular media that interpreted widespread penury, the impoverished farms and overcrowded tenements, as a sign of the Irish male's inability to set his home in order and, by extension, of the Irish race's supposedly innate inability to govern itself.[22] Nationalist discourse responded by valorizing images of the well-kept peasant home — "to make your room as dainty as possible," the female readers of *Sinn Féin* were reminded, "is a step in nation-building"[23] — and by extolling the virtues of dutiful, self-sacrificing Irish "mothers and hearth-keepers."[24]

Particular importance was attached to the ability of the peasant wife to keep herself and her family well dressed,[25] with fine clothes indicating both an ordered home and an ordered nation, a land from which — in a particularly revealing example of the significance attached to the domestic woman's national duty in the face of widespread emigration—the youth of Ireland would be loath to depart: "Oh! The delightful, the triumphant feeling of walking out, knowing that every article on one's person has been made by a pair of Irish hands . . . and that every shilling we have spent on our clothes has helped to keep some Irish boy or girl at home in the dear land."[26] The fact that the Gillane family can now afford "grand clothes" marks Bridget as a fit overseer of the private sphere and evokes a broader sense of domestic harmony that is entirely consistent with nationalist images of the "true" peasant home, thereby establishing a theatrical relationship with the audience in which representation accords directly with prevailing notions of the real. Indeed, Joseph Holloway, who would later castigate John Synge's peasant comedy *The Playboy of the Western World* (1907) for its "libellous falsehoods," describes this peasant scene as "nature's own image," singling out "the industrious way [Bridget] knitted" as entirely "natural."[27]

As for Peter, his main concern is not clothes but the dowry he has secured in arranging the marriage. Prior to his son's entrance, Peter states: "I hope he has brought Delia's fortune with him safe, for fear the people might go back on the bargain and I after making it" (*VPl*, 216). When Michael arrives, proudly explaining that the village priest "was never better pleased to marry any two in his parish," Peter asks curtly, "Have you got the fortune, Michael?" (*VPl*, 217). Peter's remarks, though perhaps harsh to our ears, would likely have served initially to confirm his status as a "real" Irish peasant, for the dowry-obsessed patriarch had become an almost stock figure in Ireland's agrarian communities, where widespread poverty and limited farm acreage often resulted in the payment of a "bride price" to the male's family for taking on a female dependant. Here again, the play offers "the visible real" as confirmation of a peasant reality that precedes and follows the point of representation.[28] What goes unmarked— at once exposed and elided—is the woman's position within rural Ireland as a commodity, as a transactional object whose worth can be quantified by a bag of gold and whose limited access to economic agency, precisely because she functions as an object of exchange, goes unquestioned.

The play takes a sudden and, from a nationalist perspective, potentially problematic turn, as Bridget voices demands that are, literally, out of character for the heretofore real/ideal peasant woman. When she chides her husband for "seem[ing] well pleased to be handling the money," Peter exclaims, "I wish I had had the luck to get a hundred pounds, or twenty pounds itself, with the wife I married" (*VPl*, 217), a remark that, while perhaps humorous given the lighthearted tone of the play's first half, neatly relegates Bridget to the same position as Delia, with both females weighed in terms of their monetary value. Bridget's rejoinder is, however, far from humorous: "Well, if I didn't bring much I didn't get much. What had you the day I married you but a flock of hens and you feeding them, and a few lambs and you driving them to the market at Ballina? (*She is vexed and bangs a jug on the dresser.*) If I brought no fortune I worked it out in my bones, laying down the baby, Michael that is standing there now, on a stook of straw, while I dug the potatoes, and never asking big dresses or anything but to be working" (*VPl*, 218).

Bridget's remarks anticipate those of Synge's Nora Burke, the heroine of his controversial 1903 play, *In the Shadow of the Glen,* who chooses, much to the dismay of nationalist audiences, to depart from a marriage based exclusively upon financial security.[29] Bridget's claims also evoke the rhetoric of Ireland's increasingly prominent suffragists, such as Riobard Ua Fhloinn, who argued, in a turn-of-the-century pamphlet, that Irishmen "are as terrified at the thought of the independence of women as Englishmen are at the thought of the independence of Ireland. . . . If we consider how much boasting we have lavished on Irish women, and how little real respect we have paid them—how little real liberty we have allowed them—we need not be surprised at the degraded and denationalised condition in which we find Ireland today."[30] Bridget's comments certainly do call attention to "how little real respect" she has been paid, though it is debatable whether or not Gregory intended to exploit a nationalist attachment to the restoration of the Irish home as a means of advancing an explicitly feminist agenda.

What is clear, however, is how the performance itself, while remaining within the representational economy of conventional realism, introduces possibilities of female identity that exceed the reproduction of the normal. By establishing Bridget as "natural," as a fit overseer of the hearth who "never ask[ed for] big dresses or anything but to be working," Gregory puts the play's audience in a difficult position. They cannot dismiss Bridget in the manner that patriarchal nationalism generally reserved for suffragists and other outspoken women, those "shrieking viragoes or aggressive amazons" who had supposedly neglected their domestic duties.[31] Nor can they claim, as later nationalist audiences would of Synge's heroine, that she is a false representation of the peasant wife, for doing so would fundamentally challenge Bridget's earlier, affiliative representational value. At the same time, to view Bridget as real requires the audience to acknowledge the contradictions imbedded within the discourses of patriarchal nationalism—the disjunction between the contented, self-sacrificing peasant wife and this dramatic representation of female discontent and self-will—and it also requires them to directly confront the material conditions of peasant reality that reduce both Bridget and Delia to the status of commodity.

This tension that Gregory introduces haunts the remainder of the play, and it is in part exacerbated and in part contained by the plot's turn with the introduction of the Old Woman—Cathleen ni Houlihan—to Yeats's different, symbolic, and performative representational economy. I will explore this issue at length toward the end of this section, but first I want to call attention to how contemporary audiences responded to or, specifically, failed to respond to the heated exchange between Bridget and Peter. Significantly, this is the only scene to have been singled out for criticism among reviewers such as Edward Martyn, who, writing for *The United Irishman*, objected to "the low comedy-man air" adopted by Frank Fay (Peter): "The audience, from beginning to laugh at the few jokes that were in the text, ended by laughing at every word however serious that came out of Peter Gillane's mouth. He was not played as a Mayo peasant, perplexed and frightened by some vague terror impending, which was to shatter his pathetic little concerns, but as an optimistic Dublin jarvey [hackney driver] whose reputation for drollery secures for every remark a laugh from his fare."[32]

Martyn's claims, particularly his assertion that Fay had failed to play his character "as a Mayo peasant," are significant for two reasons. First, his comments engage with the material conditions of peasant society but shift the terms of that engagement so as to emphasize Peter's avarice over Bridget's outrage. The vexing issue of female commodification, let alone Bridget's desire for respect and acknowledgment, is displaced by a broader indictment of Peter's "pathetic little concerns," an obsession with monetary gain that, while perhaps true of the rural patriarch, would not, in any case, be displayed in this particular manner. Second, Martyn, whose misogynistic leanings were well known,[33] illustrates how the spectator might unconsciously reconcile the gender-based tensions that the play itself produces. Rather than focusing on Bridget, the peasant female who is and is not the real of patriarchal nationalist thought, or on the actual character of Peter, the peasant male whose single-minded attachment to the material increasingly casts his wife's concerns in greater relief, Martyn calls attention to the quality of the acting: "The misconception of the character [on Fay's part] went near wrecking the piece."[34]

The possibility of "wrecking the piece" involves the destabilization of what Phelan calls the "truth-effect" of the visible real, the power of representation to satisfy the audience's desire for reproduction and normalization,[35] but, because Martyn focuses on the dramatic performance itself, that issue does not need to be raised. The real, that is, patriarchal nationalism's conception of the real, remains unchallenged in the background, while any tension experienced, Martyn tells his readers, is the result of Fay's failure to reflect that real accurately, to play the rural patriarch not as a true peasant but as a "Dublin jarvey [who] secures for every remark a laugh from his fare." Indeed, Martyn's use of the word "fare" evokes precisely that which the nationalist audience cannot confront but cannot entirely dismiss: the assignment of a quantifiable value to a human being, the fact of an exchange whose object is not laughter, as Martyn's displacement suggests, but the desiring woman.

The majority of the play's nationalist reviewers, however, tended to ignore the substance of Bridget's remarks altogether, a stance encouraged by Yeats himself. As if anticipating objections to the play's realistic elements, Yeats, in a statement published in *The United Irishman* prior to the first performance, provides a means for the audience to interpret the opening section of "my" work—Lady Gregory is not acknowledged—in a manner consistent with nationalist patriarchy:

> I have described a household preparing for the wedding of the son of the house. Everyone expects some good thing from the wedding. The bridegroom is thinking of his bride, the father of the fortune which will make them all more prosperous, and the mother of a plan for turning this prosperity to account by making her youngest son a priest. . . . Into this household comes Kathleen Ni Houlihan herself, and the bridegroom leaves his bride, and all the hopes come to nothing. It is the perpetual struggle of the cause of Ireland and every other ideal cause against private hopes and dreams, against all that we mean when we say the world. (*LAR*, 82)

As with Martyn's review, Yeats's comments are revealing for what they say and fail to say concerning the dowry. Instead of addressing Bridget's claims, he emphasizes the general mood of domestic harmony established at the beginning, reading (or misreading) "the fortune which will make them all more prosperous" as a symbol of the comfortable, ordinary world that Michael is called upon to renounce. In so doing, Yeats, like Martyn, shifts the terms of audience engagement from the real to the dramatic representation of the real, though Yeats is concerned not with the quality of the acting but with the type of theatrical relationship that the play attempts to establish with the audience.

For Yeats, the chief danger of dramatic art is that the viewer is conditioned to accept representation as reality. Audiences, having grown accustomed to the "theatre of commerce" in which "the superficial appearances of nature are so closely copied" (*IDM*, 150), expect theatrical representation to confirm prevailing notions of the real and to enable the spectator to experience a sense of passive satisfaction that occurs during his or her identification with the characters on stage. As Yeats writes in 1899, mimetic art has, historically, required "no imagination to admire": "The managers made the costumes of the actors more and more magnificent, that the mind might sleep in peace, while the eye took pleasure in the magnificence of velvet and silk and in the physical beauty of women. These changes gradually perfected the theatre of commerce, the masterpiece of that movement towards externality in life and thought and Art against which the criticism of our day is learning to protest" (*IDM*, 150). Yeats's "protest" involves departing from the representational economy upon which mimetic drama is based. His "dramaturgical method," explains James Flannery, "is similar to that of Brecht in that they both attempt to break the flow of the dramatic action in order to jolt the spectators out of a conventional identification with the story line and characters."[36] Unlike Brecht, Yeats's goal is, at least at this point in his career, expressly nationalistic, the creation of plays that, in tearing aside the veil of reality, call upon the spectator to engage with a set of deeper truths that are the actual reality of the Irish people, "a community," he writes in 1903, "bound together by imaginative possessions, by stories and poems which have grown out of its own life, and by a past of great passions which can still awaken the heart to imaginative action" (*EI*, 213).

Yeats's section of *Cathleen ni Houlihan* seeks to "awaken the heart to imaginative action" by initially adopting a central convention of nationalist melodrama, the deployment of the woman as embodiment of the nation. Indeed, the Old Woman's references to "Too many strangers in the house," "My land that was taken from me," and "My four beautiful green fields" (*VPl*, 222–223) would certainly not have gone unnoticed by an Irish audience. Yet the play is not a transparent allegory, for the Old Woman's entrance signals the introduction of a new representational dynamic in which the conventions of mimetic art are strategically undermined. Specifically, Yeats disrupts the passive satisfaction that the audience experience when viewing plays that offer, as the real, "images of what we wish to be, a substance of things hoped for" (*IDM*, 116), by prompting the spectator to become aware of his (the pronoun is intentional) own position as audience member and by foregrounding the Old Woman's performative role, her function as a symbolic object that is called upon to enact the coming-into-being of the unified community.

Whereas mimetic art, according to Yeats, allows the spectator to take "pleasure . . . in the physical beauty of women"—the reproduction of the woman as object to be possessed by the (heterosexual) male gaze—*Cathleen ni Houlihan* offers an old hag whose rags conceal the celebrated beauty, Maud Gonne.[37] The play thus frustrates the usual channels of audience desire, but, more important, it employs the dramatic spectacle of the female to mark the spectator's own "lack," his failure to possess that which would make him complete: the beautiful woman beneath the veil who is the true Irish nation. Tapping into British stereotypes of the impotent Irish male, the play forces the audience member to confront his deepest anxieties, to become self-conscious of his position as heretofore passive spectator, and to recognize that the Old Woman cannot herself dramatically represent the fulfillment of his erotic/revolutionary desires: "With all the lovers that brought me their love," she tells Michael, "I never set out the bed for any" (*VPl*, 226).

If the veiling of Gonne produces sexual uneasiness and self-consciousness on the part of the spectator, the speech of the Old Woman further calls attention to the viewer's role within the performance itself. Initially, the audience member can remain in the shadows by identifying with Michael, the potent male, by virtue of his upcoming marriage, who becomes transfixed during the Old Woman's hypnotic chanting:

> They [those who go to die in the uprising] shall be remembered for ever,
> They shall be alive for ever,
> They shall be speaking for ever,
> The people shall hear them for ever. (*VPl*, 229)

Yet, the words of the Old Woman are spoken as much to the audience member as they are to Michael. In fact, accounts of the first performance indicate that Gonne, "the well-known nationalist orator[,] did not address the other actors as is usual in drama, but spoke directly to the audience, as if she was addressing them in Beresford Place."[38] Here again, the play makes explicit the spectator's position as spectator, and, as the off-stage crowd noise becomes increasingly audible, provides an alternative, deferred point of identification. For erotic and revolutionary completion to occur, the audience member must become one with the crowd, those cheering men who, as the close of the play reveals, have gathered to greet the French landing parties come to aid the Irish rebels. The spectator must, like the crowd, take up arms. Further, the viewer, in recognizing his own performative role, is called upon to register the performative role of the Old Woman. As the marker of sexual and national lack, as the public speaker who spurs men to action, the Old Woman cannot be viewed simply as a transparent symbol of the nation; rather, she represents an object through which revolutionary unity will be achieved, an object that will perform the rebirth of the nation once the spectator himself takes action. This is precisely why the climax, the unveiling of Gonne as young queen, takes place outside Bridget and Peter's cottage and out of sight of the viewer, for the play, in order to spark actual change, cannot allow the spectator to contemplate passively another gendered performance of nationhood. He must perceive the symbolic woman as a means to fulfillment and not as fulfillment itself.

In this respect, *Cathleen ni Houlihan* undermines traditional theatrical expectations in order to awaken a deeper sense of masculine desire and to channel that desire into a militant, revolutionary program. Yet this is, from a patriarchal nationalist perspective, a dangerous game. The problem is not that the audience would consciously differentiate between the implicit, gendered performance of nationhood that occurs in traditional nationalist melodrama and the more complex, explicit performance that occurs here. Indeed, the presence of Gonne, who was frequently represented in popular media as the very embodiment of the nation itself,[39] would have ensured a favorable response. "Our cup ran over," remarked W. G. Fay, "for . . . Miss Gonne was in fact what Kathleen ni Houlihan was in symbol. . . . Her promised appearance assured us of the support not only of her own society but of [the nationalist organization] Cumann na nGaedeal as well."[40] Rather, the danger is that the play, in disrupting traditional spectator identification by exposing the performative, draws attention to exactly what representation cannot do: completely reproduce the normal, completely erase the disjunction between the woman as fetishistic object and the woman as desiring subject. Yeats, ironically, seeks to contain this possibility by exploiting the audience's desire to view representation as reality, to see the woman as confirmation of prevailing notions of the real. In other words, the symbolic section of *Cathleen ni Houlihan*, even as it introduces a performative representational economy, cannot, precisely because of its larger nationalist drive, entirely abandon a more traditional representational economy. This point of internal contradiction manifests itself in the figure of Cathleen, an overdetermined signifier that represents at once the nation, lack, the promise of revolutionary/erotic fulfillment, and the real peasant wife and mother.

Before turning to this aspect of Cathleen, we need first to address the play's final treatment of Bridget, for her assertion of self-will, though perhaps easily dismissed by the audience, remains to haunt the performance as a source of anxiety that must continually be written over and displaced. When the Old Woman arrives, Bridget slips from the role of wife to mother, as she senses, with increasing foreboding, that this stranger somehow poses a threat to the safety of her child. Like the character Bridget of Yeats's earlier play *The Land of Heart's Desire* (1894), whose daughter is lured from their peasant home by faeries, she is immediately suspicious of the otherworldly Old Woman, asking, "Is she right, do you think? Or is she a woman from beyond the world?" (*VPl*, 225). Unlike in *The Land of Heart's Desire*, Bridget's wish to protect her child has direct political repercussions, for her extreme attachment to Michael disrupts her symbolic position as the mother whose true function is to raise young men loyal to the cause of Irish independence. As "Eibhlin" writes in a 1906 *Sinn Féin* publication, "It is the men of Ireland—strong of will, strong of heart and purpose . . . who shall win the Great Victory. It is the women of Ireland—fit helpmates and mothers of a nation of men—who shall help them to it."[41] The threat of "excessive" devotion to the family as a source of nationalist anxiety, in fact, should not be dismissed as another example of what we might too hastily classify as Irish provincialism. Writing sixty years later from the perspective of a colonized North African, Albert Memmi explains—with a lack of self-reflexivity concerning the position of women in a nationalist struggle—that a colonial preoccupation with the success of the immediate family often serves to diffuse a revolutionary impulse: "The young man will marry, will become a devoted father, reliable brother, responsible uncle and, until he takes his father's place, a respectful son. . . . But it is a pyrrhic victory. Colonized society

has not taken even half a step forward; for the young man, it is an internal ca-
tastrophe. He will remain glued to that family which offers him warmth and
tenderness but which simultaneously absorbs, clutches and emasculates him."[42]
The possibility of the emasculated son was as dangerous to Irish nationalists as
it is to Memmi, but this threat, unlike Bridget's demand for recognition in the
domestic sphere, is more easily reconciled. By changing Bridget's representational significance from wife to mother, Yeats now uses her to signify not the
outspoken woman who challenges nationalism's idealized image of the silent
wife, but, in Holloway's words, "the good-hearted, kindly, *motherly* housewife
in every turn [whose] love for her big, strong, manly boy, 'Michael,' was ten-
derly and beautiful [*sic*] expressed."[43] The tension that Bridget produces as desiring subject, the representation that does not transparently conform to prevailing notions of the real, is displaced as female desire becomes maternal desire.

Yet the containment process does not end here, in fact cannot end here,
for representation, to quote Phelan, "always conveys more than it intends" and
"is never totalizing."[44] Thus, the play now introduces the Old Woman who will
supplant Bridget as the real peasant mother and Delia as the real peasant wife.
Prior to the Old Woman's entrance, Bridget has been "ready[ing] the house for
the woman that is to come into it" (*VPl*, 218), the character Delia, who will become Michael's wife and eventually replace Bridget as the center of the domestic sphere. It is, however, not Delia but the Old Woman who appears. She is accorded the primary female position in the house that would have been reserved
for Delia, "by the fire" (*VPl*, 221). Though Michael is at first uneasy about
"a stranger" coming into "the house the night before my wedding" (*VPl*, 221),
a comment that subtly marks her as Delia's rival, he, in the manner of a smitten
young groom, is quickly captivated by the Old Woman. Gradually, Michael
moves from the doorway to a place next to Cathleen at the hearth. The path to
revolution, initially "outside" the domestic sphere, now begins at its very center.

At this point, as Bridget, speaking for herself and for Delia, becomes aware
of Cathleen's true purpose, the issue of money is again raised. In a direct reversal of her earlier remarks, Bridget now reminds Michael of Delia's dowry:
"The woman that is coming home is not coming with empty hands; you would
not have an empty house before her" (*VPl*, 227). The Old Woman, however,
has already stated: "It is not silver I want" (*VPl*, 226). The entire issue of female economic power, the quantification of female worth in the rural home, is
thus dismissed as frivolous in comparison to the true cause of independence.[45]
More important, Bridget, the outspoken wife, whose only weapon is the monetary value of Delia, precisely what she had previously railed against, is now
allied with the money-grubbing Peter. Thus, the play, by offering a contradictory portrait of Bridget, attempts to cast her as the false peasant wife and sets her
apart from Cathleen, the true peasant wife whose only concern is prompting

men to embrace the cause of revolution. Rather than allowing the audience to empathize with Bridget—and thus to identify with a domestic woman whose own needs run counter to those of nationalist hegemony—*Cathleen ni Houlihan* calls upon the audience to view her with a mixture of sympathy and scorn. In other words, the performance itself does result, as critics have argued, in the bifurcation of female identity, but the play conditions audience reception so that identification centers entirely on Cathleen and not on Bridget or Delia.

In moving to the hearth, the Old Woman also supplants Bridget as the proper peasant mother. Unlike Bridget, who focuses on the future, Cathleen's primary concern is the past. As a 1906 *Sinn Féin* article indicates, the ultimate role of the mother is to pass down traditions to the young people: "Shall we of this generation not strive to pass on the previous heritage of that tradition as untarnished as we get it? Yes, surely,—or we are degenerates—and not worthy of the life our generous mothers gave us."[46] It is exactly this role that Cathleen performs when she calls Michael to the hearth and tells him of "the O'Donnells from the north, and a man of the O'Sullivans from the south, and there was one Brian that lost his life at Clontarf by the sea, and there were a great many in the west, some that died hundreds of years ago" (*VPl*, 224–225). Whereas Bridget looks to the health and happiness of her son—an understandable, yet, from a revolutionary nationalist perspective, improper and excessive example of maternal attachment—Cathleen fulfills the proper symbolic and realistic role of the peasant mother by reminding her surrogate son of Ireland's heroic past and by setting him on the path toward revolution. As both wife and mother, Cathleen becomes the true guardian of the home, as the "home" comes to be defined as Ireland itself. When Michael asks, "What hopes have you to hold to?" Cathleen replies, "The hope of getting my beautiful fields back again; the hope of putting the strangers out of my house" (*VPl*, 226).

The play's conclusion completes the transformation of the Old Woman from signifier of lack to signifier of promised fulfillment as well as the transformation of Bridget and Delia from sources of potential identification to objects of pity. As the Old Woman, Cathleen is the mother of all Ireland, at once ideal and real. As "a young girl," she is the wife of all Ireland, the true domestic partner who calls her husband to fight and die for Ireland. Indeed, it is she, not Bridget or Delia, who actually takes on the role of the bereaved matriarch and spouse who mourns the losses that will occur—"Many that are red-cheeked now will be pale-cheeked"—but she recognizes the greater good that will come through revolution: "They shall be speaking for ever, / The people shall hear them for ever" (*VPl*, 229).

In its effort to contain female agency, the play reveals the profound tension present in a nationalist performance designed to interpolate fundamentally unequal subjects into an overarching narrative of communal unity. Bridget and Delia remain on stage, relegated to the position of bystanders in this na-tional drama. Bridget clings desperately to her now hollow position as center of the home, lamely referring to the clothes that had once marked her sym-bolic power—"Look here, Michael, at the wedding clothes. Such grand clothes as these are!"—while Delia, now literally a stranger in the house, an object that has no position in the true world of revolutionary Ireland, clings to her role as wife: "Michael! (*He takes no notice.*) Michael! (*He turns towards her.*) Why do you look at me like a stranger?" (*VPl*, 229–230). Their basic irrelevance, their func-tion as simply objects of pity, exposes the extent to which the play, as national-ist performance, can never completely erase the actual, desiring woman. They remain as corporeal reminders of the metaphoric and actual injustice visited upon the individual subject by a movement bent on unity at all costs, "the re-jected from which," as McClintock writes of the "abject" in imperial discourse, "one does not part,"[47] the leftover traces of those women whom Cathleen/ Gonne, as an idealized vision of the nation itself and of the true peasant wife and peasant mother, has not entirely supplanted.

As is the case with *Cathleen ni Houlihan*, feminist discussions of *Deirdre* have generally centered on the eponymous heroine's representational value, with critics arguing that she embodies the "dual character of helpless woman and *femme fatale*"[48] found in *Cathleen ni Houlihan* and other revivalist works or, more frequently, that she signals a departure from Yeats's earlier, decidedly roman-tic notions of femininity. Evidence can be marshaled to support either posi-tion, though it would be difficult to overlook what Andrew Parkin describes as Deirdre's "steely calculation" in outwitting Conchubar—the Irish High King who betrays and murders her true beloved, Naoise—and her "sheer physical courage" in choosing heroic suicide over a forced marriage with the King.[49] It would also be difficult to overlook the similarity between Yeats's protagonist and the mythic "heroines, queens, and martyrs" often celebrated in the dis-courses of Ireland's then emerging suffrage movement.[50] In contrast with the complacent guardians of the home popularized in the rhetoric of conventional nationalism, Deirdre and the play's "wandering" female musicians are likely intended to represent both the "lawless women without homes and without children" whom Yeats, as he notes in *Reveries over Childhood and Youth* (1915), admired as a young man (*Au*, 80) and the "new women" friends and associates whom he encountered in the theater, such as the actress and suffragist Florence Farr, who served as the model for the First Musician.[51]

While labeling Deirdre a "Celtic feminist," as some critics have done, might be stretching the point, the play itself certainly does contain a feminist impulse, but if our goal is to offer a postcolonial feminist reading that analyzes dramatic representation without ultimately reaffirming the essential—the gendered image that is, in this case, a signifier of "positive" female identity—we must attend to the performative labor of representation in the play itself, that is, we need to examine what goes marked and unmarked in the play's construction of the real. According to Phelan, "Within the history of theatre the real is what theatre defines itself against, even while reduplicating its effects. . . . Each real believes itself to be the Real-real."[52] *Deirdre* overtly follows this logic by carefully establishing Conchubar's nation, Ulster, as a "false Real." Yeats evokes a world strategically divorced from contemporary Ireland in which the willful, desiring female is called upon to perform the legitimacy of the state. In the case of the Musicians, this entails sanctioning the domestication of Deirdre, while in the case of the heroine, it involves playing the role of the submissive woman who silently embraces her position as guardian of the home. By foregrounding representation as performance and by making explicit the extent to which performances of nationhood are contingent upon the forcible suppression of female desire, Yeats seeks to awaken a potentially feminist response in the audience by turning their critical gaze to the High King's patriarchal state.

In place of the false real of Conchubar's world, Yeats attempts to establish a "true Real," an imagined Irish nation whose ethos is given expression in Deirdre's noble sacrifice. Because, for Yeats, "tragedy must always be a drowning and breaking of the dykes that separate man from man" (*EI*, 241), the goal is nationalistic in the sense that the audience, contemplating the heroine's suicide, might become of "one mind" (*Mem*, 215), a people who, while retaining their own individuality, are momentarily cognizant of those deeper truths that bind a community together. "We feel," Yeats writes of tragic art, "our minds expand convulsively or spread out slowly like some moon-brightened image-crowded sea" (*VPl*, 1298–1299).[53] Considered from this angle, the play enacts that which it critiques: the deployment of the tragic and heroic female as an object designed to establish and embody national unity. By directing the audience's gaze specifically toward Conchubar's nation—and thus not toward the play's own performance of nationhood—Yeats struggles to contain the play's contradictory drives. Yet this process of containment cannot remain unrevealed. The fact that the play must divorce its real from that of contemporary Ireland is itself symptomatic of Yeats's fundamental inability to reconcile a potentially subversive critique of the patriarchal discourses of nationhood with his own nationalistic ends. Further, the construction of Deirdre as signifier of the true real exposes Yeats's desire and ultimate failure to account for a specific form of female identity that exceeds his own gendered performance of the nation: the "ordinary," desiring woman who is not the spiritual guardian of an idealized domesticity.

Yeats departs from other contemporary dramatic versions of the Deirdre legend[54] in a number of different ways, two of which are designed to mediate the relationship between audience and representation: the introduction of the Musicians as chorus and the inclusion of a group of "dark-faced men with strange, barbaric dress and arms" (*VPl*, 349) who serve as Conchubar's minions.[55] According to Yeats, tragic art seeks "to diminish the power of that daily mood," which the audience experience when contemplating the mimetic, "to cheat or blind its too clear perception. If the real world is not altogether rejected it is but touched here and there, and into the places we have left empty we summon rhythm, balance, pattern, images that remind us of vast passions, the vagueness of past times, all the chimeras that haunt the edge of trance" (*VPl*, 1298). The chorus, in their guise as storytellers and interpreters of the events unfolding on stage, help to awaken in the audience a sense of "the vagueness of past times," but they also introduce a level of distance between audience and dramatic image. Prior to the entrance of Fergus, the aged former King of Ulster, the First Musician begins to narrate the Deirdre legend, describing her mysterious birth, her adoption by Conchubar, the High King's love for Deirdre when "she put on womanhood" (*VPl*, 346), and Deirdre's subsequent flight with Naoise. The tale concludes in the present, as the spectator is called upon to recognize that the play itself will dramatize the outcome. Yeats, however, exploits the audience's awareness of the legend's tragic climax, reinforced through the chorus's ominous reference to the "secrets" of the High King (*VPl*, 347), in order to shift attention from plot to performance, from theater to meta-theater. Each character will play a role, and the trick for the spectator is to recognize that certain performances are false, such as Conchubar's feigned benevolence, while others are true, such as Deirdre's final decision to embrace her role as tragic heroine.

The "dark-faced men" function to disrupt traditional audience expectations by evoking those "chimeras that haunt the edge of trance." They are also, of course, an example of orientalism, the dark, "barbaric" Other who transports the audience from the mundane world of Western reality to an "exotic" world at the psychic and geographical margins of the civilized. That a nationalist artist and intellectual would display this type of imperialist mindset is not surprising, for, as Frantz Fanon and others have argued, it is the "Western bourgeoisie . . . from whom [the "national bourgeoisie"] has learnt its lessons."[56] Yeatsian orientalism, however, typically manifests itself in the form of idealized depictions of the East,[57] reflecting his tendency to project onto other "primitive" nations the cultural unity that he believed had once characterized Celtic Ireland. Something entirely different is going on here. The men silently "pass by the doors and windows" (*VPl*, 349), as the First Musician and Fergus debate Conchubar's intentions. The former, in keeping with her belief that Conchubar aims to betray Naoise and marry Deirdre, claims that they are assassins, noting their "murderous and outlandish-looking arms" (*VPl*, 349), while the latter, having secured Conchubar's forgiveness for the two lovers, uneasily dismisses them as Eastern merchants.[58]

An Irish audience, familiar with the legend, would likely consider the First Musician's interpretation to be the correct one — indeed, as I will later suggest, the play's nationalist drive is contingent upon the audience embracing the view of the chorus — yet a level of uncertainty remains, in part because these figures do not appear in previous tales and in part because they are racialized. They are, to quote the First Musician, "dark men," not "dark-faced men" (*VPl*, 349). When Fergus asks of these silent figures, "What are you?" (*VPl*, 349) — not "Who are you?" — he voices the anxieties of the Western audience encountering the Eastern Other who is, necessarily, always more than he seems, an opaque signifier whose ultimate meaning can never be entirely fixed. Thus, the incorporation of the exotic does more than simply cheat the daily mood. It immediately works to disrupt a transparent relationship between the image and the real, thus creating a theatrical experience in which representation cannot be viewed simply as reproduction. Yeats exploits the set itself to emphasize the mystery of these figures, having them pass in silence by the windows at the rear of the stage without actually entering the cottage until later in the play.

If Yeats is aware of the extent to which these dark men raise the issue of performance within the play itself, he is, I believe, equally cognizant of how the discourses of nationhood must repeatedly perform the stability of the nation. Here again, the opening discussion is significant. Although Yeats's Fenian days, when he had attacked England as "an Empire built on the rapine of the world,"[59] were behind him, and although it would be many years until "The Ghost of Roger Casement," a poem that mocks British "fame and virtue," Yeats has Fergus describe these "merchants" in terms that would seem to evoke not ancient Ireland, but contemporary Britain:

> Conchubar's fame
> Brings merchandise on every wind that blows.
> They may have brought him Libyan dragon-skin,
> Or the ivory of the fierce unicorn. (*VPl*, 350)

The First Musician counters, "If these be merchants, I have seen the goods / They brought to Conchubar, and understood / His murderous purpose" (*VPl*, 350). While Fergus speaks with the naïve certainty of the colonial administrator, claiming several times during the play, "I have known [the High King's] mind as if it were my own" (*VPl*, 351), the First Musician plays the role of the experienced nomad:

> Forgive my open speech, but to these eyes
> That have seen many lands they are such men

As kings will gather for a murderous task
That neither bribes, commands, nor promises
Can bring their people to. (*VPl*, 350)

The play, however, is certainly not a colonial allegory, for the prompts commonly found in nationalist melodrama—an emphasis on geographical conquest, a clear division between (British/Protestant) colonizer and (Irish/Catholic) colonized, or the presence of stock figures, such as the informer—do not appear. Moreover, the positioning of the merchants/assassins as Other, the introduction of the outsider whose actions, unlike those of the British agent, cannot be anticipated with any assurance, creates a tension not commonly experienced in the nationalist theater where representation can always be read within the terms of nationalism's binary logic.

Yeats provides a clear focal point for the audience's anxiety. The subtle references to colonization—the fact that Conchubar requires men from outside the nation to engage in acts that would repel his own people, the fact that an Irish high king adopts the tactics of an imperial despot—help to transport the audience to an abstract world whose legitimacy is not assumed, a space in which a nation, but not *the* nation, is struggling to consolidate itself. Indeed, when one of Conchubar's "dark slaves," as Deirdre describes them, appears later in the play to announce that "Supper is on the table" (*VPl*, 368–369) and to reveal Conchubar's true intentions, the scene again evokes a colonial society similar to but not identical with contemporary or historical Ireland, a realm of clear racial hierarchies in which the Other plays the role of butler and speaks with the "iron tongue" of his master: "I am Conchubar's man, / I am content to serve an iron tongue" (*VPl*, 370–371).

In shifting the real of the play from Ireland's "actual" past to a decidedly imagined, ahistorical time, Yeats attempts to contain the possibility that the audience might read the performance as a direct commentary on contemporary Ireland or upon his own nationalist project. This is particularly important, given that the play, beginning with the dialogue between Fergus and the Musicians, introduces a topic otherwise likely to raise the suspicions, if not the anger, of a nationalist audience: the performative function of female identity in the discourses of nationhood. During the period when Yeats composed and revised *Deirdre*, his theater essays repeatedly return to this theme. Not unexpectedly, given his steadfast defense of Synge's work, Yeats notes, with tongue in cheek, that morally correct images of female identity—calculated to reinforce the belief that "Irish women" are "more chaste than those of England and Scotland"—have played "a valuable part of our National argument" (*IDM*, 54): "Someone said to me a couple of weeks ago, 'If you put on the stage any play about marriage that does not point its moral clearly, you will make it difficult for us to go on attacking the English theatre for its immorality.' Again, we were disordering the squads, the muskets might not all point in the same direction" (*IDM*, 38).

Perhaps less expectedly, Yeats is also conscious of a deeper relationship between normative representations of female identity and the legitimation of the bourgeois state, arguing that British playwrights, with one eye on the bottom line and one on the censor, provide these constructions as a means of galvanizing communal identity. Plays that offer "a view of the world as sexually unexciting as possible always displayed as if it were reality" (*IDM*, 121), that invariably close by "ring[ing] down the curtain on . . . marriage bells" (*IDM*, 30), do more than simply reaffirm patriarchy or provide images of reality that men "bring their wives and daughters to admire" (*IDM*, 30). They enable "certain opinions [to remain] always in force" (*IDM*, 121), producing in the audience that feeling of complacency that arises from perceiving the reproduction of a stable community whose outward expression is "conventional love-making and sentimental domesticity" (*IDM*, 110).

For Yeats, the moral imperatives of Irish nationalism and of imperial British culture are, in this respect, essentially two faces of the same patriarchal coin. Just as "English critics" denounced the works of Henrik Ibsen, "our more hysterical patriots," writes Yeats, "continually attack in the interest of some point of view popularized by Macaulay and his contemporaries, or of some reflection from English novelists and the like, Irish emotion and temperament discovered by some writer in himself after years of labour" (*IDM*, 116). The intolerant Irish priest, in decrying supposedly immoral works, "has never understood that his new puritanism is but an English cuckoo" (*IDM*, 31). Within the play itself, however, this specific critique does not emerge. Instead, the hazy, loosely imperialistic, unstable nation that Yeats evokes provides a clear target for the audience's now critical gaze. Like Conchubar's followers, the Musicians are not Irish—"We have no country but the roads of the world" (*VPl*, 348)—and, like the dark men, they constitute a threat to the stability of this expressly imagined nation. For Fergus, who expects the tale to conclude with the wedding of Deirdre and Naoise and thus to confirm Conchubar's benevolence and the legitimacy of the state, the Musicians are dangerous because they refuse to "speak the welcome and the joy / That I lack tongue for" (*VPl*, 348). They refuse to play the role that Fergus, lacking both a suitable voice and the proper gender, cannot enact—a female celebration of domesticity.

The deeper problem, however, is that the Musicians, by introducing the potential for betrayal, make Fergus conscious of that which he (and the audience) would prefer to ignore, the potential for an *explicit* performance in which the individual desiring female will be sacrificed to the patriarchal dictates of the nation. Fergus responds by commanding, "Be silent, or I'll drive you from the door" (*VPl*, 350)—a statement that subtly equates the nation with the domestic sphere—and by reminding the women that "slander [upon] the High King" is punishable by "prison, or death, or banishment" (*VPl*, 351). Yet, what Fergus requires is not silence but, quite literally, performance. After dismissing their claims as the product of "wild thought / Fed on extravagant poetry" (*VPl*, 351)—an out-of-character assertion, given Fergus's mythic status as poet king, that further divorces the play's reality from Irish reality—he calls upon the Musicians to begin a song, ironically choosing the tale of Lugaidh Redstripe, who, along with "his lady[,] perished wretchedly" (*VPl*, 351) in this same cottage and under similar circumstances. Thus, during this exchange the performative function of gender in the discourses of nationhood is at once exposed and erased. The play calls attention to (the clearly deluded) Fergus as the representative of an abstract, patriarchal state while strategically eliding any references to the "role" of the woman in contemporary Irish society and, more important, as we shall see, to the role of the chorus in the play's final celebration of Deirdre's heroism.

The climactic debate between Deirdre and Conchubar follows a similar pattern, and it is useful to examine that discussion in light of theorist Claude Lefort's comments on representation and ideology. Addressing the discourses of nationhood in modern societies, Lefort argues:

> In Ideology the representation of the rule is split from the effective operation of it. . . . We encounter [this] ambiguity of the representation as soon as the rule is stated; for its very exhibition undermines the power that the rule claims to introduce into practice. This exorbitant power must, in fact, be shown, and at the same time it must owe nothing to the movement which makes it appear. . . . To be true to its image, the rule must be abstracted from any question concerning its origin; thus it goes beyond the operations that it controls. . . . Only the authority of the master allows the contradiction to be concealed, but he is himself an object of representation; presented as possessor of the knowledge of the rule, he allows the contradiction to appear through himself.[60]

I quote at length because, as Homi Bhabha notes, this passage underscores the tension that haunts any attempt to represent and thus to perform the nation as homogeneous entity. As High King, Conchubar recognizes that he can never completely embody the authority of the state, can never transparently signify national unity. Rather, he must continuously perform his own legitimacy before the people. As the nation's patriarch, he further recognizes that the status of his own home mirrors that of the nation, and he explains to Naoise, with false kindness, that the abduction of a king's intended is rarely forgiven:

> There is no king
> In the wide world that, being so greatly wronged,
> Could copy me, and give all vengeance up.
> Although her marriage-day had all but come,
> You carried her away; but I'll show mercy. (*VPl*, 379)

Naoise's response is both ironic and poignant, "You have many words" (*VPl*, 379); but words alone will not fulfill the High King's need. Conchubar requires Deirdre to perform that which he himself cannot: the ordering of his home, the ordering of the state. Though he would achieve this through force, promising to release Naoise if Deirdre acquiesces, he knows that her performance must appear to be freely given. He tells Naoise,

> You may go free,
> If Deirdre will but walk into my house
> Before the people's eyes, that they may know,
> When I have put the crown upon her head,
> I have not taken her by force and guile. (*VPl*, 379)

Conchubar's words, spoken for the audience's ears and before their eyes, do not represent, in Lefort's terms, the articulation of the rule itself. They represent the ideological labor that any enunciation of the rule always seeks to contain, the patriarchal imperatives that, in this case, underpin Conchubar's desire for a public wedding ceremony. Hence, the play, in addition to exposing representation as performance, again exposes the extent to which performance is itself bound up with power, the nation's drive to establish the appearance of unity by visibly setting the High King's house in order.

Like Conchubar, Deirdre recognizes that appearance, and not essence, is what matters to the state. When her beloved is killed, Deirdre plays upon that desire, hoping to view Naoise's body alone in order to end her life with a concealed dagger. Initially, she adopts a persona, indicated by the dramatic pause, calculated to affirm conventional notions of female desire:

> Let me go to [Naoise's body].
> (*Pause.*)
> King Conchubar is right.
> A single woman is of no account,
> Lacking array of servants, linen cupboards,
> The bacon hanging — and King Conchubar's house
> All ready, too — I'll to King Conchubar's house.

It is but wisdom to do willingly
What has to be. (*VPl*, 383)

Deirdre's words are and are not about a contemporary Ireland where "a single woman," unable to own property, "is of no account," where access to social and economic status, for the Irish female, is contingent upon marriage. The repetition of "King Conchubar's house" directs the attention of the spectator toward the patriarch who demands that Deirdre (appear to) "do willingly / What has to be." The High King, however, remains suspicious. Thus, Deirdre quickly shifts roles, becoming the wanton whose loyalty and love can turn on a whim. "You'll stir me to more passion than he could," she tells Conchubar, suggesting that this will occur more quickly if she, having gazed upon the High King's living body in all "your strength," can now look upon "the soiled body" of Naoise, "All blood-bedabbled and his beauty gone" (*VPl*, 385).

Conchubar does not relent until Deirdre performs, before his dark-faced minions and the chorus, the role of (white) aristocratic woman. Deirdre is cognizant of the fact that the establishment of domestic harmony cannot appear to be coerced, particularly given the threats to national stability posed by the presence of the outspoken female chorus, who have questioned Conchubar's intentions, and the racial Other, whose own intentions are never certain. Thus, she greets the High King's denial with scorn: "But he must drag me to his house by force. / If he refuses [my request] he shall be mocked of all" (*VPl*, 386). Responding to Conchubar's fears of a concealed knife, a phallic prop that suggests the High King's own lack, his fundamental impotency as patriarch, Deirdre argues:

>   Have me searched,
> If you would make so little of your queen.
> It may be that I have a knife hid here
> Under my dress. Bid one of these dark slaves
> To search me for it. (*VPl*, 386)

Her request cannot be obeyed and her larger argument cannot be refused because she calls upon the High King to cross a set of racial, sexual, and class boundaries that cannot be violated. The possibility of "dark slaves" (race) groping beneath the "dress" (sex) of a "queen" (class) is, quite simply, unthinkable. Such a move would expose, before the eyes of Conchubar's nation, the fact that his position as patriarchal leader is not essential but contingent upon power dynamics that must remain hidden, that literally and figuratively cannot appear to touch the female body.

The audience—witnessing this exchange—are thus made acutely aware that Conchubar and Deirdre are playing a series of parts in the false reality of the High King's patriarchal nation, this realm where performances of domestic harmony are explicitly bound up with power and the consolidation of the nation. Yet the audience, beginning with the entrance of Deirdre and Naoise, are also called upon to acknowledge the existence of a "correct" performative role for Deirdre, which she does, in fact, embrace "willingly." Throughout this process of construction, a set of alternative roles for the heroine are introduced and rejected, as the play at once reveals and conceals Yeats's own desire for performance, his own desire for Deirdre to enact national unity. When Deirdre appears, she, like the Musicians, is immediately suspicious of Conchubar's intentions, while Naoise, like Fergus, hastily dismisses her claims: "I will not weight the gossip of the roads / With the King's word" (*VPl*, 363–364).

We can read this parallelism on two levels, both with and against the grain of the play's own codes. On the one hand, the audience are asked to recognize that Naoise is under the same delusion as Fergus, with each man believing not simply the King's word but also the fundamental logic of the patriarchal state. The woman who, as Naoise claims of Deirdre, "has the heart of the wild birds that fear / The net of the fowler or the wicker cage" (*VPl*, 364)—the "untame" woman who does not embrace the domestic sphere—speaks without reason and poses a threat that must be contained. Thus, Naoise's response directly echoes Fergus's earlier command, "Be silent if it is against the King [you speak]" (*VPl*, 363)—"What frenzy put these words into your mouth?" (*VPl*, 365). On the other hand, Naoise's own words are consistent with Yeats's own veiled desires, though the threat that Deirdre represents is not a rejection of the domestic but an embracing of the common, that is, in order for Deirdre to perform the nation, she cannot continue to play the part of the "wild" female, "bred . . . in [a] mountainous place" (*VPl*, 364), but must act the part of a highborn, aristocratic woman.

This desire is a product of Yeats's anxieties concerning class, specifically his consistent attempts, as Michael North has argued, to reconcile a fundamental contradiction embedded in a nationalist project designed to celebrate the Anglo-Irish aristocracy, usually associated with colonization, as the true expression of the Irish nation.[61] The important point for *Deirdre*, however, is that the class issue is displaced—though again, not entirely erased—by an emphasis on female beauty. Although the play identifies the Musicians as "comely" (*VPl*, 345), when Deirdre herself attempts, as a means of frustrating Conchubar's desires, to become like the Musicians and thus to transgress class hierarchies, the play calls attention to the physical cost of this transgression. Explains Deirdre,

> Then there is but one way to make all safe,
> I'll spoil this beauty that brought misery
> And houseless wandering on the man I loved.
> These wanderers will show me how to do it;
> To clip this hair to baldness, blacken my skin
> With walnut juice, and tear my face with briars.
> O that the creatures of the woods had torn
> My body with their claws! (*VPl*, 367–368)

Deirdre's words provide a clear image of what the heroine might become, bald, blackened (a point I will return to momentarily), and torn, as Yeats, in exploiting the audience's tendency to equate external beauty with true images of female identity, asks the spectator to view this potential transgression as an "unnatural" marring of the heroine's body. Indeed, the link between beauty and class, (un)marked in the play itself, is explicit in Yeats's letters from this period. Initially, he was apprehensive about "Mrs. Patrick Campbell" playing the role of Deirdre because she "and her generation were trained in plays like [Pinero's] *Mrs. Tanqueray*, where everything is done by a kind of magnificent hysteria. . . . This school reduces everything to an emotional least common denominator. It finds the scullion in the queen, because there are scullions in the audience but no queens. It gives the scullion grace and beauty, but it must be the grace and beauty that the scullion dreams of " (*L*, 475).

Yeats's comments are certainly elitist, but my point is not to indict the playwright but to use his words as a means of highlighting how beauty is bound up with class in the play. When Deirdre explains to Naoise, "Whatever were to happen to my face / I'd be myself" (*VPl*, 368), Yeats, I believe, both wants and does not want this to be true. If Deirdre is indeed the very embodiment of Irish "grace and beauty," the very embodiment of the real nation, then, regardless of the roles she performs for Conchubar, she will remain the real heroine. At the same time, the play itself, by emphasizing the physical costs of this transgression, suggests that were Deirdre to perform the role of the wild "woman," were she to soil her external self, an essential change would take place. The tension here makes transparent a tension in the play as a whole—Yeats's attempts, at once, to expose and to conceal the performative—and it is symptomatic of Yeats's own need for a specific, class-based form of performance, the representation of a heroine who is not the common woman, who is not the "scullion" but the ideal of whom the scullion dreams.

This is why Deirdre's list of self-mutilation includes "blacken[ing] my skin." Just as the High King, if his desired performance of nationhood and domesticity is to continue in the correct manner, cannot permit his dark slaves to come in contact with the queen, the play, if its own performance of nationhood is to continue in the correct manner, cannot permit Deirdre to become like the Musicians and, their negative counterpart, the dark-faced men. Were this to occur, the power dynamics that structure the play's nationalist drive would be made manifest, for Deirdre, as the dark Other, would come to represent that which exceeds Yeats's reproduction of the woman as nation, the abject that marks the fundamental inability of nationalist discourse to account for all forms of (female) identity. In other words, the heroine would become the Other against which the nation defines itself and not a "positive" signifier of communal harmony. Yeats attempts to assuage this tension by once again drawing attention to Fergus's explicit patriarchal bias—"What, wilder yet!" (*VPl*, 368)—and by giving Naoise the last say, punctuating his comments with the arrival of a figure who represents the "true" Other: "Leave the gods' handiwork unblotched, and wait / For their decision, our decision is past. / (*A Dark-faced Messenger comes to the threshold.*)" (*VPl*, 368). The reintroduction of the Other at the threshold—significantly, neither inside nor outside the home—makes Yeats's investment in the beautiful aristocratic woman as the embodiment of the real nation all the more anxious. Deirdre's threat of physical/class-based transgression is answered by the return of the Other, the signifier of commonality—the darkening of the (female) body—that Yeats certainly cannot embrace yet cannot quite dismiss.

If Deirdre cannot become the common woman, what is her true performative role? When the messenger departs, Deirdre immediately proposes that she and Naoise do battle with Conchubar's men: "Let's out and die, / Or break away, if the chance favour us." But Naoise argues:

> They would but drag you from me, stained with blood,
> Their barbarous weapons would but mar that beauty,
> And I would have you die as a queen should—
> In a death-chamber. You are in my charge.
> We will wait here, and when they come upon us,
> I'll hold them from the doors, and when that's over,
> Give you a cleanly death with this grey edge. (*VPl*, 372)

Like Conchubar, Naoise believes that the proper role of the woman is to remain under the charge of her husband, and, given the fact that Fergus has, after voicing identical (patriarchal) sentiments, been proven wrong, the members of the audience recognize, if they have not already, that Naoise too is deluded. Yet, his delusion is of a very specific type. While Conchubar's men cannot touch Deirdre, the play itself cannot allow their "barbarous weapons"—the phallic threat of the savage Other—to "mar that beauty." Deirdre must die "as a queen should," but this will not occur, as Naoise mistakenly assumes, by his own hand. Rather, as the play makes clear in the end, it will occur by an act of will on the part of the heroine.

According to Elin ap Hywel, the fact that Deirdre's suicide is a calculated act sets Yeats's play apart from other nationalist retellings of the legend that treat her death as a "hysterical" moment of passion,[62] an implicit "forewarning of what happens to silly, pretty little girls who stray from the paths prescribed by a paternalistic family unit."[63] Hywel is correct up to a point, but it is important to recognize that an expression of thoughtful, female self-will does not necessarily amount to a rejection of nationalism's patriarchal logic. Consider, for example, Irish cultural nationalism's increasing emphasis, beginning roughly at the turn of the century and continuing through the 1916 Easter Rising, on the noble, bereaved wife and mother at the hearth who has tragically and heroically sacrificed her own needs, generally represented as a "womanly" desire to protect a husband or son from harm, to the revolutionary needs of the community.

In part, the emergence of this image is explained by the fact that, while relatively few women had lost their sons and husbands in the Easter Rising as compared to the Great War, the figure of the bereft woman — of Grace Gifford exchanging wedding vows with Joseph Plunkett on the eve of his execution — quickly became a standard trope in revolutionary mythology. During the 1918 election campaign, Sinn Féin pamphlets frequently appealed to voters by evoking Margaret Pearse, mother of the revolutionary leader Patrick Pearse who was executed shortly after the Rising.[64] In part, however, the promulgation of these images, even before 1916, by nationalists such as Pearse (and, in different ways, by Yeats) can be understood as a response to the increased visibility of women in Irish public life: suffrage groups who rejected, to quote the proto-feminist journal *Bean na hEireann*, the "bleak and colourless life of endless drudgery" facing many Irish women,[65] outspoken revolutionaries who demanded a place within Ireland's exclusively male nationalist groups,[66] and, as Britain militarized, a growing number of working women who, lured by the high wages paid in British munitions factories, became the primary breadwinners in their families. What distinguishes the image of the heroically suffering woman from earlier images of motherly, peasant storyteller at the hearth is that the former accounts for the possibility of female desire, while the latter assumes a silent woman who unself-consciously fulfills her motherly duty. In this sense, patriarchal nationalism, through the valorization of the bereaved woman, acknowledges and works to contain the existence of individual female desire by marking self-sacrifice, a *conscious* choice to renounce desire, as the hallmark of the ideal woman who stoically bears witness to the parallel self-sacrifice of the men in her family.

Yeats attempts to account for female desire in a similar manner, though I am not suggesting that he secretly embraced the patriarchal imperatives of conventional Irish nationalism. Rather, the play reaches this end by different means because, as a nationalist text, it cannot do otherwise. Having brought the question of female self-will to the fore, having validated the individual desires of the Musicians and Deirdre over those of Conchubar's patriarchal state, the play must not offer a heroine devoid of individuality. When Naoise suggests, prior to Conchubar's entrance, that he and Deirdre follow the lead of Lugaidh Redstripe and his wife, nobly playing a game of chess as their doom approaches, he once again indirectly foreshadows Deirdre's proper end: "I have never heard a death so out of reach / Of common hearts, a high and comely end" (*VPl*, 373). The adjective "comely" now clearly signifies the aristocratic death that Naoise (and Yeats) would have Deirdre perform. Yet Deirdre, her "veins being hot," does not embrace this exact performance: "I cannot go on playing like that woman / That had but the cold blood of the sea in her veins" (*VPl*, 374, 375). Her death will not be "common," but what separates her from the ordinary is her individuality, her ability to outwit Conchubar and to achieve a heroic death in a manner that has not been preordained.

At the same time, Yeats, in order to fulfill the play's larger nationalist drive, in order for the heroine to embody the real community, must represent the ultimate expression of Deirdre's desire as self-sacrifice. To represent desire in another way would turn the play's critique of the patriarchal state back upon itself, introducing into the true real of the play the woman whose own desires, because they are not directed toward a specifically identifiable end, would remain, so to speak, free-floating, unidentifiable and thus unpredictable. Within the play's own codes it truly is "but wisdom" for the heroine "to do willingly / What has to be" (*VPl*, 383). Deirdre does not, like Synge's Nora, depart with the Musicians for the road, nor does she attack Conchubar's men, an action likely to cause the audience to view her as a representation of those suffragists who had begun to demand more than "a purely supportive role" in Ireland's national struggle.[67] Instead, her courage and intelligence, her ability to exploit the performative demands of Conchubar's nation, are designed to fulfill Yeats's own performative demands. Indeed, Deirdre's suicide is itself a performance of domestication, an affirmation of the woman's role as guardian of the spiritual health of the nation. Although the High King believes that her final words signify his triumph, Deirdre, the Musicians, and, crucially, the audience know instead that she is celebrating her own triumph as Naoise's eternal wife:

> Now strike the wire, and sing to it a while,
> Knowing that all is happy, and that you know
> Within what bride-bed I shall lie this night,

And by what man, and lie close up to him,
For the bed's narrow, and there outsleep the cock-crow. (*VPl*, 386–387)

In embracing her true "bride-bed," Deirdre willingly sanctions a form of domesticity that is not of Conchubar's nation but of the true nation, a home/death
chamber that, in transcending the physical, becomes the symbol of an Irish nation whose house is now set in order.

Like *Cathleen ni Houlihan*, ordinary women remain on stage as signifiers of female self-will that exceeds the reproduction of the woman as nation.
Unlike *Cathleen ni Houlihan*, *Deirdre* does not attempt to dismiss them as ir-
relevant "strangers" in the communal home. Rather, *Deirdre* incorporates the
Musicians—in precisely the manner once demanded by Fergus—as those who
bear witness to the triumph of domesticity, common women whose ultimate expression of self-will is singing the aristocratic woman's heroic sacrifice: "They
are gone, they are gone. The proud may lie by the proud. . . . / Into the secret
wilderness of their love. . . . / Eagles have gone into their cloudy bed" (*VPl*,
387). The realm of the Musicians, once a place of "wildness," now becomes the
"wilderness" of Deirdre and Naoise's "love." Moreover, the chorus, as speakers
of the truth throughout the play, provide a focal point for audience identification, incorporating the spectator into the celebration. They speak the audience's satisfaction at witnessing the completion of the true performance, even
as they mark Yeats's contradictory desire to reject and to affirm the gendered
discourses of nationhood. They celebrate Deirdre's final transformation from
common woman to heroine, from wild "Eagle" to, as Yeats's own comments on
the play ironically suggest, "a wild bird in a cage" (*VPl*, 1299).

In both *Deirdre* and *Cathleen ni Houlihan*, Yeats undermines conventional forms
of nationalist representation, highlighting the extent to which representation
as performance is bound up with the discourses of nationhood. Yet, because
the plays are ultimately designed to "engender" communal unity, he cannot entirely abandon the gendered symbolic economy upon which those discourses
depend, the erasure of difference and the reproduction of the woman as "true"
signifier of the nation. From a postcolonial feminist perspective, his heroines
can thus be described as neither "progressive" nor "regressive," neither the
"false" women of traditional nationalist melodrama nor the "true" women of
feminist resistance. Rather, they remain the ambiguous, conflicted dramatic
images of an ambiguous, conflicted playwright. Cathleen, Bridget, Delia, the
female chorus, and Deirdre, instead of transparently embodying the nation,
embody the tensions and internal contradictions of Yeats's own theatrical project. They mark his desire to conceal and to reveal the performative labor of
representation in plays that attempt to subvert the conventions of traditional

nationalist drama and that, at the same time, work to fulfill the larger imperatives of (patriarchal) nationalism.

When Yeats claimed in 1914 that "Ireland is no longer a sweetheart but a house to be set in order," his words thus echo the vision of community anxiously expressed in *Deirdre*, yet they also speak to a change in his understanding of nationalist drama. During the first decade of the 1900s, Yeats sought to create a theater that would have broad-based appeal, providing on the stage images designed to express heroic Irish individuality and, simultaneously, to evoke those deeply rooted thoughts and emotions that bind a community together—Cuchulain plunging into the waves, Deirdre slumped over the body of Naoise. By the early 1910s, however, his growing frustration with audiences who demanded bourgeois realism and patriotic nationalist melodrama prompted Yeats to adopt a new strategy. Instead of struggling to condition audience reception in the popular theater, Yeats takes the radical step of controlling the type of audience that will view his plays, thereby embracing, as he has famously written, "an unpopular theatre and an audience like a secret society where admission is by favour and never to many" (*IDM*, 131).

Staged in "some great dining-room or drawing-room" (*IDM*, 131), performed for a select group of Irish artists and intellectuals, and presided over by an "accomplished hostess" (*IDM*, 132), such as Lady Gregory, Yeats's theater is unabashedly aristocratic. It is also, on the levels of class and gender, fundamentally conflicted. In plays such as *The Only Jealousy of Emer* he organizes communal Irish identity around an image that expresses the heroic individuality that Yeats believed characterized the Anglo-Irish as a distinct class: Emer, the noble, self-sacrificing domestic heroine who—like the grand drawing room, the sophisticated audience, and the brilliant courteous hostess—completes his vision of an Ireland whose house has been set in order. In this respect, the ambiguities that we have examined in *Cathleen ni Houlihan* and *Deirdre* become, in his later drama, more pronounced, as Yeats's stance hardens into a reactionary—and some might argue, escapist—pose. At the same time, though Yeats the dramatist was content with his "unpopular theatre," Yeats the poet, living in the aftermath of Easter 1916, could not remain aloof from the realities beyond the door of the big house—the realities of an Ireland in the grip of violent transition from colony to Free State. And it is this chaotic, incoherent Ireland that will form the historical context of the next two chapters, as we explore Yeats's conflicted responses to the discourses of imperialism and nationalism in his finest collection of poetry, *The Tower*.

THREE

Rewriting History in a Time of Violence

"Nineteen Hundred and Nineteen" and "Meditations in Time of Civil War"

The one duty we owe to history is to rewrite it.

——Oscar Wilde, *The Critic as Artist*

the problem after any revolution is what to do with
your gunmen
as old Billyum found out in Oireland

——Ezra Pound, Canto LXXX

For those engaged in bringing postcolonial theory to bear on Yeats studies, *The Tower*, a collection often read within the context of British high modernism, offers a tempting point of entry. Published in 1928, *The Tower* contains poems mostly written during the nine-year period that saw the drafting of the Irish Declaration of Independence in 1919, the passage of the Government of Ireland Act in 1920 as well as the Anglo-Irish Treaty in 1921, and the creation of the Irish Free State in 1922, a period that, viewed from one angle, marked Ireland's emergence from the shadow of imperialism into the light of postcolonial independence.[1] Published "after the post," after this supposed instant of transition, *The Tower* itself, arguably Yeats's most important collection, may allow critics to position him as a postcolonial poet, an attractive move given the current scholarly cachet attached to the postcolonial and given the potential that such a characterization would afford for counterbalancing the attacks on Yeats's politics that have gained prominence since the 1980s.

Yeats scholars have, however, been suspicious of the temptation to make broad-based, prematurely celebratory, postcolonial readings of Ireland in the 1920s or of Yeats's work from that period.[2] Echoing the cautionary remarks of theorists Ella Shohat, Anne McClintock, and others, they have argued that such readings, in assuming a clean break between an oppressive colonial past and a liberated postcolonial present, obscure the complexities and unique features of the Irish situation, fail to examine in detail the transitional period itself (one in progress to this day), and, most important, ignore empire's crippling economic, political, cultural, and psychological legacies.[3] Accordingly, critical studies of *The Tower* and of the late poetry have frequently emphasized the degree to which Yeats's verse remains bound in empire's Manichean logic, idealizing those aspects of Irish culture and those apparently essential qualities of the Irish race that imperial discourse had used to mark the former colony as Other.[4]

If, as Donald Torchiana, Conor Cruise O'Brien, Terry Eagleton, and Seamus Deane have argued, Yeats's early cultural nationalism worked to romanticize, and thus to reinscribe, these outmoded forms of Irish identity, his late verse engages in an equally regressive nationalist project. Experiencing an increasing sense of disconnection from bourgeois Ireland, Yeats retreats into myth, presenting, in the manner of his "unpopular theatre," a model for a new Ireland rooted in an Ascendancy past when Catholic peasant and Protestant landlord existed in supposed harmony. "At the very moment of its demise . . . the Ascendancy," writes Eagleton, "was able to turn round upon itself and, in the person of Yeats and his colleagues, rewrite this often inglorious political history as high cultural tradition. . . . All those rumbustious lords and randy earls were now suddenly imbued with mythic status, spiritual heroes in some imposing drama."[5]

Looking broadly at Yeats's evolving project of cultural nationalism as it is represented in his most bitterly nostalgic works from the 1930s,[6] we would find it difficult to defend Yeats against the charge that, in Deane's words, "he distorted history in the service of myth,"[7] and it is not my intention to do so here. Deane and Eagleton are certainly correct when they argue that Yeats's postrevolution nationalism remains grounded, at least in part, in an ultimately conservative attachment to an imagined past, an attachment that, according to Deane, "clearly harbours the desire to obliterate or reduce the problems of class, economic development, bureaucratic organization and the like, concentrating upon the essences of self, community, nationhood, racial theory, Zeitgeist."[8] For Deane, Yeats's "myth of history . . . is a subtle and adaptable figure of thought, as a careful reading of 'Nineteen Hundred and Nineteen' or of 'Meditations in Time of Civil War' reveals."[9] He does not proceed to elaborate upon that reading, but, based upon his more general claims and the earlier, equally critical arguments of Torchiana,[10] we may surmise that "Meditations," viewed from this perspective, functions as a kind of elegy: a glorification (or, more accurately, a wholly idealistic reconstruction) of an older, nobler Ireland, a lament for its having passed, and an implicit call for those cultural and political leaders in the present to recapture "the inherited glory of the rich" and to be again those "Bitter and violent men [who] might rear in stone / The sweetness that all longed for night and day" ("Meditations in Time of Civil War").

While I agree to some extent with these general claims, I differ with Deane and Eagleton concerning "Meditations in Time of Civil War" and "Nineteen Hundred and Nineteen." My primary objection involves their critical reliance upon a traditional Marxist reading of historical false consciousness, now adapted to the postcolonial, whereby these poems are viewed as expressing a retreat from the material present into an imagined past. Rather than emphasize those historical narratives that would displace a concrete engagement with history (as if that displacement occurs seamlessly, one narrative simply erasing another), I intend, in keeping with more broad-based deployments of postcolonial theory, to focus on the moment of displacement itself, a transitional moment when, to quote Homi Bhabha, "the language of culture and community is poised on the fissures of the present becoming the rhetorical figures of a national past."[11]

Where a strictly Marxist reading would see a dialectical shift from an engagement with history unfolding in the present to a glorification of history in the past, our reading will center on this ambivalent moment in war-torn Ireland when history is becoming History, when the heterogeneous scraps of individual experiences are transformed and translated through the discourses of nationalism into homogeneous narratives of national history and national identity. By shifting our gaze to this transitional moment itself and to Yeats's engagement with these nationalist constructions of history as they are being formulated, we begin to perceive a more complicated Yeats whose poetic meditations on an Ireland gripped by war may not be so readily dismissed as romantic idealism or naïve historical myth-making. Rather than offering a means either to celebrate Yeats as a writer whose verse somehow transcends the legacy of imperialism[12] or to attack him for his admittedly aristocratic and authoritarian politics, the postcolonial, considered in this light, provides a new vantage from which to reinvestigate Yeats's verse within the contexts of an Ireland in transition.

This chapter will focus specifically on constructions of history during a period of militant nationalism. After briefly analyzing the discourses of Irish nationalism in the early 1920s, I will argue that in these two key poems from *The Tower*, Yeats is indeed exercising his "one duty" to rewrite history.[13] But far from reinscribing an outmoded nationalist mindset that idealizes one form of Irish identity, eighteenth-century or otherwise, Yeats pointedly challenges former and current nationalist narratives of history by focusing instead upon instances of rupture and the chaos of the present. In so doing, he undercuts those stable narratives of a unified heroic nation that were central to the political and cultural nationalists' agendas in the 1920s and that helped to perpetuate, in Deane's words, a "colonialist mentality" even after the establishment of the Free State.[14]

In the late 1910s and early 1920s, the period during which Yeats wrote "Nineteen Hundred and Nineteen," the rhetoric of Sinn Féin drew heavily upon a type of nationalism popularized in the previous century by Thomas Davis.[15] Characterized by appeals to Ireland's heroic past of imperial resistance, such rhetoric stressed both the duty of the patriot to continue that struggle and the duty of the historian and artist, in the words of Davis, "to hallow or accurse the scenes of glory and honour, or of shame and sorrow; to give to the imagination the arms, and homes, and senates, and battles of other days; to rouse, and soften, and strengthen, and enlarge us with the passions of great periods; to lead us into the love of self-denial, of justice, of beauty, of valour, of generous life and proud death; and to set up in our souls the memory of great men who shall then be as models and judges of our actions."[16] During their ultimately successful 1918 election bid, Sinn Féin campaigned upon a platform of "separatism," the final goal being not simply Home Rule but also a distinct, and increasingly Catholic, Irish Republic, an imagined community sanctified through the discourse of Sinn Féin nationalism as that state for which former insurrectionists had given their lives. Not surprisingly, "the memory of Easter week," as historian D. George Boyce notes, was consistently "held up for approval" by Sinn Féin, but, more important, it was a distinctly "historical" Easter week, one couched as the climactic date in a revolutionary calendar whose highlights included 1798, 1848, and 1867 and which affirmed, as the *Sinn Féin General Election Manifesto* (1918) proclaimed, "the fact that in nearly every generation, and five times within the past 120 years our people have challenged in arms the right of England to rule this country."[17]

At the time of the election, 1916 was marked by most Republican leaders as the conclusion of violent resistance, a past that would in itself serve to invigorate a political struggle in the present. But that position changed during the years of the Anglo-Irish War, as increased violence and revolutionary resistance in what came to be known in Irish Republican Army (IRA) discourse as the "four glorious years" of 1918 to 1921 readily provided for, indeed demanded the articulation of, a living history of heroic struggle. Responding to this crisis, Sinn Féin obliged by again offering a narrative of the present, readily grafted upon earlier nationalist constructions, through which acts of violence—the burning of homes, the killing of informers, the deaths of fellow insurrectionists—might be read within the context of a larger revolutionary mythology.[18] While certainly understandable during a period of armed resistance, the continuous elaboration of a unified national history centered on a tradition of heroic sacrifice served to support the normalization of violence and helped (we can say with admitted hindsight) to lay the groundwork for a reactionary and an oppressive politics after liberation occurred. The hasty execution by the IRA of accused spies and the killing of innocent civilians during surprise attacks were forgotten, while the deeds of men such as Tom Barry, leader of a celebrated ambush attack in Kilmichael, readily became the stuff of folklore, significantly altering the landscape of nationalism for years to come and giving, in the opinion of Boyce, "political violence a new lease of life in Ireland."[19]

The Yeats of this period must be understood against this backdrop of nationalist sentiment. Conor Cruise O'Brien has written that "the conception of history as a series of blood sacrifices enacted in every generation . . . is most essentially a literary invention. The great propagandist of this notion, as far as Ireland is concerned, was the poet Yeats."[20] But as early as 1918, Yeats seems to have been acutely aware of the practical impact of inflaming "the old historical passion" (*L*, 649); and during the debates that followed the passage of a British bill (March 1918) authorizing conscription of Irish soldiers for service in the Great War, Yeats, though publicly opposed, carefully tempered his opposition.[21] Writing to Clement Shorter concerning an upcoming lecture on Irish poetry, he explains: "Times are too dangerous for me to encourage men to risks I am not prepared to share or approve. If the Government go on with conscription there may be soon disastrous outbreaks. . . . The old historical passion is at its greatest intensity" (*L*, 649). As a letter to Lord Haldane written later that year reveals, Yeats's primary concern was not simply violence in itself but also what that violence might become in both imperial and national historiography: "There will be incidents that will become anecdotes and legends. . . . Each side will have its wrongs to tell of and these will keep England and Ireland apart during your lifetime and mine. England will forget the anecdotes in a few years, but the legends will never be forgotten."[22]

In "Nineteen Hundred and Nineteen," Yeats offers a response to such potential constructions of history by articulating a vision of the present that steadfastly refuses to conform to the contours of Republican historiography. This is not to say that Yeats peers through the haze of Republican nationalism to discover or articulate a "true" history of the Anglo-Irish War, nor, as Deane would argue, does he attempt to replace one idealized history with another. Rather, as so often happens with Yeats, he begins anew. He fundamentally questions those positivistic histories developed by most forms of Irish nationalism. He indicts himself for having blindly participated in the construction of previous national histories and, in an attempt to lay the foundation for a new history of Ireland rendered in art, plunges into the "foul rag and bone shop" of war, exploding the gap, to borrow Enda Duffy's remarks on *Ulysses*, "between the horror of actual violence and the explanations of overtly political discourse," between the actual community and the imagined community, between a history waiting to be written and a history that has been written.[23]

"Nineteen Hundred and Nineteen," as Curtis Bradford's compilation of Yeats's manuscripts indicates, underwent numerous revisions, two of which, central to our reading, occurred after its original publication in *The Dial* (1921) and *The London Mercury* (1921). The title was changed from "Thoughts upon the Present State of the World" and the postscript date "1919" was added, though, as a letter to Olivia Shakespear reveals, Yeats was still working on the poem in April 1921 (*L*, 668). These changes nicely highlight the issue of historiographic desire that I see at the core of the poem, as Yeats, in a move designed to heighten its ultimate irony, initially seems to present a poem that will give order and meaning to history as it unfolds. The original title serves to indicate the subjective position of the author, an artist simply reflecting upon a series of events passing before his eyes. In sharp contrast, both the formal title "Nineteen Hundred and Nineteen" and the postscript date resonate with a sense of objective truth and the weight of history and historiography. It is as if Yeats, in the manner of the prophetic romantic artist, perceives the historical importance of that year as it happens.

Furthermore, by seeming to announce the centrality of that year in his title, Yeats asks the reader to view the poem as a representation of history, a point in time that must then be considered within the context of other significant historical moments. This is true of Yeats's whole canon, as the title inevitably brings to mind other key dates such as 1913 and 1916, demanding the contextualization of the poem within, at the very least, his individual literary history and suggesting an evolutionary trajectory in which the sacrifices of 1916 would be (re)validated by the revolutionary heroes of 1919. Historical contextualization is also demanded on a broader level, for, as numerous critics have noted, "Nineteen Hundred and Nineteen" signals the beginning of a new era after the Great War and, in terms of the Irish situation, clearly sets the poem within the context of the Anglo-Irish War, marking the first year of that struggle when, in January, the Dáil formally declared secession from the United Kingdom. Indeed, during the 1921 treaty debates, 1919 was, according to nationalist leaders such as Eamon De Valera, the year when the Republic envisioned in 1916 actually came into being.[24]

Viewed in this light, Yeats's decision to alter the title and to add the postscript date would appear to support the type of reading initially advanced by Torchiana: the act of grounding the poem in a historical moment that must be read within the broader context of larger historical narratives pointedly heightens the poem's fundamental irony.[25] Instead of offering a linear progression, an unbroken positivistic history as the title might suggest, the poem turns upon itself, profoundly critiquing the present state of disorder and looking back with a mixture of bitterness and nostalgia toward an idealized Ascendancy past. Yet a rejection of the present does not necessarily entail a desired return to a more stable—that is, colonial—moment in Ireland's past. Rather, the poem itself is doubly ironic in that the expected progression evoked by the date is undercut by a chaotic vision of the present, which is in turn further undercut by the poem's refusal to sanction any concrete historical narrative as a means for comprehending (and, in turn, valorizing) that present.

The poem, in other words, plays upon historiographic desire—the desire to use temporal markers as a means for constructing order in the present—by continually frustrating that desire, revealing that the old, particularly nationalist and imperialist modes for ordering time must be cast aside before new histories of Ireland may be articulated in this transitional period. Though direct analogy between the African and Irish colonial and nationalist situations must not be readily assumed, Frantz Fanon's words concerning the truly revolutionary national poet are applicable here: "It is not enough to try to get back to the people in that past out of which they have already emerged; rather we must join them in that fluctuating movement which they are just giving a shape to, and which, as soon as it has started, will be the signal for everything to be called into question."[26] While Yeats's own earlier cultural nationalism would seem to find answers in history, in "Nineteen Hundred and Nineteen" he finds only questions that all point to a profound need to (re)join the Irish people with a new, fluctuating present.

The poem opens, in a manner not unlike that practiced by Ezra Pound in the *Cantos*, with a lamentation for what has passed, an Athenian world of artistic triumphs, "ornamental bronze and stone / An ancient image made of olive wood— / And . . . Phidias' famous ivories" (*VP*, 428). Yet the tone is not one of nostalgia—these "ingenious lovely things are gone"—but grim acceptance, not one of a desire to return to that past (or to recreate that past in the present) but a need to perceive the dangers of attempting to do so. With the line, "We too had many pretty toys when young," the poem shifts to a more recent past, and here we begin to see the root of this acceptance. The compulsion to establish a seamless relationship between past and present and to assume that the supposed greatness of the past has continued unabated into the present has led to historical myopia, an idealization of what had gone before and naïve confidence in what was to come:

> . . . habits . . . made old wrong
> Melt down, as it were wax in the sun's rays;

Public opinion ripening for so long
We thought it would outlive all future days.
O what fine thought we had because we thought
That the worst rogues and rascals had died out.

As a younger man, Yeats dreamed that the Irish were beginning "to recognize the right of the individual mind to see the world in its own way," to cast
aside those "habits of thought and feeling come down from [the Young Ire-
land] party, for the seasons change, and the need and occupation with them"
(*IDM*, 113). The poem, however, reveals that the seasons have not changed.
"Habits"—established modes of reading the past—have continued to limit
historical perception and have helped to perpetuate blind faith in the stability
of "future days."

Elizabeth Cullingford reads this section as a bitter commentary upon
nineteenth-century values, faith in "Victorian stability, peace, and [a] belief in
progress," and clearly the passage is designed to capture a mood of naïve certainty.[27] A trace of the Irish context, though, is recognizable in the drafts, as the
lines concerning "public opinion" originally contained a more local reference:
"A speedy remedy for obvious wrong; / No swaggering soldier on the public
ways / Who weighed man's life lighter than a song."[28] Likely a direct allusion
to the Black and Tans,[29] the British forces sent to occupy Ireland in 1920, these
lines suggest a more pointed historical narrative that would align directly with
nationalist historiography. The Victorian values espoused by British cultural
imperialism—Britain as the paradigmatic modern, civilized nation fostering
the evolutionary journey of the colony toward a similar state of civilization—
were simply hollow rhetoric, a set of beliefs that, during the Anglo-Irish War, no
longer concealed the true goals of imperialism: political subjugation, economic
exploitation, and cultural domination. Yeats's use of the term "swaggering"
would likely have had strong and direct connotations for an Irish audience all too
familiar with Royal Irish Constabulary (RIC) and Black and Tan atrocities—
the burning of Balbriggan, the sacking of Cork, and the Croke Park massacre—
and with popular representations of these troops as proud, heartless, and, in the
words of British Brigadier General F. P. Crozier, "drunken and insubordinate."[30]
Significantly, Yeats immediately does away with this image in the next draft, pre-
ferring the much more ambiguous "public opinion." In so doing, he moves from
a clearly nationalistic history—one that would immediately sanctify 1919 and,
by extension, the Anglo-Irish War as another chapter of heroic sacrifice—to a
broader indictment of historical desire. Public opinion, be it British or Irish, has
led to blind faith in historical progress, that which "made old wrong / Melt
down," and the return of that faith leads to a state of profound violence in
the present.

The two stanzas that follow look Janus-faced toward both sides of the Irish Sea. As several critics have noted, the phrase "Parliament and king" refers to the British Empire prior to the Great War, a world of imperial certainty soon to be undone,[31] while the stanza that follows, characterized by some of the most bitter language in *The Tower*, centers upon Black and Tan attacks during the Anglo-Irish War:

> Now days are dragon-ridden, the nightmare
> Rides upon sleep: a drunken soldiery
> Can leave the mother, murdered at her door,
> To crawl in her own blood, and go scot-free;
> The night can sweat with terror as before
> We pieced our thoughts into philosophy,
> And planned to bring the world under a rule,
> Who are but weasels fighting in a hole.

Yeats's vivid description of the murdered mother again smacks of nationalist historiography, British confidence in its own evolutionary imperial project now exposed as simple tyranny, the wanton killing of an innocent woman. The mother referred to is Ellen Quinn,[32] who was, as Augusta Gregory's journals reveal, "shot dead . . . with her child in her arms" in November 1920.[33] Lady Gregory used this incident as the basis for her *Nation* article "Murder by the Throat" (1920), one of many nationalistic works decrying Black and Tan atrocities.

Yeats too wrote an explicitly nationalistic poem on the subject. In "Reprisals" he imagines the deceased Robert Gregory, Augusta's son, looking upon the current state of Ireland and finding that "Half-drunk or whole-mad soldiery / Are murdering [his] tenants there." The poem goes on to ask with bitterness:

> Where may new-married women sit
> And suckle children now? Armed men
> May murder them in passing by
> Nor law nor parliament take heed. (*VP*, 791)

According to A. Norman Jeffares, Yeats chose not to publish "Reprisals" for fear of upsetting Robert Gregory's pro-British widow, a claim that R. F. Foster has since countered by demonstrating that it was in fact Augusta Gregory, concerned that Yeats had "dragg[ed]" her son "from his grave to make what I think a not very sincere poem," who urged suppression of the piece.[34]

Regardless of Yeats's motives for withholding publication, the poem offers a useful contextualization for his handling of the same incident in "Nineteen Hundred and Nineteen." In the former, agency is quite clear, as these "armed men," the minions of a coldly detached British "parliament," move about the countryside — the traditional site in nationalist historiography of evictions, burning of homes, and summary executions — "murdering" the Irish peasantry, Gregory's former "Kiltartan . . . tenants."[35] In the latter, though certainly evocative of Black and Tan "murder[s]," agency is somewhat clouded. The death of the mother is viewed as part of a more abstract whirlwind of chaos and violence, and the local Kiltartan time and setting are replaced by a broader vision of "days" that are now "dragon-ridden."[36] More important, the pronoun "we," so rarely used by Yeats, abounds in this section, suggesting no clear demarcation between Irish victim and British aggressor. The two, bound together in their desire to find stability in time and to discover in the past validation for deeds in the present, be they in the service of an imperial or national cause, have tragically failed to perceive the violent ends of such desires: "We pieced our thoughts into philosophy, / And planned to bring the world under a rule, / Who are but weasels fighting in a hole."

Sections two and three of the poem are less overtly concerned with specifically nationalist or imperialist narratives of time, but they too play upon this same theme of historiographic desire. The second section begins with "Loie Fuller's Chinese dancers," a line that would seem to anticipate a high modernist move practiced by Pound, and at times by Yeats, in which a Western present looks for a structuring aesthetic in an Eastern past. The expected temporal link, though, is displaced by a much broader vision of history: "So the Platonic Year / Whirls out new right and wrong, / Whirls in the old instead." The compulsion to find order in the past leads only to an awareness of time as profoundly uncontrollable, a Platonic span of 25,000 years in which the planets return to their original positions, change without change, the whirling of Fuller's dancers replaced by the whirling of time itself in which "All men are dancers and their tread / Goes to the barbarous clangour of a gong." This move into a more abstract understanding of time is itself undercut, as Yeats plays ironically upon his own "Platonic" sense of history. The "solitary soul" is compared to "a swan," an allusion to Yeats at a slightly earlier stage, the "moralist or mythological poet" who, in *The Wild Swans at Coole* (1919), first wrote poems based upon the famous (or infamous) visionary system that he derived from automatic writing sessions with his wife, Georgia Hyde-Lees, whom he had married in 1917. The eponymous opening poem of that collection employs the swans — "All suddenly mount / And scatter wheeling in great broken rings / Upon their clamorous wings" — as a metaphor of cyclical history, the wheeling of gyres whose true nature the poet in his tower, as the character Michael Robartes sees in "The Phases of the Moon," "seeks in book or manuscript" but "shall never find."

In "Nineteen Hundred and Nineteen," in time of war, such attempts to garner a broader comprehension of history have taken on an added sense of urgency, yet here again the fulfillment of historiographic desire never occurs: time viewed politically, artistically, or, in this case, philosophically remains profoundly uncontrollable. History whirls onward. A man remains "lost amid the labyrinth that he has made / In art or politics," while the dreams of those, including the poet, who sought "to mend / Whatever mischief seemed / To afflict mankind" have gone unfulfilled:

> The swan has leaped into the desolate heaven:
> That image can bring wildness, bring a rage
> To end all things, to end
> What my laborious life imagined, even
> The half-imagined, the half-written page:
> O but we dreamed to mend
> Whatever mischief seemed
> To afflict mankind, but now
> That winds of winter blow
> Learn that we were crack-pated when we dreamed.

The swan has departed, fading, as with all things in this poem, into a whirlwind of dust and chaos, a "desolate heaven." Such knowledge tempts the poet to despair, "to end / What my laborious life imagined," yet that individual sense of bitterness is again linked with a broader "we," a people on both sides of the Irish Sea whose faith in history as evolutionary is now revealed as "crack-pated."

In section four, which seems to address the confident mindset of the British (and perhaps the Anglo-Irish) before the Great War, Yeats returns to the weasel metaphor:

> We, who seven years ago
> Talked of honour and truth,
> Shriek with pleasure if we show
> The weasel's twist, the weasel's tooth.

The phrase "seven years ago," though certainly evocative of prewar Britain, speaks equally to Ireland's recent past. The years 1912–1914, alluded to in "Easter, 1916" with the lines "For England may keep faith / For all that is done and said," marked a period of debate concerning the final prerevolution Home Rule Bill introduced in the British Parliament in April 1912.[37] That bill, designed to grant Ireland a separate parliament with jurisdiction over internal affairs, was, after two years of heated argument,[38] placed on the statute books in 1914 but not enacted because of the outbreak of war. The subsequent Easter Rising, the British government's hard-line response, and its later attempts to conscript

Irish forces all led to a climate in which support for constitutional Home Rule in Ireland gave place to more extreme demands for complete autonomy.

In this context, the section tantalizingly evokes a pointedly nationalist reading of history: imperial commitments, talk of "honour and truth," have given way to the reassertion of imperial might. Yet, the pronoun "we" is again of central importance. Like most nationalists, Yeats supported the 1912 Bill, and it is particularly telling that he referred to the weight of history when expressing that support to a group of southern Protestants: "The clear verdict of the history of civilised nations in modern times is that the responsibilities of self-government and the growth of political freedom are the most powerful solvents for sectarian animosities."[39] Adopting a key trope of imperialist historiography — "the history of civilised nations" as the field from which "positive" historical truths may be harvested — Yeats recasts the evolutionary certainties of the modern imperial nation in Irish terms, establishing those certainties as the basis of his faith in moderate constitutional nationalism. In "Nineteen Hundred and Nineteen," such faith is dismissed as another component of the labyrinth, a form of historical myopia pervading both sides of the colonial binary; however, rather than replicate that binary by simply attacking imperialism's rhetoric of "honour and truth" and by positioning himself as an Irish nationalist who perceives clearly the betrayal that imperial discourse would belie, Yeats indicts all who have participated in the construction of sanctioning historical narratives. What remains is not the aloof comfort of gazing upon a historical narrative proven false but the bitter "shriek" of "pleasure" that comes with perceiving the hollow core of historiographic desire.

In the poem's concluding section, Yeats moves quickly from a chaotic present in which there are no heroes (the "few . . . handsome riders . . . break and vanish"), no clear villains, only "Violence upon the roads," to an imagined vision of the distant past, a final ironic play upon historiographic desire:

> But now wind drops, dust settles; thereupon
> There lurches past, his great eyes without thought
> Under the shadow of stupid straw-pale locks,
> That insolent fiend Robert Artisson
> To whom the love-lorn Lady Kyteler brought
> Bronzed peacock feathers, red combs of her cocks.

These lines look back to "The Second Coming," with Robert Artisson — a fourteenth-century "evil spirit much run after in Kilkeeny," as Yeats notes (*VP*, 433) — occupying the same position as the "rough beast," a pitiless figure who, gazing "without thought," does not trouble to look upon unimportant local human time, his visage "stupid" because he is simply an agent of cyclical history. This section, however, is not without a local Irish trace. In Raphael Holinshed's *The Historie* [sic] *of Ireland* (1577), Artisson is the spirit with whom the witch, Dame Alice Kyteler, "was charged to have nightly conference . . . [and] to whom she sacrificed in the high way ix red cockes, & ix peacocks eies [*sic*]."[40]

The image of a "love-lorn" woman making a sacrifice, as I discussed in the preceding chapter, had served in Yeats's early nationalist drama to evoke a harmonious blending of individual and collective desire. Here, however, the image functions as a bitter trope, indirectly evoking Yeats's belief that "Nationalist abstractions [are] like the fixed ideas of some hysterical woman" (*Au*, 192) and directly recalling those women, such as Maud Gonne and Constance Gore-Booth, who sacrificed all (or, at least, what Yeats considered as "all") to the cause of extreme nationalism. For such women, "Too long a sacrifice," as Yeats wrote in "Easter, 1916," "Can make a stone of the heart." As so often occurs in Yeats's later writings, the woman, in this case the sacrificing witch, now becomes a symbol of his own nationalist desires and frustrations. The desire to find a structuring object in Ireland's folk past and to construct a homogeneous narrative of an Irish history that might evoke an Ireland worthy of sacrifice, meets with its ironic, frustrating fulfillment. If blood sacrifice is the ultimate goal of cultural nationalism, blood sacrifice is what Yeats discovers in this journey back into Ireland's folk past, but in this poem it is a sacrifice utterly devoid of heroic overtones: the sacrifice of animals to an evil spirit, a fitting commentary on an Ireland where human lives continue to be sacrificed for historical causes.

The postscript date that follows these lines is thus entirely ironic. The historical certainty that it seems to evoke, the historiographic desire to order time in an evolutionary manner, has been foreclosed in the poem proper. Confidence in linear history, be it in the service of an imperial or national program, has conspired to produce days that are "dragon-ridden" and a world in which men and women have, like Dame Kyteler's peacocks, sacrificed their eyes, their capacity to "see" the violence that all have produced, to historical certainty. For the cycle to break—for 1919 to not be read as simply another "glorious year"—history, in the fluctuating world of a colony becoming a nation, must be viewed anew.

As with "Nineteen Hundred and Nineteen," "Meditations in Time of Civil War," a sequence of poems that Yeats composed while residing in his restored stone tower during the summer and autumn of 1922, may be productively studied in light of nationalist discourse, particularly in light of Republican and Free State appeals to Ireland's noble past during the Anglo-Irish Treaty debates and ensuing Civil War.[41] Not surprisingly, both groups adopted the rhetoric of pre-independence nationalism, though with different ends in mind. While Free State supporters tended to promote the treaty as the climactic moment in a centuries-old struggle, an ultimate validation of the heroic actions undertaken by previous generations, Republicans characterized it as a fundamental betrayal, "a surrender," according to Republican leader De Valera, "of the ideals for which the sacrifices of the past few years were deliberately made and the sufferings of these years consciously endured."[42] Following the Republican seizure of the Four Courts government buildings in Dublin, the act that precipitated the Civil War, De Valera issued an "Easter Proclamation," a revolutionary declaration designed to construct a clear historical trajectory extending from 1916, through the current "uprising," and toward the imagined future Republic, "the destiny God has in mind for Ireland the fair, the peerless one. You are the artificers of that destiny. Yours is the faith that moves mountains, the faith that confounds misgivings. Yours is the faith and love that begot the enterprise of 1916. Young men and young women of Ireland, the goal is at last in sight—steady, all together forward. Ireland is yours for the taking. Take it."[43] The Free State responded in kind:

> For forty-eight hours the soldiers of your army have unflinchingly borne the brunt of battle against the forces of anarchy in your capital. Some of them have given their lives, and many others have been wounded in the defence of your rights as citizens. You are faced with a conspiracy whose calculated end is to destroy the Treaty signed by your representatives and endorsed by yourselves. Under that Treaty the government and control of your own country and its resources have been surrendered back to you after centuries of usurpation. You are asked to reject this surrender and engage in a hopeless and unnecessary war with Great Britain. The people in the Four Courts say they are fighting for a Republic. In reality they are fighting to bring the British back.[44]

Here the weight of history is brought to the fore, though the emphasis is on a specific historical narrative. Although the word "surrender" refers grammatically to the governmental control and resources that will be restored to Ireland, the term, on a rhetorical level, carries broader connotations, as if this compromise amounts to military surrender on the part of the British. In this respect, the Free State's pronouncement implicitly characterizes the settlement as a military "victory," thereby positioning it within a nationalist tradition of armed resistance, heroic sacrifice, and martyrdom as opposed to a more moderate tradition of constitutional nationalism. Accused by Republicans of securing merely a "political" triumph akin to the supposed triumph of the 1914 Government of Ireland Act, this Free State pronouncement places the Anglo-Irish Treaty within history as the end for which previous generations and those engaged in the current battle "have given their lives." To reject the treaty would amount to an invalidation of those sacrifices and a return to a "hopeless" war against the British, a curious twist of logic given that the British had apparently "surrendered."

Written in the whirlpool of violence that followed the treaty split, Yeats's "Meditations in Time of Civil War" can be viewed as engaging with and responding to these competing narratives of an Irish present and past. Again, though, it is important to recognize the fundamental instability of these ideologically driven narratives. As both Fanon and Bhabha emphasize, the articulation of a new national history along a progressive linear axis necessarily remains an ongoing and essentially temporal process. Throughout that process fissures are constantly erupting as the national "intellectual" is called to graft the amorphous, uncertain, and chaotic present of which he or she is a participant onto nationalism's more stable master narratives. This, explains Bhabha, is the central difficulty facing those who would write the history of a people: "The present of the people's history, then, is a practice that destroys the constant principles of the national culture that attempt to hark back to a 'true' national past, which is often represented in the reified forms of realism and stereotype. Such pedagogical knowledges and continuist national narratives miss [in the words of Fanon] the 'zone of occult instability where the people dwell.'"[45]

Like other public figures struggling to articulate a unified, stabilizing vision of a new Irish nation during the profound instability of the Civil War, Yeats, as his critics have suggested, did much to promulgate a brand of nationalism intent upon "hark[ing] back to a 'true' national past," a desirably pre-modern Ireland set against a present driven by self-interest and hatred. In "Meditations in Time of Civil War," however, we find a more complicated engagement with nationalism. Writing in the "zone of occult instability" that was the Civil War, Yeats attempts to construct a space in which a new vision of Ireland might emerge and in which the deeds of the present—Irish turned against Irish, violence now bereft of the underpinning sanction of imperial resistance—cannot and must not be contained by or reconciled with what had been sustaining nationalist narratives. As with other more recent postcolonial writers who focus on time, Yeats questions stable narratives of and from the past that can be controlled by any one nationalist (or imperialist) agenda; emphasizes violence as rupture, moments to be understood, not as the culmination of a series of past events, but as profoundly engendering the unknowable (or for Yeats partially knowable) future; and, most important, confronts his reader with the senseless violence of the living present.

Yeats opens "Ancestral Houses" by positing a split between a supposedly culturally unified Ireland in the past and a fundamentally debased Ireland in the present, but the tone of this section, as with the opening of "Nineteen Hundred and Nineteen," is one of uncertainty, less a call for a return and more a meditation upon the viability of deploying narratives derived from that past as a means for comprehending the present. Here, unlike the remaining poems, the focus of historiographic desire is initially not a nationalist past but a distinctly Anglo-Irish past in which cultural unity, "The sweetness that all longed for night and day"—a phrase out of Matthew Arnold—emerges ironically from "violence" and "bitterness" (*VP*, 418). Yeats wrote in 1910 that "all noble things [including "great nations and classes"] are the result of warfare" (*EI*, 321), but in the present of 1922, a present saturated with violence, that possibility seems foreclosed from the start, the product of an utterly naïve idealism. The age of noble ancestral homes has ended. The "abounding glittering jet," a symbol of the "self-delight[ing]," creative spirit of that age, has dried up, leaving only "some marvellous empty sea-shell / . . . which / Shadows the inherited glory of the rich." In every home once occupied by an important person resides "the great-grandson of that house" who, for all the "bronze and marble" of his surroundings, is "but a mouse," a useless creature living among halls constructed by men long since dead. The "levelled lawns and gravelled ways," physical reminders of individuals who tamed their natural surroundings, remain merely for "slippered Contemplation," emblems of a society now devoid of both greatness and bitterness.

With violence on all sides, why has not the spirit of Ireland's Anglo-Irish past reawakened? A letter written in October 1922 from Yeats to Olivia Shakespear holds one possible clue:

> I spent the summer correcting proofs and writing a series of poems called "Meditations in time of civil war" which I shall send to the *Mercury*. . . . The situation here is very curious—a revolt against democracy by a small section. . . . I have met some of the ministers who more and more seem too sober to meet the wildness of these enemies; and everywhere one notices a drift towards Conservatism, perhaps towards Autocracy. I always knew that it would come, but not that it would come in this tragic way. . . . Perhaps there is nothing so dangerous to a modern state, when politics take the place of theology, as a bunch of martyrs. A bunch of martyrs (1916) were the bomb and we are living in the explosion. (*L*, 689–690)

This is Yeats the privately outspoken Free State supporter (he was less so in public and when addressing his more Republican-leaning friends such as Lady Gregory), but his words provide an important local context for reading "Ancestral Houses." The current Free State leaders of Ireland, unlike their mythical predecessors of "a haughtier age," are "too sober to meet the wildness of these enemies." At the same time, what Yeats goes on to emphasize is not the cowardice of such individuals but the very pervasiveness of violence, the seemingly inevitable slide toward "Autocracy" in an Ireland where political agendas, on both sides, are advanced with religious fervor, an Ireland "living in the explosion" of revolution.[46]

This contrast between past and present, between a past in which violence leads to greatness and a present in which violence yields only further violence, is evident in the opening stanza. The spirit of Ascendancy Ireland is characterized as a jet of water that "rains down life," choosing "whatever shape it wills / And never stoop[ing] to a mechanical / Or servile shape, at others' beck and call." In an Ireland gripped by the Civil War, those who embrace violence and bitterness certainly do so in a "mechanical" manner, obeying the "beck and call" of their Republican leaders with the blind zeal of martyrs. But an awareness of the gap between past and present on the part of the poet offers little comfort, only the knowledge, as the poem's closing lines suggest, that Anglo-Ireland's noble past cannot be recreated in the present: "What if those things the greatest of mankind / Consider most to magnify, or to bless, / But take our greatness with our bitterness?"

Marjorie Howes, in discussing the link between greatness and bitterness/violence in the previous stanza, suggests that the verb "take" in the phrase "But take our greatness with our violence" holds two possible connotations: *take away* and *take on*.[47] The same holds true for the closing stanza, though here the focus is very much historiographic desire. Those who would "magnify" or "bless" the outward trappings of Ascendancy Ireland and would retreat from the ever-encroaching chaos of the present into "great chambers and long galleries, lined / With famous portraits of our ancestors," *take away* greatness with bitterness. "Pacing to and fro on polished floors," they remain caught in comfortable, impotent nostalgia, failing, like the leaders of contemporary Ireland, to take decisive action in the present. Those who perceive the necessary link between violence and greatness and who comprehend fully the root of Anglo-Irish greatness are faced with the awareness that the past contained within itself the seeds of its own demise. A world built from bitterness and violence has regressed into violence, the past has again yielded its ironic harvest, and the speaker is left to confront a present in which the choice to *take on* further violence will merely perpetuate the cycle.

In the second poem, "My House," Yeats turns to the old tower itself, a hybrid image—derived in typical Yeats fashion from British literary culture ("*Il Penseroso*'s Platonist toiled on / In some like chamber") and Irish local culture[48]—that might serve as a physical reminder of some preexisting unity, a period in Yeats's own past when a strategic blending of imperial literary tradition and colonial folk tradition provided the basis for a vibrant cultural nationalism. Struggling against the ever impinging real, Yeats opens each of the first two stanzas by detailing the physical characteristics of his tower, "A winding stair, a chamber arched with stone, / A grey stone fireplace with an open hearth," as if to rebuild it in art, to create a monument linking past and present. Yet the "wall is loosening." The tower is crumbling, the Civil War is at hand, and, as Yeats writes in a letter from 1922, "One wonders what prominent man will live through it. One meets a minister at dinner, passing his armed guard on the doorstep, and one feels no certainty that one will meet him again. We are entering on the final and most dreadful stage" (*L*, 690).

Evidence of that final stage is what Yeats finds as he gazes from the tower. Here again the emphasis is self-consciously upon historiographic desire, the drive to graft an unstable present upon a more stable past, and the regressive practical effects of attempting to do so. This accounts in part for the oddly "dated" reference in the first stanza to the surrounding "acre of stony ground / Where the symbolic rose can break in flower." Drawing upon a symbol from his earliest phase of cultural nationalism, Yeats aligns his own personal "literary" history with that of the nation. Just as the nineteenth-century nationalism of Thomas Davis had sought to find deeds in the past, which, correctly "magnified" and "blessed," would serve to energize a popular front in the present, Yeats in poems such as "To Ireland in the Coming Times" had adopted the rose as a symbol of, among other things, a once and future Ireland, a symbol designed to evoke the essence of an Irish state always poised to be again. Indeed, the symbolic rose had and continued to serve as a standard trope in more directly political nationalist art, the red rose of Ireland blooming from ground soaked by the blood of martyrs. Thus proclaimed Joseph Plunkett in "The Little Black Rose Shall Be Red At Last," a poem written on the night before his execution in 1916: "Praise God if this my blood fulfills the doom / When you, dark rose, shall redden into bloom."[49] In "The Rose Tree," published in 1920, Yeats imagines Patrick Pearse expressing the identical sentiment: "There's nothing but our own red blood / Can make a right Rose Tree."

In "Meditations" this tradition of martyrdom is evoked, the "Old ragged elms" and "old thorns innumerable" suggestive of Christ-like sacrifice, but the repetition of the word "old" and the use of the term "innumerable" indicate a fundamental need to question that tradition in which violent death has led to a sterile cycle of further violence, the barren landscape of "stony ground" littered with thorns a fitting metaphor for Ireland in the grip of the Civil War and nationalist fervor. The rose too functions quite differently, as Yeats now draws our attention not to what might be evoked but to the very process of evocation, not to what might be signified but to the "artificial" operation of the signifier—the rose marked as the "symbolic" rose, the rose of sacrifice become tired cliché.[50] The ambiguous verb "break"—suggesting both the difficult birth of a rose and the destruction of a flower already in bloom—highlights the gap between past and present. Those who would assert the will, in this case the poetic will, are called to embrace violence, the repetition of an "act of founding" that, writes Marjorie Howes, "does not institute a self-sustaining genealogy" but only further blood sacrifice, while those who are cognizant of the ironic return of the past are left to confront a present in which the rose of independence has given way to the thorns of war, the flowering of a new Ireland broken in blossom.[51]

Yeats gazes from his tower, hearing, in a line that echoes "A Prayer for My Daughter," the "sound / Of every wind that blows," and seeing a "stilted water-hen / Crossing stream again / Scared by the splashing of a dozen cows." Like the water-hen disturbed by a herd of cows, the solitary "stilted" artist—the word "stilted" perhaps indicative of his own sense of disconnection from those taking direct action—is left behind in the wake of change, searching tirelessly for some clear evidence of purposeful bitterness, a mode of representing the present in history that moves beyond the cycle of blood sacrifice and that might sustain future generations, "Befitting emblems of adversity" hammered into history that "My bodily heirs may find, / To exalt a lonely mind."

Upon Yeats's table rests one such emblem, "Sato's gift, a changeless sword." At once an art object and an instrument of war, the sword represents an Eastern past identical to the previously envisioned Anglo-Irish past in which greatness is born from violence and bitterness, "a changeless work of art" produced by an individual who possessed "an aching heart." The sword, one of many "marvellous accomplishment[s]" passed "From father unto son," sparks a renewed desire for historical continuity, but such hopes are quickly dashed: "it seemed / Juno's peacock screamed." In the 1925 version of *A Vision*, the scream of Juno's peacock is linked with the full expansion of the primary gyre and the inevitable slide of civilization as a whole, signaled by the abandonment of individual thought, toward mob rule: "The loss of control over thought comes towards the end; first a sinking in upon the moral being, then the last surrender, the irrational cry, revelation, the scream of Juno's peacock" (*V1*, 180).[52]

Although Yeats's esoteric claims are, in *A Vision*, applicable not simply to the history of Ireland but also to history in general, the stanza that follows in "Meditations" immediately shifts the focus to a more local Irish context:

Life scarce can cast a fragrance on the wind,
Scarce spread a glory to the morning beams,
But the torn petals strew the garden plot;
And there's but common greenness after that.

We are again in the garden of the Big House, a garden littered with "torn petals," confirmation that the rose of Ireland has indeed been broken. The closing image suggests a potential and ironic connection with "Easter, 1916," in which the heroes of revolution, "Now and in time to be, / Wherever green is worn, / Are changed, changed utterly." Though by no means devoid of irony itself, "Easter, 1916" presents violent historical change as a "terrible beauty," the flowering of independence from the graves of martyrs. Here, in contrast, we have violence without growth, a landscape in which an image of temporal progression, dawn, gives way to "common greenness."[53]

In section five, "The Road at My Door," Yeats, for the first time in the poem, meditates directly upon the Civil War itself:

> An affable Irregular,
> A heavily-built Falstaffian man,
> Comes cracking jokes of civil war
> As though to die by gunshot were
> The finest play under the sun.

Here, Yeats ironically evokes a British theatrical tradition in order to indict a Republican ideological project built upon nationalist dramatic representations of the noble, self-sacrificing Irish warrior. The reference to Falstaff evokes the braggart soldier, Shakespeare's comic antihero, yet the tone falls somewhat short of outright condemnation, expressing rather a curious mixture of tragedy and farce. In a letter from December 1922, Yeats adopts the same tone to describe the burning of a friend's home: "I have just heard that when Mrs. Campbell's house was burnt . . . she appealed to the irregulars not to turn her children out in the night. The irregulars cried but said they could not help themselves, the new orders. Presently one of them went up stairs with Mrs. Campbell to fetch down—the house was I think already burning—the children's Xmas toys" (L, 695). In each case, the Irregular—a figure who might easily have been depicted as the stereotypical embodiment of heartless cruelty, the callous burner of homes—is rendered with surprising sympathy, less a political dissident to be executed by the Free State government and more a deluded follower.

The true focal point of the stanza is thus representation itself, the capacity of nationalist rhetoric to render violence as heroic, killing as fulfillment of a cause, death as noble sacrifice, duty as blindly following "the new orders." By characterizing the Irregular as "Falstaffian," Yeats does more than simply indict the soldier for indifferent cruelty, "cracking jokes of civil war," and implied cowardice, another Falstaff, another British-type soldier come, like the Black and Tans, to swagger about after destroying homes. Rather, the characterization points to Falstaff's primary flaw, his ability to exploit those inexperienced soldiers for whom war has been represented as glorious and to the Irregular's own tragic belief that "to die by gunshot were / The finest play under the sun." By emphasizing the theatrical, Yeats roots the tragic-comic return of violence in a supposedly "liberated" Ireland precisely in a nationalist Republican project that would represent war as heroic theater.

In the same December 1922 letter, Yeats touches upon this theme when he continues, "Strange tragedy of thought that creates for such men such crimes but I don't suppose that these men were conscripted rebels" (*L*, 695). The men who burned his neighbor's house were not conscripted, but they were fired by the same passion that fuels Yeats's "affable Irregular," the same passion that fueled Plunkett to write "The Little Black Rose," the same passion that fueled, to take an example from nationalist drama, Patrick Pearse's revolutionary hero in his play *The Singer*: "One man can free a people as one Man redeemed the world. I will take no pike, I will go into battle with bare hands. I will stand up before the Gall as Christ hung naked before men on a tree!"[54] The call to suffer and die for the cause of Ireland, for each individual to become a Christ, had produced revolution, but in the transitional moment of the Civil War, Yeats challenges his readers to reconsider that narrative and to imagine an Ireland in which such calls are recognized as simply words designed to perpetuate bloodshed.

Yeats turns, in order "To silence the envy in my thought," from this world of violence toward the solitude of his tower. The poet's envy is directed at a "moor-hen" who "guides" her chicks "upon the stream," an image of natural harmony set in contrast to Ireland's self-destructive present and, ironically, toward the soldiers themselves, men capable of action because, unlike the contemplative Yeats, they remain happily and dangerously true to nationalism's progressive myths. For Yeats, "caught / In the cold snows of a dream"—the verb "caught" and the adjective "cold" indicative of a mind forced to fully confront violence simply as violence—such comfort is impossible. The tower has become a prison: "the key is turned / On our uncertainty." Violence reigns on all sides, "somewhere / A man is killed, or a house burned," but this is violence without meaning, devoid of history's structuring myths: "no clear fact [can] be discerned." Indeed, the seemingly optimistic plea for "honey-bees" to "Come build in the empty house of the stare" merely highlights the divide between the natural world, where decay and death give way to growth and rebirth, and Ireland's "empty" present, where Yeats is forced to bear witness to the surrounding violence: "Last night they trundled down the road / That dead young soldier in his blood."

John Unterecker suggests that Yeats is referring here to a soldier who "had actually been dragged . . . down a nearby road, his body so battered that his mother could recover only his torn disembodied head."[55] Yeats does mention such an incident, complete with the gruesome detail of the head, in an October 1922 letter to J. C. Grierson,[56] but there Yeats is describing earlier Black and Tan violence. A more plausible reference is the death of a "National soldier" described in a letter to T. Sturge Moore written while Yeats was working on the "series of poems about this Tower and on the civil war," which would become "Meditations": "A motor has just passed with a National soldier and a coffin up on end and what I suppose were the relatives of the dead man" (*LSM*, 46). In either case, what is important to note is the absence of agency in the poem itself, the refusal to identify the soldier's affiliation and thus the affiliation of his killers. For Yeats, tempting as it may be, this moment must not be made into another tale of heroic martyrdom readily inscribed onto a Republican narrative designed to further revolutionary bloodshed or onto a Free State narrative designed to justify violent reprisals. Rather, this is meaningless violence served to a people who, including the poet, "had fed the heart on fantasies." To represent this death as part of a broader fantasy of heroic sacrifice would be to contribute even more to a current state in which "The heart's grown brutal from the fare; / More substance in our enmities / Than in our love."

"Meditations in Time of Civil War" concludes with images of chaos and violence that abruptly shift the setting from Civil War Ireland to eighteenth-century France, as cries now resound calling "For vengeance on the murderers of Jacques Molay." Generally regarded as an emblem of the coming apocalypse that Yeats dramatized in "The Second Coming," outlined in *A Vision*, and saw proof of in world events such as the Bolshevik Revolution, few critics, with the notable exception of Elizabeth Cullingford,[57] have analyzed this section at any length in light of the local Irish context. A Grand Master of the Knights Templar, Jacques de Molay was executed, with the tacit approval of Pope Clement V, by Philip the Fair of France in 1314. During the eighteenth century, French Freemasons, at odds with both the Catholic Church and the monarchy, symbolically linked their ancestral founder, Hiram Abif, executed for refusing to divulge the society's secrets, with Molay. From the perspective of anti-Masonic French historians, the desire of Freemasons to avenge the death of Molay helped to fuel the anti-monarchy and anti-Church sentiments of the French Revolutionaries, the "class-hatred" that Yeats cryptically refers to in his note on Molay in "Meditations."[58] Within the poem itself, the drive to avenge a supposedly clear political wrong is rendered as anything but clear, a whirlwind of violence:

> The rage-driven, rage-tormented, and rage-hungry troop,
> Trooper belabouring trooper, biting at arm or at face,
> Plunges towards nothing, arms and fingers spreading wide,
> For the embrace of nothing.

According to Cullingford, this concluding section, which seems to move us beyond the local Irish context, is in fact a fitting commentary on the Civil War: "What began as the struggle to avenge a genuine wrong, and to gain Ireland's independence from England, has degenerated into fratricidal strife."[59]

To this perceptive analysis I will simply add that the stanza is not concerned merely with violence born from "revenge" but with the core ideological component driving the compulsion for revenge in Civil War Ireland: nationalist historiographic constructions of martyrdom. According to Yeats, "A cry for vengeance because of the murder of the Grand Master of the Templars seems to me [a] fit symbol for those who labour from hatred, and so for sterility in various kinds" (*VP*, 827). Vengeance for Molay is a "fit symbol," but it is so because Molay has himself been appropriated symbolically within Masonic historiography as an emblem of all who have given their lives to combat the influences of secular and religious tyranny, the foundational martyr whose death, so to speak, pre-sanctions subsequent extremism and unchecked violence. If, as I have suggested, "Meditations in Time of Civil War" functions to disrupt precisely those same types of constructions in Republican and Free State discourse, narratives spawned during a colonial period to counterbalance imperial historiography and the tyranny it would legitimate, these "Monstrous familiar images [that] swim to the mind's eye" are more than fitting, more than "familiar." They provide a complementary tale of chaotic violence and hatred in a present that has seemingly remained locked in the past, a tale that comments directly upon a transitional Ireland ceaselessly replicating the initial wrong perpetrated by imperialism during colonization, a physically liberated Ireland struggling to become a truly postcolonial Ireland.

FOUR

Discovering a "New Vintage," a New Vantage

The Tower and Imagined Exile

Told him the shortest way to Tara was via *Holyhead.*

—Stephen Dedalus, in *A Portrait of the Artist as a Young Man*

If you . . . were born in a small Italian principality in the Middle Ages . . . you would be in exile with a price on your head.

—J. F. Taylor to W. B. Yeats, *Autobiographies*

This is an indescribably lovely place—some little Greek town one imagines. . . . Here I shall put off the bitterness of Irish quarrels, and write my most amiable verses.

—W. B. Yeats, Letter to Augusta Gregory

Yeats never did quite manage to "put off the bitterness of Irish quarrels," though the Nobel Prize-winning artist and former Irish senator who wrote these words in 1928 from "some little Greek town" certainly had good reason for wishing to do so. During the previous nine years, Yeats had borne witness to the bloodshed of the Anglo-Irish War, a sharp contrast to the romantic struggle he had once imagined, and to the ironic return of violence in the Civil War. While serving as a senator in the Irish Free State from 1922 to 1928, he also watched in dismay as the new government, with his vociferous opposition, enacted a host of conservative measures, ranging from the censorship of film and literature to a standing order effectively banning divorce, designed to appeal to Ireland's Catholic majority. Thus, while Yeats's literary reputation and political influence had never been stronger, we find in his private letters from this period repeated references to "bitterness" and a longing, rarely apparent in his early writings, to be done with Ireland entirely. "I feel now that all may be blood and misery. If that comes," he wrote to Olivia Shakespear in 1921, "we may abandon Ballylee to the owls and the rats, and England too (where passions will rise and I shall find myself with no answer), and live in some far land" (L, 675). He frequently traveled to the Continent during these years, stating on one occasion: "I say goodbye sadly . . . but I shall have the mountains of Rapallo in exchange. It will be a delight to get there for quiet winters — here all is storm" (L, 743). And, just after the publication of The Tower: "Once out of Irish bitterness I can find some measure of sweetness and of light, as befits old age — already new poems are floating in my head, bird songs of an old man, joy in the passing moment, emotion without the bitterness of memory" (L, 737).

Although these expressions of both frustration and a desire to depart from the land of his birth are consistent with the sentiments voiced by a host of other Irish writers who embraced exile as a means to artistic and political freedom,[1] critics have rarely addressed exile as a theme or issue in Yeats's writing.[2] Whereas earlier scholars celebrated a high modernist Yeats whose verse engages with universal themes that transcend local Irish politics,[3] postcolonial scholars, in keeping with Frantz Fanon's two-step model of decolonization, present a Yeats who, in every sense of the phrase, remained behind. When he appears in larger discussions of Irish literature and exile, Yeats frequently plays a bit part as the hopelessly romantic nationalist[4] or the aloof modernist, representing, in either case, the colonial-cum-postrevolution intellectual and artist who fails to move beyond Fanon's regressive "national consciousness." Thus, Richard Kearney, after outlining Yeats's repeated attempts to integrate Ireland's rapidly shifting present into a larger mythic structure, turns with approval to Samuel Beckett and other Irish "cosmopolitan exiles" who "possessed no motherland" and "refused to drop through the escape-hatch of myth."[5] Matthew J. Lamberti repeats these assumptions, labeling Yeats "a starting point" distinct from those Irish modernists in exile who sought "alternative responses to the colonial situation" that did not "replicate the nationalist systems they hope[d] to undermine. . . . Whereas Yeats positions his literary movement specifically within the Irish land and race, Joyce positions his in flight, in the name of Dedalus — a literary exile which allows him to view Ireland as a sort of cultural tourist."[6]

James Joyce clearly does not exhibit the mindset of the nationalist in exile who, according to Andrew Gurr, constructs a "static" and idealized vision of his or her homeland,[7] nor does his work bear any resemblance to the discourses of imperial travel writing. The phrase "cultural tourist," however, indirectly reminds us that exile is more than simply a geographic move, that embracing physical departure does not necessarily amount to adopting an alternative or progressive cosmopolitan consciousness. The obverse is also true. The artist who remains behind is not necessarily doomed to adopt or perpetuate a regressive national consciousness. In this sense, exile represents an epistemological stance available both to those who depart and to those who do not,[8] the assumption of a metaphorically external vantage from which the artist might call into question the hegemonic drive of postcolonial nationalism without abandoning a commitment to the difficult process of nation-building. This is a particularly useful perspective for considering the Yeats of the 1920s who addressed issues ranging from the role of the judiciary in the new government, to coinage and "compulsory" Gaelic, to the education of children—a Yeats who continually adopts the mask of the outsider, casts a skeptical eye on the conventional discourses of nationalism, yet remains deeply invested in Ireland's struggle to define itself as an independent nation.

This Yeats who expresses a desire for departure and a simultaneous commitment to reengagement represents, I want to suggest, an example of those nationalist and postcolonial artists who exhibit "the consciousness of exile" but do not depart, those writers for whom exile remains a viable option only in the realm of the imagination—a type of "intellectual exile."[9] As Seamus Heaney muses at the close of "Singing School,"

> I am neither internee nor informer;
> An inner émigré, grown long-haired
> And thoughtful; a wood-kerne
>
> Escaped from the massacre,
> Taking protective colouring
> From bole and bark, feeling
> Every wind that blows.[10]

For Heaney and other "inner émigrés"—a group that, Chelva Kanaganayakam notes, includes Sri Lanka's Jean Arasanayagam, Maori authors in New Zealand, and Aboriginal writers in Australia—exile does not mean a celebration of cosmopolitan "placelessness."[11] Rather, "Exile for the intellectual in this metaphysical sense," as Edward Said states, "is restlessness, movement, constantly being unsettled, and unsettling others,"[12] an intellectual and imaginative shift in perspective that enables the artist to critique the failures of nationalism while struggling to fulfill the ultimate goal of nationalist decolonization, what Fanon describes as "the all-embracing crystallization of the innermost hopes of the whole people."[13]

Placing Yeats among this tradition of "imagined exiles," artists who gaze with suspicion upon nationalism as a cultural and political program without abandoning a fundamental commitment to the process of nation-building, helps to bring to light a key shortcoming evident in the standard, Fanon-based approaches. While many postcolonial Irish critics have been suspicious of all forms of nationalism, an understandable stance given the lingering effects of nationalism in contemporary Ireland,[14] Fanon himself does not dismiss it entirely. His critique emerges within the specific contexts of the Algerian struggle for independence, and he is careful to distinguish between the "bourgeois nationalism" of native elites and a type of broad-based, popular, and international nationalism that Neil Lazarus, drawing upon the work of Anouar Abdel-Malek, terms "nationalitarianism."[15] While the former, as Lazarus neatly summarizes, served "the interests of the elite indigenous classes, and was aimed at the (re)attainment of nationhood through means of the capture and subsequent appropriation of the colonial state," the latter, advanced by Fanon's own Front de Libération Nationale party, represents a form of "national consciousness that does not merely mobilise 'the people' but actively registers and articulates their aspirations."[16] Yeats's relationship with nationalism must similarly be understood within the contexts of postwar Ireland. Although his rejection of bourgeois Irish nationalism was motivated in part by class hatred, and although he was, at times, guilty of dismissing one form of regressive nationalism only to replace it with another, both his critique of the Free State and his desire for communal unity are closer to Fanon's nationalitarian position than critics have allowed or even considered.

What is striking about Yeats's public remarks from this period is that he consistently focuses upon the nationalist ideological compulsion underpinning Free State conservatism. While quick to adopt the pose of the aristocrat—and Yeats, as Elizabeth Cullingford has shown, was certainly conscious of adopting that pose, especially during the divorce debates—his objections center on the Free State's attempt to impose hegemonic rule upon a diverse population by appealing to prior, nativist conceptions of Irish identity.[17] Just as Fanon rejects the bourgeois leader who "asks the people to fall back into the past and to become drunk on the remembrance of the epoch which led up to independence,"[18] Yeats begins his Senate career by announcing: "The past is dead not only for us but for this country. . . . I suggest we are assembled here no longer in a Nationalist or Unionist sense, but merely as members of the Seanad" (*SS*, 18). Similarly, his objection to the Censorship of Publications Bill (1928) centers not on the drive to foster communal unity but on the provincial belief that Irish culture, by banning English newspapers and other works that might "excite the imagination," "would return" to some prior state of "innocence" (*SS*, 167). Playing the role of the outsider, he cautions, in an early Senate speech, against reviving "the old form of wild, wasteful historic idealism" (*SS*, 33), and, in a version of his "Divorce Speech" (1925) delivered to George Russell, then editor of the *Irish Statesman,* he calls upon the Free State to recognize the shortcomings of thoughtlessly perpetuating a political and cultural agenda spawned during a period of armed conflict: "For the last hundred years Irish Nationalism has had to fight against England, and that fight has helped Fanaticism, for we had to welcome everything that gave Ireland emotional energy, and had little use for intelligence so far as the mass of the people were concerned, for we had to hurl them against an alien power. The basis of Irish nationalism has now shifted, and much that once helped us is now injurious, for we can no longer do anything by fighting" (*SS,* 149).

Yeats's political thought from this specific period can be described as nationalitarian and not simply, in the manner of Cullingford, as "liberal,"[19] in that he rejected the imposition of an exclusively nationalist agenda from above without dismissing the ultimate goal of nationalism—the creation of a new, viable, independent community. Building upon his earlier conception of cultural nationalism, he perceived the government's role to be the transformation of individual consciousness into communal consciousness "by creating a system of culture which will represent the whole of this country and which will draw the imagination of the young towards it" (*SS,* 76). Where Fanon advocates a political program that tries "relentlessly and passionately, to teach the masses that everything depends on them; that if we stagnate it is their responsibility, and that if we go forward it is due to them,"[20] Yeats, when arguing for the adoption of new Irish, as opposed to traditional British, judicial robes, explains: "We all want the people to realise that the law is now their own creation, their own instrument, and any external change which marks that fact will in some degree . . . help the people to understand that the judges are their own judges and not judges imposed upon them from without" (*SS,* 116–117).[21] Just as Fanon argues that to "educate the masses politically is to make the totality of the nation a reality to each citizen,"[22] Yeats, when talking about the education of children, argues that Ireland should adopt a holistic approach, concentrating upon the child's immediate surroundings: "The tendency of the most modern education . . . is to begin geography with your native fields, arithmetic by counting the school chairs and measuring the walls, history with local monuments, religion with the local saints, and then to pass on from that to the nation itself. . . . That which the child sees—the school—the district—and to a lesser degree the nation—is like the living body. . . . If your education therefore is efficient in the modern sense, it will be more national than the dreams of politicians" (*SS,* 158–159).

My goal in introducing the concept of imagined exile and in highlighting Fanon's distinction between bourgeois nationalism and nationalitarianism as they apply to Yeats is not to offer a new defense of the poet's politics during the

1920s. Rather, my aim is simply to establish an alternative theoretical context for reading *The Tower*, a collection that Yeats's postcolonial critics have, often only in passing, discussed in terms of its nostalgia for an imagined (colonial) Irish past and that more traditional critics generally examine in terms of its broader modernist themes: the sterile, fragmented nature of modern life, the slide of civilization toward violence, old age and the decay of the body, the pangs of memory, and the longing for order and meaning in art. In this chapter, I will argue that *The Tower* charts a cycle of imaginative disengagement followed by reengagement, through which Yeats gains perspective on Ireland's unfolding present. Far from a move designed to escape from the violence and intolerance of the present, Yeats in *The Tower* attempts to reimagine Ireland's recent past as personal narrative in order to repossess it, "to build a future" for himself and the nation upon "the past without returning to it."[23] In short, the journey enacted in *The Tower* is one of imagined exile, of the poet attempting to move outside of a regressive national consciousness that had come to dominate Ireland in the 1920s in order to create a space of isolation from which the recent past may be meditated upon and new forms of communal unity, always presented in his verse as possibilities rather than certainties, might be envisioned.

Many of the poems, particularly the early poems, provide a sustained critique of bourgeois nationalism—which Yeats equates with complacency, blind idealism, an unwillingness to question the traditions of the past, and the desire to impose unity upon a heterogeneous population in the name of an essential, Catholic Ireland—as he struggles (at times, but only at times, in a reactionary manner) to discover an alternative foundation upon which to build a new, unified Ireland. The middle poems, most important "Among School Children," exhibit a nationalitarian impulse, as Yeats articulates in art a self-consciously idealized vision of the state, at once diverse and united, where communal consciousness emerges organically as, in a progressive sense, national consciousness. Finally, the middle and late poems, increasingly informed by Yeats's visionary system—another example of his desire to discover an alternative vantage for contemplating history unfolding—represent a move toward further detachment, the creation of a space from which the Irish nation might be contemplated, critiqued, and imagined anew.

The opening section of *The Tower*, from "Sailing to Byzantium" through "The New Faces," explores the desire for imagined exile, the need for a critically detached reexamination of Ireland's violent past and present, and the disquieting possibility of forced exile, the possibility that the aged Yeats no longer has a viable role to play in postrevolution Ireland. Underlying each of these increasingly historically engaged poems—the first four, strategically arranged in reverse order of their publication dates, taking us backward through the early years of the Free State, to the Irish Civil War, and finally to the Anglo-Irish War — is a critique of bourgeois nationalism and of Yeats's own failings as a nationalist artist.

"Sailing to Byzantium," first published in the 1927 collection *October Blast* and one year later in the journal *The Exile,* opens *The Tower* with a call for departure in the first line: "That is no country for old men" (*VP,* 407). Most critics read the poem as a meditation upon the transience of the natural and the desire for permanence in art, beginning and ending any discussion of the historical context by glossing "That" as a direct reference to Ireland.[24] Richard Finneran has questioned even this connection, suggesting that the opening stanza's images of natural fecundity run counter to the common historical readings of a "Catholic Ireland of the 1920s [that] was hardly dominated by sensuality."[25] Finneran's point about the Free State is certainly correct, but Yeats's emphasis on sensuality is explained when we read the opening stanza as a metaphoric rather than a mimetic representation. This is the liberated folk Ireland that Yeats the romantic nationalist had once imagined, a land — deliberately reminiscent of the insular, spiritual world depicted in "The Lake Isle of Innisfree," "Who Goes with Fergus?" and "The Stolen Child" — of "The young / In one another's arms," of "salmon-falls" and "mackerel-crowded seas." As such, the stanza includes a pointed critique, for, as so often occurs in *The Tower,* past dreams of the ideal nation have given way to ironic fulfillment. Physical liberation has produced a culture transfixed by change in the present, complacent with what has been achieved, and seemingly incapable of growth. Concern for future generations and a broader perspective on history unfolding, precisely what is needed during this period of transition, have been supplanted by a deadening self-absorption: "all neglect / Monuments of unaging intellect." As Yeats argues in a Senate speech from 1925, "The children, everybody will tell you, are individually intelligent and friendly, yet have so little sense of their duty to community and neighbour that if they meet an empty house in a lonely place they will smash all the windows" (*SS,* 160). The imagined, sensual Ireland evoked in the poem, once regarded as an idealized image of pre- (and post)revolution Ireland, is now exposed as an unstable foundation for building community. Modernity, in the form of revolution and civil war, has brought utter change, and, just as the speaker must reject the world of the young, so too must Yeats turn from "that sensual music."

The closing stanza of "Sailing to Byzantium" presents the antithesis of the first. The speaker imagines himself in the final lines as a timeless monument, a golden bird "set upon a golden bough" that will sing from its aloof perch "Of what is past, or passing, or to come." The desire expressed here is for a new comprehension of time and of self-willed exile. If Ireland represents self-absorption, Byzantium offers an external perspective from which past, present, and future might be reexamined. If Free State nationalism represents complacency and a return to older, restrictive notions of Irish identity, Byzantium functions as an imagined homeland where old identities might be purged.

The stanza, though, is tinged with uncertainty, expressing a not entirely comfortable state of exile. The moment of transformation is set in the future, "Once out of nature," the object that the speaker would become is presented in ambivalent terms, with the word "Or" indicating two possible metaphoric states, and the speaker in one transformed state is represented as a being entirely devoid of agency, "*set* upon a golden bough to sing / To lords and ladies of Byzantium" (emphasis added). The absence of agency is particularly important, indicating that the "triumph" achieved comes, in the words of Declan Kiberd, "at the cost of mobility and growth."[26] The desire for an external vantage might easily become a desire for complete detachment, escape an end in itself, the longed-for monument the plaything of a "drowsy Emperor." Indeed, though Yeats's conception of imperial Byzantium is markedly different from his understanding of imperial Britain, his characterization of Byzantium as a languid imperial world should give us pause. It is not that the speaker in exile would simply become a servant of imperialism; rather, this highly qualified triumph indicates that exile as a political move contains within itself the possibility for a new form of stagnation—an uncritical celebration of what George Lamming ironically terms the "pleasures of exile," the temptation for Yeats to abandon Irish bitterness altogether. The poem is placed at the opening of *The Tower* to announce the desire for exile, yet its complex final lines suggest that exile is for Yeats more a process than an end in itself. Like the souls of the dead in Yeats's mystical philosophy, the Irish artist in exile must dream back his life—he must, from the vantage of imagined exile, relive the recent past in order to imagine a new future, a new Ireland.

"The Tower" thus returns us immediately to Free State Ireland. In the first section, Yeats revisits the theme of old age, further undercutting the supposed triumph achieved at the close of "Sailing to Byzantium," while in the second section he delves into the folk past of the area surrounding Thoor Ballylee, recalling local myths and his own rendering of the character Hanrahan in the *Stories of Red Hanrahan* (1904). These folktales, though comic, provide an ironic commentary on the costs of worshiping images, which critics have highlighted as a central theme in the collection, and, I will add, on the costs of an atavistic cultural nationalism. The lines concerning Mary Hynes, a peasant woman celebrated in the verse of the early nineteenth-century Gaelic poet Anthony Raftery, focus not upon the actual beauty of this woman but upon poetic constructions of ideal beauty: "A peasant girl commended by a song" (*VP*, 410). For an audience familiar with the Young Ireland movement—when individuals such as James Clarence Mangan equated the pursuit of the female beloved with the pursuit of independence[27]—and with Yeats's own representations of the woman as nation in his early verse and drama, the tale's tragic-comic outcome resonates on the level of nationalist politics:

> And certain men, being maddened by those rhymes,
> Or else by toasting her a score of times,
> Rose from the table and declared it right
> To test their fancy by their sight;
> But they mistook the brightness of the moon
> For the prosaic light of day—
> Music had driven their wits astray—
> And one was drowned in the great bog of Cloone.

Death as the result of misapprehension, of mistaking an ideal image for reality, is a theme that Yeats, as I have previously argued, develops more fully in the war poems, where he links the perpetuation of violence with the belief that martyrdom is so much heroic theater. Indeed, "Meditations in Time of Civil War," which employs images of myopia, "the eye's complacency," to suggest destructive rage, provides an ironic recontextualization of the Hynes myth, as the pursuit of an ideal beloved's "embrace" becomes a metaphor for "senseless" violence perpetuated by Free Stater and Republican alike: "Trooper belabouring trooper, biting at arm or at face, / Plunges toward nothing, arms and fingers spreading wide / For the embrace of nothing."

The abbreviated reference to Red Hanrahan—who, as the *Stories* reveal, grew mad in old age, deluded by one of the fairy Sidhe into forsaking his earthly love, Mary Lavelle, and pursuing an ideal, and thus unobtainable, image of beauty—operates in a similar but more complex manner. The tale immediately follows Yeats's assertion that poetry itself, beginning with Homer and his depictions of Helen of Troy, is predicated upon the construction of ideal images that others pursue:

> the tragedy began
> With Homer that was a blind man,
> And Helen has all living hearts betrayed.
> O may the moon and sunlight seem
> One inextricable beam,
> For if I triumph I must make men mad.

This conception of the aloof artist who creates objects of desire that "must make men mad" is complicated by the introduction of Hanrahan, for Yeats's fictional poet is both agent and victim of his own idealism. In the original story,

Hanrahan, after writing lines celebrating Mary Lavelle in the guise of Venus, misapprehends his verse as reality. Driven by an image he has created, Hanrahan blindly seeks to embrace not Mary but Venus, not the real but the ideal. Yeats too had devoted much of his poetry to the construction of an ideal beloved, and his "imagination" had certainly "dwel[t] the most / Upon a . . . woman lost"; but the tale's placement points to a larger issue: the link between poetic triumph and delusion, the creation of an imagined object that transfixes both audience and artist. This is a serious, politically relevant concern given Yeats's self-deprecating admission in "Meditations in Time of Civil War" that he and others "had fed the heart on fantasies."

In recounting the Hanrahan story, Yeats emphasizes his own, almost sadistic control as the artist who feeds his fictional poet on fantasies, "I myself created Hanrahan / And drove him drunk or sober through the dawn," and subtly hints, with the words, "I thought it all out twenty years ago," of a new, more critically detached relationship with an earlier cultural nationalist project rooted in Irish folklore. Significantly, Yeats halts the tale at precisely the moment when Hanrahan is about to plunge recklessly into delusion, as if the story itself has taken on a life of its own, threatening, in the retelling, to overwhelm Yeats himself: "Hanrahan rose in frenzy there / And followed up those baying creatures towards — // O towards I have forgotten what — enough!" This final moment of strategic amnesia, this denial of a tragedy that has already occurred, introduces an element of anxiety over the role of the national artist that will emerge in the war poems. The danger in "The Tower" involves becoming lost in "the labyrinth of another's being," lost in the image of the beloved, but in "Nineteen Hundred and Nineteen," the danger is extended to include another, self-created labyrinth: "A man in his own secret meditation / Is lost amid the labyrinth that he has made / In art or politics."

Because memories of Ireland's folk past have only exposed the costs of worshiping an atavistic, folk Ireland created in art, Yeats, in the third section, evokes an alternative Irish past. Here the poem's immediate historical contexts fully emerge, as Yeats attempts to establish a foundation for cultural unity linking past, present, and future:

> It is time that I wrote my will;
> I choose upstanding men
>
> .   .   .   .
>
>   I declare
> They shall inherit my pride,
> The pride of people that were
> Bound neither to Cause nor to State,
> Neither to slaves that were spat on,

Nor to the tyrants that spat,
The people of Burke and of Grattan
That gave, though free to refuse—
Pride.

This passage echoes his remarks during the Senate divorce debates when he celebrates Edmund Burke, Henry Grattan, Jonathan Swift, Robert Emmet, and Charles Stewart Parnell as representatives of a Protestant tradition that, according to Yeats, has "created the most of the modern literature of this country" and "the best of its political intelligence" (*SS*, 88). As a number of scholars have correctly argued, both speech and poem are characterized by a reactionary retreat into a mythic past. Writes W. J. McCormack, "The evocation of Grattan's magnanimity, and the assumed empathy with Burke, are part of Yeats's transformation of history into symbol."[28] But how exactly does this desire to celebrate a Protestant past and to connect that past with Ireland's present and future relate to bourgeois nationalism as it manifests itself in postrevolution Ireland?

To answer that question it is helpful to examine more broad-based discussions of nationalism among postcolonial scholars. According to Sangeeta Ray, bourgeois nationalism, "as a 'derivative discourse' . . . forever straddles the quicksand of a negation of the discourse of power that is colonialism and the assertion of a new discursive order of national power in the alien image of that which it seeks to replace."[29] Yeats, who, as a Protestant outsider, had borne witness to the Irish government's drive toward Catholic hegemony and toward what R. F. Foster describes as "self-definition against Britain," both "cultural and political,"[30] was certainly aware of the pitfalls of an essentially derivative nationalist project that tirelessly seeks to define the new nation in opposition to its former colonial ruler. At the same time, his affirmation of a counter, Protestant-minority tradition merely replaces one mythic foundation, one derivative discourse, with another.[31] But Ray is referring to a deeper and more specific Manichean relationship between nationalism and imperialism whereby "nationalist thought," to quote Partha Chatterjee, "becomes the particular manifestation of a much more general problem, namely, the problem of the bourgeois-rationalist conception of knowledge, established in the post-Enlightenment period of European intellectual history, as the moral and epistemic foundation for a supposedly universal framework of thought which perpetuates . . . colonial domination."[32] Although bourgeois nationalism "asserts the autonomous identity of a national culture," it also lays claim to the status of modernity, a nation of individuals who possess the "universal" rights enjoyed by all free peoples, and in this sense bourgeois nationalism "accepts the claim to universality of this 'modern' framework of knowledge."[33]

Considered from this angle, poem and speech reveal the difficult position of the postcolonial artist who seeks to affirm the nation as both unique and modern, without fetishizing the unique—a "true," insulated Ireland—or hastily embracing the modern—an Ireland that is simply another England, another "civilized," rational, materialist nation. In the speech, Yeats attempts to achieve balance by citing a Protestant tradition—"one of the great stocks of *Europe*" (*SS*, 88, emphasis added)—that is at once distinctly Irish and broadly European. For Yeats, Protestant Ireland recognized what the Free State, in attempting to ban divorce, does not: "Among modern communities . . . men and women who are held together against their will and reason soon cease to recognize any duty to one another" (*SS*, 86). He further argues that, were the divorce prohibition to pass, Ireland would return to a stagnant past and would, in short, fail to become modern: "You are going to invite men and women in the prime of life to accept for the rest of their existence the law of the cloisters" (*SS*, 86).

Yeats's argument is, of course, highly problematic. In addition to obscuring the imperial roots of the Ascendancy, the extent to which class hierarchies worked to perpetuate colonialism, his ideal conception of this Protestant past—this past in which the modern and the unique are harmoniously balanced—clearly represents a regressive model for the new state. Indeed, this specific model illustrates, in Fanon's sense, one of the pitfalls of bourgeois nationalism, for Yeats's appeals to the modern in the face of Irish provincialism are designed to legitimate the perpetuation of old colonial hierarchies in new forms, with Protestant aristocrats such as Yeats remaining to guide the nation. The same appeal to this aristocratic past occurs in the poem, as Yeats, Ireland's national poet, chooses "upstanding men" drawn from peasant Ireland, "That climb the streams until / The fountain leap," who will inherit the "pride" of the Ascendancy, "The pride of people that were / Bound neither to Cause nor to State." The community that Yeats imagines is thus a harmonious combination of the modern (Protestant leaders) and the unique (peasant followers).

Speech and poem, however, are not identical. Whereas Ascendancy Ireland represents, in the speech, the model for a new Ireland, it represents, in the poem and in the collection, only one of many models, one stance that gives way, in the poem's close, to a need for further detachment. In addition, as Yeats turns from "pride" to "faith," we perceive a more complex engagement with the problem of modernity and Enlightenment thought not evident in the speech:

And I declare my faith:
I mock Plotinus' thought
And cry in Plato's teeth,
Death and life were not
Till man made up the whole,

Made lock, stock and barrel
Out of his bitter soul,
Aye, sun and moon and star, all,
And further add to that
That, being dead, we rise,
Dream and so create
Translunar Paradise.

Yeats's placement of this philosophical meditation in a section of the poem that begins by focusing on the creation of national community is explained when we recognize that "nationalist thinking," in Chatterjee's words, "is necessarily a struggle with an entire body of systematic knowledge [that is, post-Enlightenment rationalism]. . . . Its politics impels it to open up that framework of knowledge which presumes to dominate it, to displace that framework, to subvert its authority, to challenge its morality."[34] Here, Yeats returns to one of the foundations of Western thought, the writings of Plato and Plotinus, in order to reject the domination of that thought.

His point is not to dismiss these two philosophers themselves. Indeed, in a note to the poem he quotes Plotinus's assertion that the "soul is the author of all living things, that it has breathed the life into them all, whatever is nourished by earth and sea, all the creatures of the air, the divine stars in the sky" (*VP*, 826). Rather, Yeats is attacking the larger development of Western rationalism, belief in the finite and the immediate, a mechanical and decidedly modern view of the world, suggested by the phrase "lock, stock and barrel," that creates the world in its own image. In other words, the modern, rational human produces a modern, rational reality where life gives way to death, where notions of progress yield to war, and, in the Irish context, where nationalist dreams of returning to a precolonial, ideal nation come to naught. Yeats's mockery, his affirmation "That, being dead, we rise," is thus actually a return to Plato and Plotinus in the face of Enlightenment, post-Enlightenment, and nationalist thought.[35]

Yeats's faith in the creative power of the human soul, the potential of the soul to shape a world that is not based upon the rational, qualifies his earlier celebration of Ireland's Ascendancy past. Whereas he willed "pride" in that past to his heirs, he now wills this "faith," his belief in humanity's living power to recreate the world in new forms. This sense of openness, this willingness to think outside the rational, represents an alternative stance that counterbalances the reactionary pose adopted earlier in the poem, as Yeats now "leave[s] both faith and pride." Having worked to subvert modern rationalism, he returns to the issue of community building, comparing the soul's creation to natural creation:

As at the loophole there
The daws chatter and scream,
And drop twigs layer upon layer.
When they have mounted up,
The mother bird will rest
On their hollow top,
And so warm her wild nest.

This is a form of creation that is not mechanical. The birds instinctively build according to a pattern that has not been "learned," that has not been preordained by the rational mind. The type of creation momentarily evoked here will emerge later in the collection as a nationalitarian vision of community, a vision of the future nation that will manifest itself according to a pattern that is, paradoxically, specific but not predetermined, that is neither a retreat into the past nor an unqualified affirmation of the modern.

This vision does not materialize here, though the final stanza seems to conclude triumphantly, "Now shall I make my soul, / Compelling it to study / In a learned school," as if the journey begun in "Sailing to Byzantium" has reached its close. Yet, the war poems still loom ahead. The concrete realities of change begin to intrude, and Yeats, drawing upon an image from earlier in the poem, a swan "Float[ing] out upon a long / Last reach of glittering stream," again expresses a longing for perspective, a romantic retreat into the imagination whereby the possibility of "worse evil [to] come" momentarily

Seem[s] but the clouds of the sky
When the horizon fades
Or a bird's sleepy cry
Among the deepening shades.

"Worse evil" will come in the next two poems, as Yeats returns from imagined exile to contemplate, with the new insight of one who has temporarily achieved detachment, the violence of the Civil War and, dreaming back through time, the Anglo-Irish War.

"Meditations in Time of Civil War" and "Nineteen Hundred and Nineteen" begin that process. As I argue in chapter 3, Yeats indicts both British imperialism and Irish nationalism (Free State and Republican) for clinging to progressive notions of history. Belief in the historical right of empire has resulted in an ironic culmination, the horrors of the Great War and the Anglo-Irish War, while the discourse of Irish nationalism, the legitimation of violence through appeals to Ireland's noble past and its tradition of martyrdom, has led not to postcolonial unity but to the bloodshed of civil war. Indeed, the two poems further undercut the tenuous appeals to Ascendancy identity voiced in "The Tower." Although "Ancestral Houses," the opening poem in the sequence "Meditations in Time of Civil War," looks back with longing to a self-consciously idealized past, the chaos of the present soon overwhelms, indicating again the need for the construction of a new foundation.

The poem "Youth and Age," dated 1924, follows "The Wheel," a short work concerning the individual life cycle, and the two war poems. Writes Yeats in "Youth and Age,"

> Much did I rage when young,
> Being by the world oppressed,
> But now with flattering tongue
> It speeds the parting guest. (*VP*, 434)

Read in isolation, the poem offers a bitter commentary on Yeats's status in the early 1920s, a Nobel Prize-winning artist whose best days, according to the "flattering tongue" of popular opinion, are behind him. Read within the context of the volume, "Youth and Age" and the work that follows it, "The New Faces," revisit the theme of imagined exile, forming with "Sailing to Byzantium" a frame around "The Tower" and the war poems. As an aged "guest" in the world of the young, Yeats's position in "Youth and Age" echoes that of the speaker in "Sailing to Byzantium," who, in an early draft, laments: "All that mankind think they know, being young / Cry that my tale is told, my story sung."[36] Yet, unlike the speaker in "Sailing to Byzantium," Yeats now faces the possibility of forced, as opposed to willed, exile. Having emerged from the bloodshed of war, he presents himself in 1924 as an isolated old man who may no longer have a place in the foundational project of the Free State.

"The New Faces" builds upon this theme, as he imagines a time after the death of Lady Gregory when he will never again return to Coole Park: "Neither catalpa tree nor scented lime / Should hear my living feet" (*VP*, 435). Coole Park and Lady Gregory, both emblems of the cultural revival that Yeats had helped to found, are consigned to the past, and perhaps the poet, plagued by ill health, will soon follow.[37] Yet, in typical Yeatsian fashion, he quickly adopts a contrary stance:

> Let the new faces play what tricks they will
> In the old rooms; night can outbalance day,
> Our shadows rove the garden gravel still,
> The living seem more shadowy than they.

Now, facing the ultimate exile, death, Yeats emerges with new strength. Thoughts of departure, forced or willed, again yield a return, a reengagement with an Ireland in transition, a return, in this case, to the symbolically charged space of Coole Park. Counterbalancing the anxiety expressed in "The Tower" concerning his legacy, Yeats presents an estate, despite the presence of "new faces," infused with the spirits of its former occupants and the spirit of the revival. In one sense the poem reflects a politically conservative impulse not unlike the sentiments expressed in his divorce speech, as Yeats celebrates what he earlier terms the "inherited glory of the rich" ("Meditations in Time of Civil War"), an aristocratic Ireland set against a newly emerging Ireland of individuals "play[ing] what tricks they will." But, in another sense, the poem reflects a Yeats who is never content simply to retreat into the past and who refuses to adopt the role of "parting guest." While Ascendancy Ireland repeatedly functions for Yeats as a reactionary haven, in this poem, and throughout *The Tower*, he relentlessly seeks a new understanding of Ireland in the present. Imagined exile continually yields to reengagement.

"Leda and the Swan," "On a Picture of a Black Centaur by Edmund Dulac," and "Among School Children," placed at the center of *The Tower*, follow a slightly different pattern than the opening series of poems. Here, Yeats, with the insight of his visionary system, examines the relationship between revolutionary change and knowledge, purges his former desire to mold the new nation to the form that he, as a romantic nationalist, had once imagined, and, in the final poem, articulates a momentary nationalitarian vision of Irish cultural unity.

Written in 1923, "Leda and the Swan" draws heavily upon the ideas that Yeats developed in *A Vision*, and he used the poem—without a date—to introduce the "Dove or Swan" section where he outlines his quasi-mystical theory of historical cycles, each new cycle prefigured by an "annunciation." The poem dramatizes one such annunciation, the rape of Leda and the subsequent birth of Helen marking, according to Yeats's system, the foundation of the Greek age. Analyzed in terms of *A Vision*, "Leda and the Swan" would seem to have little to do with local Irish history or politics, a suspicion apparently confirmed by Yeats's own oft-cited note to the poem when it appeared (undated) in *The Cat and the Moon and Certain Poems* (1924). Having originally conceived of the work as a depiction of Enlightenment thought giving way to "some movement, or birth from above, preceded by some violent annunciation," Yeats writes, with characteristic finality, "My fancy began to play with Leda and the Swan for metaphor, and I began this poem; but as I wrote, bird and lady took such possession of the scene that all politics went out of it" (*VP*, 828). Despite his assurances to the contrary, his eagerness to don the mask of the Romantic artist aloof from more mundane concerns, a stance that Yeats often adopted when defending his art against charges of direct political involvement, should give us pause. So should his decision to date the poem for the first time in *The Tower*, particularly as 1923 signals the end of the Civil War and the consolidation of the Free State government.

According to Kiberd, who, unlike the majority of Yeats critics, examines the poem through the lens of postcolonial theory, the inclusion of a date "leads to the possibility of interpreting the swan as the invading English occupier and the girl as a ravished Ireland."[38] As I discuss at length in chapter 2, women frequently serve in nationalist discourse, and at times in Yeats's own writing, as symbols of the nation around which other cultural and political identities are formulated. Kiberd's argument sets the poem squarely within this overtly political nationalist tradition in which the original wrong of colonization is repeatedly represented in the form of chaste Ireland defiled by the minions of empire.[39] Cullingford has similarly called attention to the poem's historical context, suggesting that "Leda and the Swan" should be read against the backdrop of gender-charged debates regarding Irish identity during the early 1920s, when Catholic groups cited with contempt "women's immodest fashions in dress, indecent dances, [and] unwholesome theatrical performances and cinema exhibitions" in an attempt to define the Irish nation against cosmopolitan England.[40] Focusing on the version of "Leda and the Swan" that appeared in 1924 in the short-lived radical journal *To-morrow*, Cullingford argues that the poem, in its explicit depiction of rape, functions as a direct challenge to these constructions of Irish identity and to Free State censorship, a radical voice in an "ideological struggle" where "sexuality, bodies, and their representations occupy center stage."[41]

In terms of the version published in *The Tower*, we can usefully complicate the readings of Kiberd and Cullingford by seeing the poem's visionary elements as crucial to its engagement with the immediate historical contexts. Just as imagined exile in "Sailing to Byzantium" leads to a more detached reexamination of Ireland's recent wars, Yeats's visionary philosophy—another form of imagined exile, another perch from which to sing of past, present, and future—offers a new means to interrogate the foundational moment of the Free State. As Simon Gikandi notes during his analysis of Ngugi wa Thiong'o's *A Grain of Wheat* (1967), postcolonial literatures consistently return to these foundational moments, but rather than offering independence as an instant when "the meaning of the past can finally be grasped in retrospect," they reveal how "the day of independence reduces nationalist eschatology into a banal event. . . . The moment of return," Gikandi continues, thus "calls into question the narrative of deliverance itself."[42] "Leda and the Swan," in its visionary detachment from the moment of national transformation, exposes the banality of nationalist foundational narratives at a time when Free State rhetoric was characterized by calls to build a future upon a "stable" conception of the past. Eschewing the temptation to commemorate or to forget, Yeats offers an ironic and profoundly destabilizing foundational myth, one that foregrounds the uncertainty of any narrative of deliverance, as he turns his gaze upon a new Ireland about to be born.

The metaphoric birth of the Irish nation depicted in "Leda and the Swan" inverts two related tropes from romantic nationalism: the Cailleac tradition, in which the woman/nation is reborn through sexual intercourse with the rightful Irish king or through the blood of martyrs; and the Speirbhean tradition, in which the chaste woman/nation passively awaits liberation. The transformational moment is presented here as violent rape, an "indifferent" god spawning a new historical cycle. As is the case with "Meditations in Time of Civil War" and "Nineteen Hundred and Nineteen," the poem steadfastly refuses to romanticize the foundational instant, setting violence itself against the mirage of positivist historiography: "A shudder in the loins engenders there / The broken wall, the burning roof and tower / And Agamemnon dead" (*VP*, 441). The initial violent act yields not stability but further bloodshed, the death of heroes (precisely what Yeats fears in "The Tower": the "death / Of every brilliant eye") and "the burning roof and tower," an image, given the volume's title, that conjures thoughts of both Troy and Ireland.

The poem's final four lines, however, represent a complex engagement with postrevolution nationalism that extends well beyond a critique of bourgeois nationalist foundational narratives:

> Being so caught up,
> So mastered by the brute blood of the air,
> Did she put on his knowledge with his power
> Before the indifferent beak could let her drop?

According to Chatterjee, nationalist thought "simultaneously rejects and accepts the dominance, both epistemic and moral, of an alien culture."[43] If, as I have argued, the poem meditates upon the violent birth of the nation, a period during which nationalist thought comes under scrutiny, Chatterjee's comments are particularly relevant, for Leda, the woman as nation, is at once "mastered" and "caught up"—a phrase that, as a number of feminist critics have argued, suggests that Yeats projects desire upon the rape victim. Considered in these terms, the final question takes on a new salience. For, if knowledge itself is tied to both culture and power, can there be a form of national consciousness that is truly autonomous? As Chatterjee asks, "Can there be knowledge which is independent of power?"[44]

The power of the poem, both aesthetically and politically, is in the very ambivalence of all possible answers. Whether or not Leda understands what has occurred, the future has been "engendered," the Trojan War will happen— knowledge is power, but it is, paradoxically and ironically, a form of power that cannot be controlled, that is at once liberating and confining. In terms of the Irish situation, the same might be true, in fact has been true. And yet, despite the almost certainty of additional violence in the future, the question is still asked. Yeats's new visionary system, his new vantage, does not spark a retreat from the ambiguity of an Ireland in flux but a renewed engagement with that ambiguous moment. Writing on an Africa in transition, Chinua Achebe claims, "We are in a period so different from anything else that has happened that everything that is presented to us has to be looked at twice."[45] Like Achebe, Yeats too calls for a figurative double-take, a relentless dreaming back of Ireland's recent past from a new perspective that, in this case, finds only questions, not answers.

"On a Picture of a Black Centaur by Edmund Dulac" serves as a bridge between "Leda and the Swan" and "Among School Children." The opening section, addressed to the centaur, recalls the mythic violence of the previous poem, though here the "victim" of violence is the poet's own work:

> Your hooves have stamped at the black margin of the wood,
> Even where horrible green parrots call and swing.
> My works are all stamped down into the sultry mud.
> I knew that horse-play, knew it for a murderous thing. (*VP*, 442)

The images—"green parrots" and "sultry mud"—evoke a tropical setting that would hardly seem indicative of Ireland. Traces of a more local context can be discerned when we note that the poem, written in 1920, was originally placed in *Seven Poems and a Fragment* (1922) immediately after "Leda and the Swan" and directly before "Nineteen Hundred and Nineteen." The theme of violence runs through each, with the phrase "a murderous thing" picked up in the latter poem when Yeats, meditating upon the Anglo-Irish War, writes: "a drunken soldiery / Can leave the mother, murdered at her door." The word "murderous," coupled with the centaur image, also suggests, as John Unterecker insightfully notes, a passage from "Four Years: 1887–1891," the section of Yeats's *Autobiographies* composed during the Anglo-Irish War: "I thought that all art should be a Centaur finding in the popular lore its back and its strong legs. . . . One thing I did not foresee, not having the courage of my own thought: the growing murderousness of the world" (*Au*, 165–166). "Horse-play" is thus a particularly apt phrase, describing Yeats's own cultural nationalism, a vehicle of revolutionary change rooted "in the popular lore," that has, in Free State Ireland, grown dangerously intractable, a force of violence and intolerance that has "stamped down" the "works" of one who had (naively? arrogantly?) sought to control it. Like the centaur, Yeats too has become something other than he had imagined, a "half insane" mystic, a ghoulish nationalist who has searched among the dead, among the past, for "old mummy wheat" that he thought would provide cultural sustenance for the new nation:

> yet I, being driven half insane,
> Because of some green wing, gathered old mummy wheat
> In the mad abstract dark and ground it grain by grain
> And after baked it slowly in an oven. . . .

Although the first section of the poem is consistent with the themes expressed in "Nineteen Hundred and Nineteen"—disillusionment, the plunge toward violence, the failings of bourgeois nationalism in general and of cultural nationalism in particular—the second section is not, and this is perhaps one of the reasons why Yeats chose to move the poem to a later position in the 1928 collection. Indeed, the second section provides a new response to Irish violence that again brings to the fore the issue of detachment and return, as "abstraction"—for Yeats, always a negative term and one that he often associates with nationalist extremism—gives way to an alternative mode of perception:

> but now
> I bring full-flavoured wine out of a barrel found
> Where seven Ephesian topers slept and never knew
> When Alexander's empire passed, they slept so sound.
> Stretch out your limbs and sleep a long Saturnian sleep;
> I have loved you better than my soul for all my words,
> And there is none so fit to keep a watch and keep
> Unwearied eyes upon those horrible green birds.

The "seven Ephesian topers" were, as Finneran notes, Christian martyrs who, entombed by the Roman emperor Decius in A.D. 251, rose from their "sleep" to confirm Theodosius II (A.D. 401–450) in the Christian faith.[46] Yeats broadens the myth to include the passing of Alexander's empire in 323 B.C. This larger view of time indicates the underpinning logic of Yeats's visionary system, a new perspective from which to view, significantly, the passing of empires and "those horrible green birds," a phrase that recalls "the indignant desert birds" of "The Second Coming," harbingers of violence, and perhaps, with the third repetition of the adjective "green," the "terrible beauty" of "Easter, 1916," here more terrible than beautiful. Having achieved an alternative perspective, Yeats himself replaces the Centaur, that emblem of cultural nationalism, which he has "loved . . . better than my soul for all my words." Because Yeats is no longer confined to the "backward" gaze of the cultural nationalist, the gatherer of wheat from graves, "there is," indeed, "none so fit" as the poet "to keep a watch and keep / Unwearied eyes upon those horrible green birds."

This is not to claim that Yeats's gaze is simply a passive one, the gaze of the poet reveling in the artistic freedom of imagined exile. The phrase "Unwearied eyes" contrasts with "the eye's complacency"—an expression used in "Meditations in Time of Civil War" to indict those who perceive "the Coming Emptiness" yet do nothing—and with the lines from "Nineteen Hundred and Nineteen": "They fixed old aching eyes, / They never saw how seasons run, / And now but gape at the sun." Unlike those who have failed to gain a broader perspective, those who, locked in the violence of the present, simply "gape at the sun," unlike, in fact, the poet himself who had "turn[ed] away and shut the door," seeking refuge in his tower, Yeats will now "keep a watch," turning his attention to "those horrible green birds," those "daemonic images" of hatred and intolerance. The ironic juxtaposition of the poem's title, which seems to indicate passive mimesis, as if the poet is simply putting into language a visual image, together with the fact that there is no such picture by Dulac,[47] serves to affirm the active, shaping power of the detached poet, and of the nationalitarian intellectual, for whom keeping a watch means not recording but transforming. The poet does not merely sing of what is "past, or passing, or to come," but turns his critical and artistic glance upon the canvas of history unfolding, aware of the need to examine history anew, wary of returning violence, and alive to the possibilities of alternative futures.

"Among School Children" shifts the focus directly back to "That country," as the poet become senator and inspector of public schools literally keeps a watch on the development of Irish culture in the Free State. Typical of the collection as a whole, wisdom born in detachment gives way to a more complex and difficult engagement with the present. The artist who dreamed of actively guarding against "those horrible green birds" has become an impotent shade of his imagined self, "a comfortable kind of old scarecrow" (*VP*, 443). No longer the one who keeps a watch, he has become the "sixty-year-old smiling public man" upon whom the students gaze, a shift in perspective that briefly reintroduces the theme of forced exile, recalling the "aged man" of "Sailing to Byzantium" and "the parting guest" of "Youth and Age":

I walk through the long schoolroom questioning;
A kind old nun in a white hood replies;
The children learn to cipher and to sing,
To study reading—books and history,
To cut and sew, be neat in everything

In the best modern way—the children's eyes
In momentary wonder stare upon
A sixty-year-old smiling public man.

As with "Sailing to Byzantium," this opening stanza offers a subtle and ironic critique of Ireland's present, though the irony does not arise, as some critics have
suggested, from the disjunction between the exaggerated certainty of the phrase
"In the best modern way" and Senator Yeats's own assertion "that the schools in
Ireland are not fit places for children. They are insanitary [sic], they are out of repair, they are badly heated, and in Dublin and Cork they are far too small"
(SS, 157). "Among School Children" was occasioned by a visit to St. Otteran's
in Waterford,[48] a "modern" Irish school run by the Sisters of Mercy, which Yeats
in one speech cites as a "model to all schools" (SS, 98). Given Yeats's enthusiasm
for St. Otteran's and given too his almost obsessive emphasis on the "filthy"
condition of most Irish classrooms (SS, 98),[49] the fact that the children are encouraged to "be neat in everything" suggests that this school does indeed represent "the best modern way."

Irony emerges when we recognize that throughout his Senate speeches,
Yeats employs the word "modern" to denote two distinct, even contradictory
forms of education. On the one hand, he uses it in a positive sense to indicate
the type of Montessori-based educational system practiced in Italy and adopted
by St. Otteran's, in which the children learn a range of interrelated disciplines
("to cipher and to sing"), are taught a variety of directly useful tasks (such as
sewing), and are prompted to consider larger concepts by examining their immediate surroundings. On the other hand, he often uses "modern" to indicate a
type of educational system whereby the student is subordinate to the dictates of
the bourgeois nationalist state:

> In the modern world the tendency is to think of the nation; that it is more
> important than the child. In Japan, I understand, the child is sacrificed to
> patriotism. I have seen education unified in America, so that the child is
> sacrificed to that of unified Americanism, and the human mind is codified.
> We are bound to go through the same passion ourselves. There is a ten
> dency to subordinate the child to the idea of the nation. I suggest that
> whether we teach either Irish history, Anglo-Irish literature or Gaelic, we
> should always see that the child is the object and not any of our special
> purposes. (SS, 101–102)

Both connotations of "the best modern way" are evident in the poem, particularly
when we note that Yeats punctuates the phrase not with a period but with a dash,[50]

suggesting that it modifies what comes before and, significantly, what comes after: "In the best modern way—the children's eyes / In momentary wonder stare." Their gaze is "modern" in the sense that they are passive individuals momentarily transfixed by Yeats the "public man," a representative of the state. His emphasis on their "eyes" again recalls the unsettling link, repeatedly evident in the collection, between "eyes without thought" and the recurrence of violence and intolerance. The children's stares of innocent wonder, molded to the dictates of the nation, might readily become the myopia of the "rage-hungry troop," the prying eye of the censor, the blind idealism of the nationalist politician.

As the public Yeats repeatedly asserts, the education of the child, like the creation of the unified nation—in fact, precisely like the creation of the nation—cannot be directly prescribed, particularly when child and state are subordinated to a cultural and political agenda formulated during a period of armed struggle. "It sometimes seems to me," explains Timothy, a character in Yeats's dialogue "Compulsory Gaelic" (1924), "that there must be a kind of politics where one need not be certain. After all, imitation is automatic, but creation moves in a continual uncertainty. If we were certain of the future, who would trouble to create it?" Such idealism is all well and good, but, as the character Paul reminds Timothy, "I cannot see any means whereby a Parliament can pass uncertainty into law" (*LAR*, 176). This neatly encapsulates the dilemma of the nationalitarian artist and politician, how to invent a unified and truly postcolonial nation without imposing a preformed vision of that future nation—how, in short, to embrace uncertainty while clinging to the ideal. For Yeats, one possibility involves a dreaming back and a purging of the desire for idealism. Thus, the next six stanzas move to the personal while retaining a trace of the political, as Yeats examines the cost of idealism, the cost of worshiping images. The lover ("passion"), the nun ("piety"), and the mother ("affection") put faith in images that, in this life, cannot be actualized:

> O Presences
> That passion, piety or affection knows,
> And that all heavenly glory symbolise—
> O self-born mockers of man's enterprise. . . .

The final line recalls the "mockery" of "Nineteen Hundred and Nineteen," the mockery of the poet who perceived the hollow core of nationalist desire and now perceives the vanity of all idealistic human endeavors. The ideal itself, that which is "self-born," makes a mockery of those who labor to create the ideal, including those who desire to mold the nation and the child—we are still among schoolchildren—according to a preestablished design.

The poem does not, however, give way to despair and the immediate need for further distance, as is the case with the war poems. The process of purging idealism leads, paradoxically, to a new nationalitarian idealism:

Labour is blossoming or dancing where
The body is not bruised to pleasure soul,
Nor beauty born out of its own despair,
Nor blear-eyed wisdom out of midnight oil.

The romantic vision of communal unity that Yeats presents here can be described as "nationalitarian," as opposed to blindly nationalistic or uncritically modern, because of where it occurs in this carefully ordered collection.

Having rejected bourgeois nationalism's romantic idealism and modernity's rationalism, Yeats now momentarily asserts a new image of totality that is, within the terms of the text itself, self-consciously idealistic, self-consciously romantic. For Yeats, the word "labour" is generally used to describe directed growth (the national body "bruised to pleasure soul"), the fostering of national culture through the type of intellectual rigor he associated with the study of mysticism ("blear-eyed wisdom out of midnight oil"), or the "mechanical" advancement of political opinion. Thus, in his early writings he notes that "we labour and labour" to rediscover those "noble types and symbols" that once energized peasant culture (*UP1*, 295), and, in a cancelled journal entry from 1909, envisions a Coole Park "slowly perpetuating itself and the life within it, in ever increasing intensity of labour,"[51] while, in a note to "Meditations in Time of Civil War," we know that he describes the "cry for vengeance" upon the murderers of Jacques Molay as a "symbol for those who labour from hatred, and so for sterility in various kinds" (*VP*, 827). The form of labor evoked at the close of "Among School Children"—at once suggestive of the labor of existence in this fallen world, the labor of birth, and, I will add, the labor of nation-making—is quite different, neither directed nor mechanical but organic: "Labour is blossoming."

An ideal, imagined nation, at once individual and collective (the pronoun "we" is now introduced), emerges precisely because the nationalist poet has abandoned the desire to fashion child and state according to a preformed design:

O chestnut tree, great-rooted blossomer,
Are you the leaf, the blossom or the bole?
O body swayed to music, O brightening glance,
How can we know the dancer from the dance?

The modern "stare" is replaced by the "brightening glance," as the stanza's final questions reveal that which is "born" from this alternative form of labor.

Initially, the community is imagined as a tree, a metaphor that, fittingly, recalls Yeats's 1925 speech, "The Child and the State," when he noted Burke's belief that "the State was a tree, no mechanism to be pulled in pieces and put up again, but an oak tree that had grown through centuries" (*SS*, 160). Once again, though, Yeats's political assertions take on an added level of complexity in his poetry, for the tree imagined in "Among School Children" is not a changeless monument to the past but a fluid, living entity. By presenting his metaphor in the form of a question, Yeats emphasizes the separate components of the tree and calls upon the reader to conceptualize those components as parts of a larger whole, precisely the opposite of a bourgeois nationalist project in which the whole completely subsumes the parts. Just as the chestnut tree is "the leaf, the blossom or the bole" as well as all of these together, Yeats's nationalitarian vision imagines, through contemplation of difference and similarity, an Ireland that is at once diverse and unified, the one and the many, as opposed to the one out of the many.

As an object that is rooted in soil, however, the tree does not quite capture a full sense of temporal change, and this is perhaps one of the reasons that the poem concludes with a dancing body. If, as Frank Kermode has noted, Yeats consistently valorized modern, nontraditional styles of dance over those practiced in the popular theater and the ballet, "the freely-moving dancer" over "the virtuosity of the ballerina's more limited range of movement," [52] Yeats's choice of metaphor is particularly apt. The nation dances to the score set by time, yet the form of the nation is continually in flux, "a lovely flexible presence" (*V2*, 279) that is a part of history but not subsumed by history, that is connected to other modern nations but, because it is an ever-changing entity, preserves its own distinct individuality. In this respect, the poem offers in art a vision of nationhood that, to recall Yeats's reflections from "Compulsory Gaelic," no act of parliament or nationalist program can legislate into being, a vision of a community that is ever-unfolding, eternally self-creating, and deeply rooted in the liberating possibilities of uncertainty.

Like Virginia Woolf's Lily Briscoe, Yeats has had his vision. But, as the arrangement of *The Tower* has brought to the fore, such ideal visions must themselves be reexamined. Thus, the collection now moves, following a series of poems concerning relationships, toward a final group of poems that reintroduce the theme of imagined exile. In "The Three Monuments," Yeats adopts the mask of the mocking outsider, as he uses the examples of Parnell, Horatio Nelson, and Daniel O'Connell—the last of whom "it was said . . . that you could not throw a stick over a workhouse wall without hitting one of his children" (*SS*, 87)— to indict Free State and unionist claims regarding the historical "purity" (both sexual and racial) of the Irish nation:

And all the popular statesmen say
That purity built up the State
And after kept it from decay;
Admonish us to cling to that
And let all base ambition be,
For intellect would make us proud
And pride bring in impurity:
The three old rascals laugh aloud.

In "The Gift of Harun Al-Rashid," Yeats returns to the mystical, celebrating, in this highly autobiographical poem, his wife, whose interest in automatic writing prompted *A Vision*. And, in a section of verse that would appear in his play *Oedipus at Colonus* (1934), a play which, appropriately enough, centers on a protagonist in exile, Yeats sings of departure: "Never to have lived is best, ancient writers say; / Never to have drawn the breath of life, never to have looked into the eye of day; / The second best's a gay goodnight and quickly turn away." One year later, following the publication of *The Tower*, Yeats sounds a similar note in a letter to Olivia Shakespear: "Re-reading *The Tower* I was astonished at its bitterness, and long to live out of Ireland that I may find some new vintage" (*L*, 742).

The wine metaphor points serendipitously to the close of *The Tower* when, in the final poem, "All Souls' Night," Yeats calls upon ghosts from his past "To drink from the wine-breath" of two glasses of muscatel, to learn of "A certain marvellous thing" he has discovered (*VP*, 471). Yeats, however, will only speak of his cryptic newfound wisdom to those who possess a

mind that, if the cannon sound
From every quarter of the world, can stay
Wound in mind's pondering,
As mummies in the mummy-cloth are wound.

We have already encountered in the previous chapter examples of minds that cannot "stay," that cannot achieve a sense of detachment when the cannon sounds, when war between Irish and Irish is at hand. Like "The young / In one another's arms" of "Sailing to Byzantium," the living in postimperial Ireland seem trapped in history, doomed to repeat the cycle of bloodshed, doomed to retell the old myths of nationalism. In contrast to the golden bird in "Sailing to Byzantium," a being devoid of agency, Yeats now stresses the active, shaping power of his detached glance (recall the "brightening glance" of "Among School Children"):

Nothing can stay my glance
Until that glance run in the world's despite
To where the damned have howled away their hearts,
And where the blessed dance. . . .

Because the living would "mock" his newfound wisdom, Yeats must imagine an audience outside the current struggles in Ireland, ghosts from his past. The "marvellous thing" itself is never revealed and, in fact, cannot be revealed because it has yet to be fully comprehended: "—such thought have I that hold it tight / Till meditation master all its parts." The implication, though, is not of bitter longing but contentment, a mind that "need[s] no other thing, / Wound in mind's wandering." This is the contentment that comes at the close of a journey when the poet, in a state of isolation, looks back upon Ireland's recent past. The poet who had in "Sailing to Byzantium" called for the sages to "Consume my heart away; sick with desire / And fastened to a dying animal" has now cast off desire to become, like the "shade" in his later poem "Byzantium," an entity wound in itself. Like the shade in "Byzantium," Yeats is poised to be anew, to purge himself by meditating upon a past that he has recreated in art.

It is in this light that we must view Yeats's call to "find some new vintage." *The Tower*, in charting a movement from hoped-for escape to a final moment of imagined isolation, a movement away from bourgeois nationalism and toward a nationalitarian conception of community, enacts the "repouring" of old wine, the recreation of Ireland's recent chaotic past as a personal narrative. Yeats closes the volume by constructing both an imagined space outside of Ireland and a time before the founding of the Free State—it is worth noting that "All Souls' Night" is set, as the postscript to several of the versions reveals, in "Oxford, Autumn 1920"—where that past now might be relived and meditated upon, where the old wine, this bitter dram that sparks a longing for some new vintage, might be sipped.

CHAPTER
FIVE

Learning "to chaunt a tongue men do not know"

Modernity, Committed Art, and the "Negative"
Language of the Early and Middle Verse

Art breaks open a dimension inaccessible to other experience, a dimension in which human beings, nature, and things no longer stand under the law of the established reality principle. Subjects and objects encounter the appearance of that autonomy which is denied them in their society. The encounter with the truth of art happens in the estranging language and images which make perceptible, visible, and audible that which is no longer, or not yet, perceived, said, and heard in everyday life.

—Herbert Marcuse, *The Aesthetic Dimension*

I too have tried to be modern.

—W. B. Yeats, "Introduction to *The Oxford Book of Modern Verse*"

When Yeats uses the word "modern," as in this somewhat coy aside from his "Introduction to *The Oxford Book of Modern Verse*" (1936) or in his more powerful and markedly different description of the present as a "filthy modern tide" in "The Statues," he generally does so to indicate not only a specific historical moment but also a type of epistemological stance, a mode of seeing (cultural, philosophical, or, most often, artistic) that is either characteristic of, or emerges in response to, the experience of modernity. In his "Introduction," Yeats focuses on the aesthetic, as he outlines two distinct strains of modern verse. The first, which he associates with the poetry of the Great War and the overtly political art of the 1930s, is characterized by a tendency "to multiply personality" (*LE*, 200). Poets such as Wilfred Owen, whom Yeats famously excluded from the anthology, adopt a series of stances in response to the tragedy of modern life that appear individualistic yet are in fact "abstract," the repetition of political opinions and "generalizations" found in "newspaper articles and government statistics" (*LE*, 195). The second, which he associates with Pound, Eliot, and with some of the poetry of Charles Madge, C. Day Lewis, and Louis MacNeice, is characterized by what Yeats terms "pure spiritual objectivity" (*LE*, 200). Echoing the theories of Eliot, he writes that for such poets "the contemplation of suffering has compelled them to seek beyond the flux something unchanging, inviolate, that country where no ghost haunts, no beloved lures because it has neither past nor future" (*LE*, 201). Leaving aside for the moment the question of where and how Yeats's own poetry fits within these broader categories, it is clear that he prefers the latter group, those truly modern artists who adopt a position of detached objectivity and "have pulled off the mask" in order to reveal "man's naked mind"—the eternal tragedy of human existence (*LE*, 200).

In "The Statues," Yeats combines an aesthetic focus with a broader consideration of culture and myth in order to imagine a distinctly Irish response to the transformational pressures of modernity. In the opening stanzas, he posits an ideal aesthetic evident in the statuary of different pre-modern civilizations. According to Yeats, Grecian statues "lacked character," lacked realistic traits, because they were based on the mathematical ratios that "Pythagoras planned," yet "boys and girls pale from the imagined love / Of solitary beds knew what they were" (*VP*, 610). Children, individuals who think in ideal terms because they have not experienced physical love, apprehended the harmonizing beauty of the ratios expressed in these abstract works of "marble" or "bronze" and "pressed at midnight in some public place / Live lips upon a plummet-measured face." After considering the later statuary of ancient Greece, where the "Calculations" of Pythagoras took on "casual flesh," and of the East, where the "Empty eye-balls" of the Buddha gaze upon the "unreality" of physical existence, Yeats turns to modern Ireland. Evoking both the cyclical understanding of history that he outlines in *A Vision* and the cultural connections that supposedly link Ireland with other pre-modern civilizations, he imagines a new, specifically Irish manifestation of the ideal aesthetic emerging out of the Easter Rising:

> When Pearse summoned Cuchulain to his side,
> What stalked through the Post Office? What intellect,
> What calculation, number, measurement replied?
> We Irish, born into that ancient sect
> But thrown upon this filthy modern tide

And by its formless, spawning, fury wrecked,
Climb to our proper dark, that we may trace
The lineaments of a plummet-measured face.

The danger, for Yeats, is that the Irish, though "born into that ancient [that is, pre-modern] sect," will not be able to give artistic expression to the ideal because they have been "wrecked" by the "filthy modern tide"—this new age in which art has become abstract, heterogeneous, "formless." In an introductory essay written in 1937 for the unreleased "Dublin Edition" of W. B. Yeats, an essay that would be published several decades after his death under the title, "A General Introduction for My Work" (1961), Yeats expresses a similar fear: "When I stand upon O'Connell Bridge in the half-light and notice that discordant architecture, all those electric signs, where modern heterogeneity has taken physical form, a vague hatred comes up out of my own dark" (*LE*, 215). If the fear, in both poem and essay, is modern formlessness, the hope is that the Irish, like Yeats on Dublin's O'Connell Bridge, will "Climb to our proper dark." The word "dark" suggests a form of racial consciousness,[1] an awareness of those cultural and (for Yeats) mystical connections that bind a community together and, crucially, that link that community with other pre-modern civilizations—an awareness that "behind all Irish history hangs a great tapestry" composed not simply of Irish myths but also of the myths that unite all humanity (*LE*, 207). In this sense, embracing racial consciousness means, paradoxically, embracing objectivity, a position from which both artist and society might apprehend and give aesthetic form to what Yeats terms "that Unity of Being Dante compared to a perfectly proportioned human body, Blake's 'Imagination,' what the Upanishads have named 'Self'" (*LE*, 210). By retreating from the "half-light" of modernity into the "dark" of racial consciousness, from a passive acceptance of modern abstraction to an active, objective awareness of that tapestry that binds past and present, the Irish, like the Greeks before them, "indeed may trace / The lineaments of a plummet-measured face."

"The Statues" is among Yeats's finest late works, but it is also, like much of his verse from the 1930s, a politically suspect poem on a number of fronts. In addition to celebrating the childlike and pre-modern quality of the Irish mind, thereby replicating a central assumption in the discourses of British imperialism, Yeats (perhaps reflecting Ireland's ambivalent status as participant in and object of Britain's imperial project)[2] adopts the positions of both the primitivist, at the imperial center, and the nativist, at the colonial periphery—positions that, like the insular nationalism he so despised, reflect a desire to isolate post-revolution Ireland from the modern global community. The deeper problem, however, is that Yeats, because he apprehends the transformational impact of modernity exclusively on an aesthetic level, effectively removes the Easter Rising itself from history. The class-based contradictions that sparked the Rising, the failures of economic policy and of political attempts at compromise, and the sectarian divisions that have continued to haunt Ireland are all, like the dead rebels themselves, subsumed within an ahistorical meditation on culture, myth, and aesthetic form. In the poem, as in his "Introduction to *The Oxford Book of Modern Verse*," "being modern" is thus for Yeats a mode of seeing that involves resistance and recuperation, a dialectical move from the historical to the aesthetic and mythic that, from a Marxist perspective, amounts to a typically high-modernist example of historical false consciousness—the perpetuation of a bourgeois (even imperialist) mindset that would perceive the contradictions of lived reality, to use Neil Larsen's postcolonial Marxist formulation, as a crisis of (aesthetic) representation and not as a crisis in (material) representation.[3]

This is a compelling argument, and one that has informed a number of Marxist and postcolonial readings designed to address not only the relationship between class and aesthetics in Yeats's work but also the connections between Yeatsian nationalism and Yeatsian modernism. Whereas earlier scholars tended to regard nationalism and modernism as discrete, even oppositional phenomena, recent criticism has demonstrated that these two categories are interrelated and mutually reinforcing. Both positions emerge in response to an ambivalent encounter with modernity, the birth of a new age characterized by utilitarian thought, materialism, and mass political movements; both formulate that encounter as an aesthetic or cultural crisis that demands an epistemological response, a new representational mode for apprehending reality; and both positions lead Yeats to embrace supposedly transcendental categories (race, tradition, the nation, the ideal aesthetic) that contain their own set of (politically regressive) ideological imperatives. As Terry Eagleton puts it, Yeats, in turning to the aesthetic, the symbolic, and the mythic as a way of restoring "the organic unity of Irish society"—whether in his early symbolist or in his later, more recognizably modernist verse—advances a "peculiarly mandarin [form of] modernism in which . . . the archaic triumphs over the contemporary," neatly eliding the class-based contradictions of his own nationalist vision of a "new" Ireland guided by a benevolent Anglo-Irish aristocracy.[4] Similarly, Edward Said—though he lauds Yeats for "join[ing] his people to its history" and for constructing in art a vision of past and present that works to counter imperialism's ahistorical representations of the Irish "as 'potato-eaters' or 'bog-dwellers' or 'shanty people'"—equates Yeatsian modernism with national consciousness, describing his "full system of cycles, pernes, and gyres" as an attempt "to lay hold of a distant and yet orderly reality" that might provide "a refuge from the turbulence of his immediate experience."[5]

Yet, if this theoretical framework is compelling when applied to *A Vision*, to individual poems such as "The Statues," and to certain aspects of Yeats's politics, particularly his valorization of a mythic Anglo-Irish past, it is also limiting when used to consider the multiple stances that are characteristic of his art and politics and that emerge out of his ambivalent experience of modernity. Specifically, this approach prompts us to treat modernism and nationalism as monolithic terms—terms that fail to encapsulate the unique, fluid, and at times contradictory positions of Yeats the modernist and Yeats the nationalist—and it tends to promote the belief that modernism and nationalism, as mutually reinforcing categories, are not simply interrelated but identical, that to adopt either position necessarily amounts to a retreat from history (whether experienced at the colonial periphery or at the imperial center) into an abstract realm of tradition, grand narratives, and ideal, totalizing aesthetic forms. In other words, this Marxist framework, when not applied exclusively to Yeats the reactionary high-modernist of the 1930s, raises as many questions as it answers.

To what extent is Yeatsian modernism, beginning with his early symbolism, reliant upon a totalizing conception of the aesthetic? In order to answer that question, it is useful to return briefly to his "Introduction to *The Oxford Book of Modern Verse*." Although Yeats clearly prefers "spiritual objectivity" to overtly political art, he does not equate his own poetry with those modern artists who retreat into an abstract, ahistorical realm, "that country where no ghost haunts." Instead, Yeats repeatedly stresses his own position as an Irish writer, a man who, "constrained by a different nationality" and "fixed to some one place," has "tried to be modern" but has usually failed, a man for whom the struggle to achieve objectivity is more important than the end itself (*LE*, 200). This reminds us, on the one hand, of the profoundly self-reflexive nature of Yeats's verse, the extent to which his poetry, in contrast with that of, say, Pound and Eliot, exposes and repeatedly undercuts its own drive toward resolution. If the fragments of the *Cantos* or "The Waste Land" are intended to evoke wholeness, shoring against the "ruin" of modernity, Yeats's poetry, throughout his career, continually evokes unity only to return to disunity.[6] Truth always yields to "counter-truth," contentment to discontentment.

It also reminds us, on the other hand, that Yeats experienced modernity at the colonial periphery, a vantage that made him acutely sensitive to the partial nature of grand narratives and universal categories. Although the discourses of cultural imperialism and conventional Irish nationalism promise to extricate the subject from the tide of modernity, presenting as models the "free" individual of civilized society or the native rooted in traditional society, both discourses merely encourage a deadening acceptance of modernity, prompting individuals to think in terms of abstractions and generalizations that deny what Yeats terms "sincerity" and "the soul's autonomy" (*LE*, 200, 201). Thus, while Yeats posits complete objectivity as a laudable goal in itself, he recognizes, as "a man of my time, through my poetical faculty living its history," that this drive toward objectivity can, for the Irish writer, readily lead toward a false sense of autonomy and a passive acceptance of modernity, that, in short, "pull[ing] off the mask" is a dangerous move at the colonial periphery (*LE*, 198, 200). As Yeats wrote in 1919 of the criticism surrounding John Synge's plays, "The outcry against *The Playboy* was an outcry against its style, against its *way of seeing;* and when the audience called Synge 'decadent'—a favorite reproach of the objective everywhere—it was but troubled by the stench of its own burnt cakes" (*IDM*, 130, emphasis added).

This leads to another set of related questions that will form the basis of this chapter: To what extent is the language of Yeatsian modernism influenced by his encounter with modernity at the colonial periphery where, as Fredric Jameson writes, "the face of imperialism is brute force, naked power, open exploitation"? How might attention to the oppositional nature of Yeats's verse—the fact that his poetry, to quote Balchandra Rajan, "proceeds from closures into that underlying openness from which endeavors at closure seek to protect themselves by the propitiation of a further succession of stances"—alter our perspective? And, most important, does Yeats's tendency to apprehend and respond to modernity on an aesthetic level necessarily amount to a flight from history, an example of nationalist escapism, false consciousness, the aestheticization of the political?[7]

In order to address these questions, this chapter will examine Yeats's early and middle phase verse (as the poems eventually appeared, in considerably revised forms, in the 1949 Macmillan edition of *The Collected Poems*)[8] through a theoretical lens that does not assume a clear link between modernism and a necessarily regressive nationalism and that does not call upon us to chart, in the manner of most current postcolonial readings of literary modernism, a stable progression from the darkness of modernism/nationalism to the light of postmodernism/liberation. Rather than considering modernism as a political, aesthetic, and theoretical dead end, I will argue that Yeats's poetry, considered in light of Theodor Adorno's conceptions of modernist aesthetics, modified so as to account for the unique features of Irish colonial modernity, evinces a specifically dialectical engagement with Irish history, as opposed to consistently displaying a (conservative modernist or liberal postmodernist) retreat from history.[9] The point is not to dismiss the escapist impulse evident in Yeats, particularly in his essays on Irish culture, nor is it to suggest that Yeats represents exactly the type of modernist whom Adorno celebrates, such as Franz Kafka, Samuel Beckett, or Thomas Mann. Rather, the goal is to use Adorno as a point of departure for examining those moments in Yeats's verse that cannot be accounted for by the standard readings of Yeatsian symbolism/modernism, moments in his early and middle poetry that register and resist the imperatives of Irish modernity.

The continual interplay of opposites in Yeats is the product of his poetry's dialectical relationship with modernity. For Yeats, "Civilization is hooped together, brought / Under a rule, under the semblance of peace / By manifold illusion" ("Meru"). This "manifold illusion" is the superficial real of modernity, of scientific rationalism and utilitarian thinking spawned during the Enlightenment and spread to Ireland via British imperial domination. And it is the superficial real of sentimental and political art, works created for "practical men who believe in money, in position, in a marriage bell" (*M*, 331). The goal of the poet is to tear the veil asunder, to expose, as he writes in "Meru," the "desolation of reality." What remains behind the real, what becomes apparent "to those who are no longer deceived, whose passion is reality," varies widely in his work, though critics have generally seized upon his references to the "true" character of the Irish race, the ethos of an imagined and decidedly idealized once and future nation (*M*, 331). Considered from this angle, the relationship between Yeats's art and Irish modernity is dialectical in a strictly vulgar Marxist sense because his poetry simply replaces one illusory real with another. Yet, considered from an Adornian perspective, the initial drive of Yeats's poetry to engage with modernity takes on a slightly different resonance.

According to Adorno, modernist art directly responds to what he terms modernity's "positivistic rationality," the belief that all things, including art, have a use value (and thus exchange value) and that "people who are no more than component parts of machinery . . . still [have] the capacity to act as subjects," that "life has [not] passed into an ideology which conceals the fact that there is life no longer."[10] Modernist art retains the potential to resist these conditions by virtue of its own autonomy and fundamental uselessness. "By congealing into an entity unto itself—rather than obeying existing social norms and thus proving itself to be 'socially useful'—art," explains Adorno, "criticizes society just by being there. Pure and immanently elaborated art is a tacit critique of the society where everything is for-other."[11] This "tacit critique," this "determinate negation of a determinate society," is evident primarily in the formal elements of modernist works that, in the words of Jochen Schulte-Sasse, direct their "entire energy toward the negation of ossified language and thought forms."[12] Modernist art, turned inward upon itself, reveals the real of modernist society that monopoly capitalism always conceals, the eradication of the autonomous subject, the quantification of language, thought, art. In other words, modernism's crucial negative feature, to quote Neil Lazarus, is that it gives "the lie to the world's ideological presentation of itself."[13]

Although Yeats's project certainly cannot be described as Marxist, his poetry, at its core, contains a similar dialectical impulse, a similar drive to "cast a cold eye" on the illusory real of modernity. I use the word "similar," however, because we must not conflate Irish modernity with Adorno's European modernity. For Adorno, the present is marked by a form of class-based domination so thorough that it is nearly always invisible and can only be apprehended, in its manifest, "objective" totality, in the fragments of modernist art. Thus, he perceives language itself as a vehicle of false consciousness, a veil of rationality, a means of knowing, classifying, and quantifying the self and the external that hide the fundamental irrationality of a world "long since crushed by the overwhelming power of an apparatus in which individuals are interchangeable and superfluous."[14] Thus, too "committed art"—art that "aims at changing the conditions underlying social ills"—is doomed to failure, for such art, because it is based upon both the assumption that art can directly change society (that is, it has a use value) and the assumption that the artist is an autonomous subject aloof from the real, simply perpetuates modernity's positivistic rationality.[15]

At the colonial periphery, however, the experience of modernity is not mediated in the same manner because the central contradiction of lived reality, the fact of imperial domination, is impossible to ignore. Indeed, for the Irish artist, the very act of writing in English underscores his or her own alienated position within imperial modernity. Stephen Dedalus knows it, as he muses upon the speech of an "English convert" come to teach in Ireland: "The language in which we are speaking is his before it is mine. How different are the words *home, Christ, ale, master,* on his lips and on mine! I cannot speak or write these words without unrest of spirit. His language, so familiar and so foreign, will always be for me an acquired speech."[16] Yeats knows it, too. Late in life, contemplating the question of "why I do not write in Gaelic," he explains:

> The "Irishry" have preserved their ancient "deposit" through wars which, during the sixteenth and seventeenth centuries, became wars of extermination; no people . . . have undergone greater persecution, nor did that persecution altogether cease up to our day. No people hate as we do in whom that past is always alive, there are moments when hatred poisons my life. . . . Then I remind myself . . . that I owe my soul to Shakespeare, to Spenser and to Blake . . . and to the English language in which I think, speak, and write, that everything I love has come to me through English; my hatred tortures me with love, my love with hate. (*LE,* 210–211)

Truly, as Yeats writes, "this is Irish hatred and solitude," the experience of a nationalist poet whose "national language" is Gaelic but whose "mother tongue" is English, whose ambivalent position allows neither blind acceptance of the language of the colonizer nor blind celebration of the language of the colonized (*LE*, 211–212). Whereas Adorno's modern subject is unaware that language—as a universal vehicle for quantifying reality, meaning that conceals its own meaninglessness—masks his or her own position as oppressed subject, Yeats, the colonial artist, cannot help but be cognizant of language's basis in imperial capitalism and its false promises of abstract equality. For Yeats, "the impersonal language" evident in contemporary realist drama "has come, not out of individual life, nor out of life at all, but out of necessities of commerce, of Parliament, of Board Schools, of hurried journeys by rail" (*EI*, 301). He continues, "One must not forget that the death of language, the substitution of phrases as nearly impersonal as algebra for words and rhythms varying from man to man, is but a part of the tyranny of impersonal things" (*EI*, 301).

If the "tyranny" of "impersonal language" is registered at the moment when the modern Irish subject speaks, the act of producing art—particularly for individuals such as Joyce and Yeats who, in very different ways, rejected nationalist cries for overtly political works—entails recognizing that one will always be read as a committed artist. The pervasive binary logic of nationalism demands acceptance or rejection, shattering the illusion of the autonomous artist standing outside of history. "In Ireland," writes Yeats, "in addition to the external art of our predecessors, full of the misunderstandings created by English influence, there is a pre-occupation of a greater part of the population with opinions and a habit of deciding that a man is useful to his country, or otherwise, not by what he is in himself or by what he does in his whole life, but by the opinions he holds on one or two subjects" (*IDM*, 119). He further argues that Irish critics, by conflating aesthetic value with political value, engage in a "half-deliberate sophistry" designed to persuade "themselves that the old tale is not true, and that art is not ruined so" (*IDM*, 120). Crucially, then, the experience of Irish modernity is one in which art is always linked with political opinions and practical value, in which power remains, so to speak, on the surface. The artist is continually faced with the imperatives of both imperial control, the compulsion to embrace Enlightenment rationalism and capitalist utilitarianism, and of nationalist conformity, the compulsion to produce explicitly political art.

These are the pressures of modernity that Yeats's poetry, as it engages with the issues of language and the political use value of art, registers and resists on the levels of form and, because of the superficial nature of power in colonial and nationalist modernity, on the level of content. The poems refuse modernity's requirement that art reinscribe the external real, as they expose the fundamental irrationality of an Irish nation dominated by the suffocating logic of imperialism and nationalism, giving the lie to a modern world that demands acceptance of its own notions of progress and of committed art. They resist, as autonomous works rooted in contraries, by evoking the possibility of closure—the possibility of pure, self-contained art that might articulate an imagined Ireland in a language yet to be written, in a language other than Gaelic or English—only to undercut that very drive, steadfastly rejecting comfortable escapism. In short, Yeats's verse always returns to this history, to this language, for, as both Yeats and Adorno recognize, art must remain bound to the now. And yet, his poetry, though the product of an age "slouching toward" further oppression, holds forth the (im)possible dream of a new Ireland, beyond the myths of imperialism and conventional nationalism, that "the poets have imagined" ("The Municipal Gallery Re-visited").

Like Gaelic revivalists before him and other postcolonial writers after him, Yeats recognizes that, in the words of Ngugi wa Thiong'o, "the domination of a people's language by the languages of the colonising nations [is] crucial to the domination of the mental universe of the colonised."[17] Throughout his life, Yeats looks back upon the near eradication of Irish and the institutionalization of English as the (re)enforcement of a distinctly imperial mindset rooted in Enlightenment notions of "direct logic" and "clear rhetoric" (*EI*, 11).[18] Yet, the solution for Yeats is not a return to Gaelic. In addition to noting the practical difficulty of grounding a nationalist project in a language that few Irish (including, to his sometime embarrassment, Yeats himself) actually spoke, he argues that an insistence upon Gaelic, particularly upon Gaelic works that privilege propaganda over aesthetics, would greatly curtail the development of those artists who express "Irish emotion and Irish thought" but write "in the English language [that they have] been born and bred to" (*UP2*, 238). Cognizant that the dream of a time "when no Irishman need write in any but his own language" is, at best, a noble but unrealizable goal for his own generation and, at worst, a vehicle for promoting a regressive, nativist hostility toward all that is not Irish, Yeats, at least in theory, embraces hybridity (*UP2*, 239). He praises Synge and Lady Gregory for adopting "our country idioms" (*EI*, 335) in plays that, to a much greater extent than "our Irish cries and grammars" (*EI*, 341), provide the basis for "a national tradition, a national literature . . . which shall be none the less Irish in spirit for being English in language" (*UP1*, 255).

In practice, though, Yeats's poems—while hybrid in the sense that they incorporate and modify traditional British forms to express Irish themes—almost never introduce the idioms of Hiberno-English. Rather, they respond to the "fallen" state of language in Irish modernity, the notion that language, as a vehicle of imperialist knowledge/power and nationalist knowledge/resistance, cannot be purified of the political, by consciously meditating upon that which nationalist poetry must tirelessly strive to achieve and can never achieve: the articulation of the ideal, unified nation, the final speech act that is the coming-into-being of the imagined community. Yeats's poetry folds back upon itself, continually exposing and undercutting its own dialectical drive toward totalization, precisely because it explicitly refuses escapism even as it explicitly desires it. For Yeats, decolonizing the mind entails turning inward, holding forth the possibility of a postimperial, postnationalist Ireland while recognizing that the medium itself, because rooted in language, can never enact the moment of closure.

Two of Yeats's earliest poems, though not set specifically in Ireland and though generally read within the contexts of Yeatsian romanticism, neatly introduce the ambivalent nature of his early modernist aesthetics by focusing specifically upon the creative function of language. In "The Song of the Happy Shepherd," the speaker, having rejected the "Grey truth" of modernity, affirms that "Words alone are certain good" (*VP*, 65) yet by this he means, as the poem makes clear, a specific kind of language. Ancient "warring kings," those "Word be-mockers" who privileged action over poetry, have been reduced to footnotes in the texts of history: "An idle word is now their glory / By the stammering schoolboy said, / Reading some entangled story." The schoolboy, "stammering" out lines learned by rote, commits a sin greater than that of his predecessors, for he "worship[s]" not actions themselves but "dusty deeds," the words of an ideal, heroic past found in crumbling tomes. This anticipates what will become a central principle of Yeatsian nationalism, the belief that Irish artists, in order to create a vital, living literature, must not parrot the sentiments of earlier writers but must realize that, as the shepherd sings, "there is no truth / Saving in thine own heart." Nor should they look to the language of modern rationalism:

> Seek, then,
> No learning from the starry men,
> Who follow with the optic glass
> The whirling ways of stars that pass—
> Seek, then, for this is also sooth,
> No word of theirs—the cold star-bane
> Has cloven and rent their hearts in twain,
> And dead is all their human truth.

The image of men looking toward the stars complements that of the boy gazing upon his book, with all searching for truth ("sooth") in the external and not the self. What is interesting about this passage, however, is the way it presents language as a vehicle for knowledge, thereby registering the extent to which rationalism (nearly always identified in Yeats's work with modern British society) pervades thought and speech. The speaker's rejection centers not simply upon the astronomers' "cold" project but also upon their words, upon the idea that modern language itself must be cast aside.

This is a difficult task, particularly given that the poem clearly does not embrace a return to the language of the past. Writing in 1908, Yeats directly confronts this dilemma:

> All literature in every country is derived from models, and as often as not these are foreign models, and it is the presence of a personal element alone that can give it nationality in a fine sense, the nationality of its maker. It is only before personality has been attained that a race struggling towards self-consciousness is the better for having, as in primitive times, nothing but native models, for before this has been attained it can neither assimilate nor reject. It was precisely at this passive moment, attainment approaching but not yet come, that the Irish heart and mind surrendered to England, or rather to what is most temporary in England; and Irish patriotism, content that the names and opinions should be Irish, was deceived and satisfied. It is always necessary to affirm and to reaffirm that nationality is in the things that escape analysis. (*IDM*, 116–117)

This passage, "one of the first Irish articulations," according to Declan Kiberd, "of the dialectics of postcolonial liberation,"[19] neatly lays out the problem anticipated on a more fundamental level by "The Song of the Happy Shepherd." If the language of the past and the language of the present must be rejected, what remains for the national poet whose craft is rooted in language? In the essay, Yeats again affirms hybridity in the face of nationalist provincialism by suggesting that Irish literature must carefully "assimilate" and "reject" foreign literary models.[20] The poem is more complicated, in part, because the focus is not literary models but language itself and, in part, because the solution does not entail the affirmation of a hybrid literature. While the "truth" clearly is the language of the heart, the poem steadfastly refuses to articulate that truth. The reader is instructed, "Go gather by the humming sea / Some twisted, echo-harbouring shell, / And to its lips thy story tell." The image suggests speech beyond speech, secret words of the heart (of the race? of the subaltern?) spoken only to the self and the "echo-harbouring shell." If "nationality is in the things that escape analysis," the language of the self—the expression of "personality," that foundation of Yeatsian nationalism—is in that which exceeds the words on the page, silent, unspoken words imagined but never enunciated.

The final section, however, is highly ambivalent, for the shepherd, despite evoking this possibility, registers the fact that he, like the poem he offers, must always remain within ordinary language. Again, we are not provided with the song itself but only the potential for a song:

I must be gone: there is a grave
Where daffodil and lily wave,
And I would please the hapless faun,
Buried under the sleepy ground,
With mirthful songs before the dawn.
His shouting days with mirth were crowned;
And still I dream he treads the lawn,
Walking ghostly in the dew,
Pierced by my glad singing through,
My songs of old earth's dreamy youth:
But ah! She dreams not now; dream thou!
For fair are poppies on the brow:
Dream, dream, for this is also sooth.

The promise of the shepherd singing to "the hapless" dead faun, singing to a pastoral world long since faded, is rife with irony, and not simply because the speaker, having rejected the schoolboy's attachment to the past, now seeks to reawaken it. Though he dreams that the faun might be "Pierced by my glad singing through," we recognize, as the shepherd ultimately recognizes, that, while "words alone are certain good," in this world they simply mark what they cannot enact: the shepherd's desire to resurrect Arcadia, the poem's desire to sing a new song, a new language beyond language. Yet the irony does not amount to a complete dismissal of the dream. Although the drive to speak the soul, soon identified in Yeats's work with the birth of a new Ireland, may be a delusion, the stuff of poets with "poppies on the brow," and though poetry must itself traffic in the language of modern life and thought, the impulse remains: "dream thou!"

The other early poem, "The Sad Shepherd," immediately introduces a further qualification, one that does not overturn the dream but places the poem's final affirmation in dialectical tension with the limitations of a project grounded in language. Shifting from first person to third, the poet offers a shepherd "whom Sorrow named his friend" (*VP*, 67). We do not know why the shepherd is mournful any more than we know why Eliot's Prufrock is paralyzed by indecision, but the poem does make clear that the difficulty for the shepherd, like that of J. Alfred, is bound up with the problem of language—the need, in the shepherd's case, to communicate the melancholy that is in his soul. He has cried his "most piteous story" to the "sea" and "to the dewdrops glistening." Neither listens because both speak in language other than language, a self-contained form in which speaker and hearer are the same: "naught they heard, for they are always listening, / The dewdrops, for the sound of their own dropping." This is the language associated later in Yeats's work with "unity of being"—when "The soul," to quote "A Prayer for My Daughter," "recovers radical innocence / And learns at last that it is self-delighting, / Self-appeasing, self-affrighting"—and with "unity of culture," a nation consisting of individuals who, in giving voice to their own hearts, paradoxically give voice to the collective mind.

"The Sad Shepherd," however, registers the fact that this moment of articulation, because it will be in words outside of words, must always remain deferred. The sad shepherd takes the advice of the happy shepherd and finds "a shell":

> I will my heavy story tell
> Till my own words, re-echoing, shall send
> Their sadness through a hollow, pearly heart;
> And my own tale again for me shall sing,
> And my own whispering words be comforting,
> And lo! My ancient burden may depart.

The poem can only imagine the point at which the soul "shall sing"—when the speaker's "sadness" and, to read the lines as anticipating Yeatsian nationalism, the race's "ancient burden may depart"—for to communicate the moment returns us to ordinary speech, to the language of the present. Thus, when the shepherd "sang softly nigh the pearly rim," the shell echoes back only the cacophony of the sea, speech that shepherd, poet, and audience, bound in this language, cannot understand: "the sad dweller by the sea-ways lone / Changed all he sang to inarticulate moan / Among her wildering whirls, forgetting him." What the shepherd hears, what the poem registers, is, in Adorno's formulation, the negative real of language in the present. The shell is the echo chamber of modernity, meaningful language returned as meaninglessness, the sound of the subject's own lack of autonomy.[21] What the poem asks is a question that haunts all writing in a postcolonial context where language is necessarily and explicitly bound up with power: Can the subaltern speak?[22] The answer here is "yes" and "no": yes, because the poem remains true to the possibility that at some future point such speech can occur; and no, because the poem reveals that language is the bind, that to articulate the imagined speech of the heart/race is not to achieve completion but only to mark completion itself as beyond the bounds of art.

Taken as a group, the two poems represent Yeats's own "fascination" with "what's difficult," the national artist's tireless desire to speak the community into being, while perceiving that the tools of his trade are precisely what subvert that (im)possible dream. Yeats's symbolism, the predecessor of his turn to modernist aesthetics, reformulates the dilemma, though critics have generally focused on the escapist elements evident in this aesthetic. His early essays repeatedly indicate that symbolic poetry, unlike realism, which offers "descriptions of nature for the sake of nature, of moral law for the sake of moral law," allows the poet to "seek out those wavering, meditative, organic rhythms, which are the embodiment of the imagination, that neither desires nor hates, because it has done with time, and only wishes to gaze upon some reality, some beauty" (*EI*, 163). To have "done with time" would seem to be the aim, yet the certainty expressed here is belied by "To the Rose upon the Rood of Time," the opening lyric in a collection that Yeats, beginning with the 1895 edition of *Poems*, entitled *The Rose* (1893).

The rose, identified in the poem with "Eternal beauty wandering on her way" and the rebirth of "old Eire and the ancient ways," is explicitly bound by time, the cross of suffering upon which it blossoms (*VP*, 101). And it is bound by the cross of language, for the mystical poet summons the rose into being, forcing essence to become signifier, in order to receive inspiration.[23] This is the rose's "own sadness," a sadness shared and embraced by the poet who, like the shepherds, would speak his own (Irish) heart, would "sing the ancient ways: / Cuchulain battling with the bitter tide; / The Druid, grey, wood-nurtured, quiet-eyed." Presumably, the volume itself will be this song, but Yeats is careful, in this opening poem, to mark the limitations of language. "Come near, come near, come near," he pleads to the rose, only to exclaim, "—Ah, leave me still / A little space for the rose-breath to fill!"

The lines are intentionally ambiguous, suggesting Yeats's own ambivalent position as both modern artist and national artist. To write, even in a quasi-mystical poem, entails embracing what Adorno terms "identity thinking," which "says what something falls under, of what it is an example or a representative" and not what it is in "itself."[24] The rose is not the song of ancient Ireland reborn but only the incomplete linguistic marker of that song, a hint of "rose-breath," aspiration that precedes language other than ordinary language. At the same time, to write as a nationalist artist is to be compelled to speak the essence of the nation, the thing "itself," which, in a world dominated by imperial and national rationalism, cannot be spoken. Thus, the poet's initial longing to merge with the rose, to achieve this moment of "pure" speech, necessarily gives way to frustration. Were the poet and the rose to become one, were the poet to speak this pure language, he would no longer be capable of writing verses, for his words would not be of this world. The poem, however, is not of despair but of hope, indeed of the only hope available to the nationalist artist who refuses complacent escapism, the compulsion to echo the dead language of the past, and who recognizes that, to be a poet, he must remain in this present of "common things that crave; / The weak worm hiding down in its small cave, / The field-mouse running by me in the grass." The hope is the always deferred dream of "learn[ing] to chaunt a tongue men do not know," a dream that is recognized but not aban-doned, as the rational mind would argue, because it is only a dream. This is all the poet can offer.

At first glance, "Fergus and the Druid," the next poem in *The Rose,* would seem to overcome the opening poem's ambivalence, as Yeats unearths an Irish legend for nationalist consumption, Samuel Ferguson's nineteenth-century tale in which Fergus, an Irish king with the soul of a poet, abdicates his throne to the more politically savvy Conchubar. Feeling the weight of the practical world, Fergus longs for and obtains the wisdom of the Druid, though this wis-dom comes at the cost of comprehending the "great webs of sorrow" that link all humanity (*VP,* 104). Yet, considered in light of the opening poem's medi-tation on language, "Fergus and the Druid" takes on a different valence that speaks directly to the relationship between language and knowledge within (Irish) modernity. For Adorno, the subject's fundamental lack of autonomy in capitalism is mediated by language, as communicative language—having be-come during the nineteenth century, to quote Astradur Eysteinsson, "instru-mentalized as an object and vehicle of knowledge"—promotes the illusion of "the subject . . . freely controlling himself, free of all concern for the empirical world and having become absolute."[25]

Bourgeois subjects, in other words, experiencing contradictions that they can sense but cannot apprehend, assume that language as a form of knowledge is the ticket to freedom. For the national artist trapped in the language of his-tory that denies the legitimacy of his own culture, the compulsion to embrace knowledge is, ironically, both enticing and superficially immediate. If his his-tory has been erased, the solution would seem to entail rediscovering the na-tion's "true" past, to know the past and to disseminate that knowledge among the people. "Fergus and the Druid" registers but does not fulfill this desire. Rather, the drive to know the past is revealed as another illusion, a dream of freedom and autonomy that conceals the subject's own lack of freedom and au-tonomy. Examined from this angle, the second poem in *The Rose* does "sing the ancient ways," as the first poem promises, yet the song is itself entirely ironic: a revelation of the inherent limitations of Yeats's nationalist project.

Fergus recognizes that he is not autonomous, but the poem rejects a type of reading that might be expected in a collection designed, as Yeats writes in the closing poem, "to sweeten Ireland's wrong" ("To Ireland in the Coming Times"): a traditional nationalist reading that would directly identify the king's lack of autonomy with imperial repression. Instead, the pressure that Fergus ex-periences is linked with the people he rules: "A king is but a foolish labourer / Who wastes his blood to be another's dream." His cry of sorrow becomes clear when we realize that Fergus, like Yeats himself—the nationalist poet laboring to fulfill the dreams of the Irish people—always remains an object of national desire charged with the impossible task of embodying or, in the poet's case, articulating what the people would become. Thus, in answer to the Druid's repeated question, "What would you, king of the proud Red Branch Kings?"—a question that essentially asks, What would you *be?*—Fergus responds,

> A king and proud! And that is my despair.
> I feast amid my people on the hill,
> And pace the woods, and drive my chariot-wheels
> In the white border of the murmuring sea;
> And still I feel the crown upon my head.

The stanza, considered in isolation, refers only to Fergus and to the pressures of an ancient Ireland where the dreamer is called upon to be the man of action, but it also contains specific allusions to other poems in the collection. The word "proud" immediately recalls the preceding poem, the "proud rose" on the cross of time. The phrase "drive my chariot-wheels" refers to "Who goes with Fergus?" in which Yeats exhorts the reader to follow the poet king who "rules the brazen cars, / And rules the shadows of the wood, / And the white breast of the dim sea." Finally, the words "white border" evoke the poet's tireless pursuit, in the collection's closing work, "To Ireland in the Coming Times," after Ireland's "red-rose-bordered hem."

These allusions subtly reinforce the link between Fergus the king and Yeats the national poet. Both feel the compulsion to fulfill the dreams of the community, a compulsion all the more urgent for Yeats because he must speak the freedom that Ireland has lost. What is important about the poem, however, is that Yeats, despite his personal commitment to mysticism, does not uncritically embrace Fergus's "solution," his desire to "learn [the Druid's] dreaming wisdom." Quite the opposite: "Fergus and the Druid" presents the dream itself as illusion, a chimera of modern rationalism. Fergus assumes that his problem is not ontological ("What would you be?") but epistemological ("What would you know?"), or, put simply, that the need he feels to embody the nation can be assuaged by discovering a new mode of thought contained in the Druid's "little bag of dreams," contained, that is, in Ireland's mythic past. Here is what he finds:

> I see my life go drifting like a river
> From change to change; I have been many things—
> A green drop in the surge, a gleam of light
> Upon a sword, a fir-tree on a hill,

An old slave grinding at a heavy quern,
A king sitting upon a chair of gold—
And all these things were wonderful and great;
But now I have grown nothing, knowing all.

Fergus becomes not the autonomous subject that he had imagined but a being devoid of subjectivity, flowing like the Druid himself "from shape to shape." Read in light of Adorno, Fergus does indeed "know all," for to obtain complete knowledge within modernity is to "have grown nothing," to register the disintegration of the subject, to become "a green drop in the surge." Read in light of Irish modernity, Fergus becomes aware that he has occupied the subject positions demanded by imperialism, "An old slave grinding at a heavy quern," or hand mill, and by nationalism, "A king sitting upon a chair of gold." What Fergus learns, what the Druid's wisdom provides, is not the knowledge of an ideal, historical Ireland but of a modern Ireland, a world in which knowledge itself always reveals the subject's position and also, by extension, the artist's position as object of imperial and national desire.

Why, then, does Fergus describe "all these things" as "wonderful and great"? One answer is that awareness of the bind and disillusion of subjectivity is at once a moment of delight and despair, the self merging with all things natural. Another answer, more relevant to the immediate historical context, is that "wonder" comes from Fergus's recognition that he is also something else, that his own identity always exceeds the master/slave subject positions demanded by colonization's binary logic. At the same time, just as the speaker's desire, in the previous poem, to be at one with the rose gives way to the realization that such closure would entail the end of poetry, Fergus's joy yields to the realization that the end of subjectivity is just that, the eradication of the self. Simply put, knowledge of the past is not the answer. A decade later, Yeats would make precisely this point when referring to Young Ireland. Because Thomas Davis and others "had taught a study of our history with the glory of Ireland for event," they introduced the notion that the proper goal of literature is knowledge (*EI*, 316). As a result, "there was no [true] literature [in their movement], for literature is a child of experience always, of knowledge never; and the nation itself, instead of being a dumb struggling thought seeking a mouth to utter it . . . had become, at best, a subject of knowledge" (*EI*, 317).

Both "Fergus and the Druid" and "The Rose upon the Rood of Time" thus take us to a border that art cannot cross. Both register that language and knowledge are embedded in the fabric of a veil that conceals the true, an imagined Ireland that escapes the signifier "rose," a language of the nation, "thought seeking a mouth to utter it," beyond this language, a form of knowledge about the self and the community that exceeds all knowledge and mystical wisdom. And yet, the poet continues to dream, producing works that expose this fallen world for what it is, a web of sorrow, and that register the compulsion to embrace imperial rationalism and nationalist escapism while remaining true to the possibility of a new Ireland. Appropriately, then, the collection ends where it began, with an affirmation of the poet's tireless desire to speak the moment of (un)realizable closure. Yeats himself, he writes in "To Ireland in the Coming Times," should not be considered "any less" than his nationalist predecessors because he refuses to articulate the instant of (postcolonial) completion, for that hope remains, must remain, in the blank spaces surrounding the words on the page:

> Nor be I any less of them,
> Because the red-rose-bordered hem
> Of her [Ireland], whose history began
> Before God made the angelic clan,
> Trails all about the written page. (*VP*, 137)

Truly, Yeats's "rhymes more than their rhyming tell." They expose a modern real in which the artist's desire for individual autonomy and national autonomy is necessarily thwarted by language and rational thought. Yet, instead of blindly turning to an imagined unity that can be directly "known" or to the dead language of the past, they hold that drive toward unity in dialectical tension, steadfastly remaining true to an ideal that art can evoke but can never speak into being. Hence, the poet continues to trail after the hem cloth of a liberated Ireland that always departs the room at the moment when the poet arrives, that remains, like the rose, a signifier bearing the trace of its essence and not the essence itself.

To this point, my focus has been confined to works usually regarded as romantic, as I have sought to demonstrate the extent to which Yeats's early verse, in its engagement with language and knowledge, exhibits a dialectical modernist impulse at odds with the escapist impulse usually identified in studies of Yeatsian symbolism/modernism. I will turn now to the more recognizably modernist poetry of Yeats's middle phase in order to examine the question of art's use value within the contexts of Irish modernity and his increased dissatisfaction with conventional nationalism. The natural starting point is "Adam's Curse," a poem that, in addition to meditating upon the "labour" of creating art, clearly represents, in its shift to more direct speech and its leave-taking of romantic love, a transitional text.

The poem—whose autobiographical elements have been discussed at length—sets the scene with Yeats, Maud Gonne, and Gonne's sister, Kathleen Pilcher, discussing poetry.[26] Yeats begins:

I said, "A line will take us hours maybe;
Yet if it does not seem a moment's thought,
Our stitching and unstitching has been naught.
Better go down upon your marrow-bones
And scrub a kitchen pavement, or break stones
Like an old pauper, in all kinds of weather;
For to articulate sweet sounds together
Is to work harder than all these, and yet
Be thought an idler by the noisy set
Of bankers, schoolmasters, and clergymen
The martyrs call the world." (*VP*, 204)

Initially, Yeats the speaker sets out to debunk the romantic notion that poetry is not the product of labor but of direct inspiration. Poems, though each "line will take us hours," must "seem a moment's thought" for a public schooled in the traditions of Romanticism. Yet, the speaker's defense, particularly when examined in light of Adorno's comments on practical art, would appear to embrace a decidedly modern conception of aesthetic use value. If poetry requires time (hours of "stitching and unstitching") and labor (work more difficult than "scrub[bing] a kitchen pavement" or "break[ing] stones"), if, in other words, poetry is composed of quantifiable factors, the product itself is necessarily quantifiable. This position hardly seems consistent with Yeats's own aesthetic theories, his tireless assertion that the "images" in art "grow in beauty as they grow in sterility," that art only becomes great when it is "separated from all the general purposes of life" (*Au*, 242). Indeed, for Yeats the central failing of European culture is that it has fostered the belief that art must include a practical function: "Had not Matthew Arnold his faith in what he described as the best thought of his generation, Browning his psychological curiosity, Tennyson, as before him Shelley and Wordsworth, moral values that were not aesthetic values?" (*Au*, 242).

To understand why Yeats the speaker advances a position incompatible with that of Yeats the artist, we need to remember the autobiographical context. Maud Gonne is the only character who does not speak, for she is the poem's direct audience, a woman who chose the man of action, John MacBride, over the poet, failing to realize that art too entails a form of practical work. We also need to recognize that the poem is decidedly ironic, though not simply because, as critics have long argued, the closing stanzas reveal the futility of romantic love. Rather, irony emerges out of the poem's apparent endorsement of aesthetic use value. The key word in the opening stanza is "martyrs." Included in a poem centered on Maud Gonne and placed in the collection directly before "Red Hanrahan's Song about Ireland," whose refrain is "Cathleen, the daughter of Houlihan," "martryrs" evokes Yeats's early twentieth-century popular image as the author of *Cathleen ni Houlihan*. "Adam's Curse" thus reminds the poem's more general audience of Yeats's own labor for the nationalist cause, linking that nationalist project specifically with his idealization of Gonne as the embodiment of an imagined Ireland. It does so in order to set the poem squarely within the contexts of Irish modernity, an Ireland in which the artist is compelled to produce practical art. The martyrs of the world and the schoolmasters whose teachings they echo consider true art the product of "idler[s]," for art in this modernity dominated by materialism ("bankers"), propaganda ("schoolmasters"), and religion ("clergymen") is consistently valorized as a means to an end and not an end in itself. In this world, the "best" art—that is, committed art—must proudly wear its use value on its sleeve.

"Adam's Curse" does precisely this, though in an unexpected manner. The production of art in the name of romantic love and nationalist idealism is linked explicitly with labor in order to expose the link itself. After "Adam's fall," there is indeed "no fine thing / . . . but needs much labouring." Notions of "love" and "courtesy," phrases "out of beautiful old books" that lovers "would sigh and quote with learned looks," are now revealed as illusory, an "idle trade" that speaks at once to Yeats's devotion to Gonne and, because of the poem's subtle evocation of the Gonne / Cathleen connection, to an ideal Ireland—"the tear and smile in Erin's eye," as Yeats mockingly puts it in 1922 (*Au*, 271–272). The poem does not, however, conclude with an escapist rejection of modernity, as if knowledge of nationalism and love's false promises allows the artist to extricate himself from the real. Instead, "Adam's Curse" dialectically opposes the real by offering an image of useful art become what it truly is, useless. Out of the dialogue emerges the voice of Yeats the poet meditating, like so many romantics before him, upon the moon:

> We sat grown quiet at the name of love;
> We saw the last embers of daylight die,
> And in the trembling blue-green of the sky
> A moon, worn as if it had been a shell
> Washed by time's waters as they rose and fell
> About the stars and broke in days and years.

The "shell" metaphor returns us to the two shepherd poems, while the fading of "daylight" recalls Yeats's *Celtic Twilight*, the dreamy prose tales of a romantic Ireland now dead and gone. What remains for the national artist bound in a modern world divorced from a prelapsarian past is to present the art object as a product divested of assumed use value, the dish of romantic, practical art served up cold and stale to a public eager to consume fresh works with clear political messages. If, for Adorno, "the idiosyncrasy of poetic thought . . . is a form of reaction against the reification of the world, against the rule of the wares of commerce over people," the idiosyncrasy of "Adam's Curse" lies in its refusal to be the art object that nationalism desires.[27] Romantic dreams that held forth the possibility of actual change metaphorically emerge out of the (Celtic) twilight in the form of the "worn" moon, an object "Washed by time's waters" and "broke in days and years." An aesthetic image, the moon is necessarily the product of labor, as the emphasis on time, by recalling the opening stanza, implicitly suggests, yet the moon's tragic beauty, its value as art, lies in the recognition that practical, romantic art ultimately does not directly spark change. By striving to love Gonne/Cathleen "in the old high way of love," the national poet had surrendered himself to modernity's promise of a life in which "all seemed happy," in which the autonomous subject could shape the world according to his desires. In the closing lines the poet now recognizes, as his beloved as well as his audience must recognize, that this vision of progressive change merely conceals his own stagnation together with the broader stagnation of a modern world dominated by nationalist idealism: "and yet we'd grown / As weary-hearted as that hollow moon." The simile becomes a metaphor for art in this Ireland, an object that registers its own roots in labor yet resists complete reification by virtue of its own profound uselessness.

Our reading of this transitional poem within the contexts of nationalist modernity helps to explain one curious feature of the 1904 collection, *In the Seven Woods*, Yeats's decision to place the seemingly transparent political poem "Red Hanrahan's Song about Ireland," a work actually written in 1894, directly after "Adam's Curse." Most critics pass quickly over "Red Hanrahan's Song," glossing it as an artifact of a romantic nationalist project that Yeats had, at this point, not entirely abandoned. Hazard Adams, however, detects in the song an "undercurrent of bitterness."[28] Recalling Yeats's always careful arrangement of his volumes, Adams suggests that the rejection of romantic love voiced in the former is paralleled by the rejection of romantic nationalism in the latter, as the Maud Gonne of "Adam's Curse" now arrives in her guise as Cathleen, a figure "powerfully idealized virtually as a religious icon . . . with similar dire results."[29]

While I agree with Adams's larger contention that the placement alters our reading of the song, I disagree with his assertion that the poem itself displays "a certain ambiguity" in its treatment of Cathleen.[30] The poem's claim that "Our courage breaks like an old tree in a black wind and dies, / But we have hidden in our hearts the flame out of the eyes / Of Cathleen, the daughter of Houlihan" (*VP*, 207) is ambiguous only insofar as all conventional treatments of the woman as nation are ambiguous, rooted in an Oedipal fear of and desire for what Patrick Keane has termed the "devouring female."[31] Rather, the poem's full irony becomes clear when we read it not as a parallel to "Adam's Curse" but as an extension of "Adam's Curse," a coda that once again offers practical art grown worn and hollow:

> The yellow pool has overflowed high up on Clooth-na-Bare,
> For the wet winds are blowing out of the clinging air;
> Like heavy flooded waters our bodies and our blood;
> But purer than a tall candle before the Holy Rood
> Is Cathleen, the daughter of Houlihan.

This is art that wears its use value as a badge of honor. Though Irish history is a tale of continual defeat, though Irish modernity is a world of people whose "bodies" and "blood" are washed in the "waters" (recall "time's waters" from the previous poem) of oppression, the nation has, with religious zeal, remained true to Eire. The image of tireless devotion directly fulfills the imperatives of committed art by instilling pride in the community, transforming defeat into heroism, and, like *Cathleen ni Houlihan*, by calling upon the audience to remain true to revolutionary idealism. Yet the previous poem has already exposed committed art as a delusion, an aesthetic that promises material change but, because it is always bound by the conditions of modernity, can never produce actual change. Thus, the lines of the song, read in isolation as an endorsement of practical art, take on an ironic charge. Steadfast dedication, suggested by the repetition of the word "low," becomes stasis, as poet and audience "have all bent low and low and kissed the quiet feet / Of Cathleen." Patriotic and religious piety, men and women lighting candles before fair Ireland, then becomes monastic seclusion, the image of a people who have not simply "hidden in our hearts the flame" of Cathleen's eyes but have hidden themselves from the truth of modernity, from the recognition that Cathleen, though "purer than a tall candle before the Holy Rood," has failed to bring about the expected resurrection. Indeed, the poem that follows, "The Old Men Admiring Themselves in the Water," neatly extends the song's irony, for adulation of practical art is adulation of modernity's false promise of the autonomous self. The old men, gazing into a pool of water in the hope of perceiving their lost beauty, are revealed as static figures, bodies become rooted in place and withered like "old thorn-trees":

> They had hands like claws, and their knees
> Were twisted like the old thorn-trees
> By the waters.
> I hear the old, old men say,
> "All that's beautiful drifts away
> Like the waters."

If "Adam's Curse" registers and resists the compulsion to produce committed art in an Ireland dominated by romantic nationalism, "Easter, 1916" provides a more complex response to a more complex situation. When Patrick Pearse, James Connolly, 1,600 Irish Volunteers, and 300 Citizen's Army soldiers seized the General Post Office and other government buildings in Dublin, proclaiming the independence of the Irish Republic, and, after several days of fighting, surrendering to the overwhelming forces of the British, Yeats, like many of his compatriots, was surprised and troubled.[32] Believing that the Home Rule Bill of 1914, though rescinded by British conservatives at the outbreak of the Great War, remained a possibility for the nonviolent restoration of at least partial Irish autonomy, he saw the rebellion as a political failure. But he was also, again like the vast majority of his compatriots, taken aback by the British government's hasty decision to execute the rebel leaders, perceiving in their deaths the rebirth of Ireland's ancient heroism. Thus, he writes to Lady Gregory with a mixture of anger, elation, and, finally, despair:

> I see . . . no reason to believe that the delicate instrument of Justice is being worked with precision in Dublin. I am trying to write a poem on the men executed—"a terrible beauty has been born again." . . . I had no idea that any public event could so deeply move me—and I am very despondent about the future. At the moment I feel that all the work of years has been overturned, all the bringing together of classes, all the freeing of Irish literature and criticism from politics. . . . [Maud Gonne's] main thought seems to be "tragic dignity has returned to Ireland." She had been told by two members of the Irish Party that "Home Rule was betrayed." She thinks now that the sacrifice has made it safe. (L, 613)

He similarly writes to John Quinn: "This Irish business has been a great grief. We have lost the ablest and most fine-natured of our young men. A world seems to have been swept away. I keep going over the past in my mind and wondering if I could have done anything to turn those young men in some other direction. . . . I chiefly dread the temptation to controversy one finds in Dublin. I knew several of the executed men, and others were familiar figures" (L, 614).

The letters neatly present the Rising itself as a form of compulsion, an event that demands response by the national artist even as it causes the poet to reconsider the practical value of art. Registering the "many miscarriages of justice" (L, 613) perpetrated by the British, Yeats immediately turns to the aesthetic as a refuge, a means of making sense of what has occurred: "a terrible beauty has been born again." Yet he remains decidedly ambivalent as to whether or not art can in fact do anything. His early attempts at "bringing together of classes" and "freeing . . . Irish literature . . . from politics"—to be sure, a disingenuous statement given the hostility toward the middle classes expressed in his previous collection, *Responsibilities* (1914)—have not brought into being the society that he had hoped to create. At the same time, Yeats clings to the belief that he was (and is) capable of controlling history, puzzling over his past actions to discover if he could have "turn[ed] those young men in some other direction." Yeats's uncertain response to aesthetic use value is, as the letters make clear, bound up with the larger conditions of Irish modernity. While the poet clearly perceives the contradictions of Enlightenment rationalism—the illusory belief that "the delicate instrument of Justice," this universal value, has been "worked with precision in Dublin"—he also clearly perceives the profound inadequacy of offering a transparently nationalist work, noting with barely concealed contempt Gonne's assertion that "tragic dignity has returned to Ireland."

"Easter, 1916" emerges out of this ambivalence. Formally, the poem, as a modernist work, appears to fulfill what the event itself demands, what the poem's nationalist audience demand, and what the title implicitly promises: meaning, a way of comprehending the actions that took place in Dublin on Easter Monday, 1916. The fragments of modernity—of life when a "world seems to have been swept away"—are assembled into an art work that restores order to the chaos of history, a committed work that validates, through the repetition of the phrase "A terrible beauty is born," the heroic sacrifice of the rebels (*VP*, 392). What the poem actually does, however, is precisely the opposite. The stanzas systematically present and reject any attempts—rational, romantic, national, or religious—to confer meaning, and thus closure, upon the rebellion. The refrain stands alone not as repetitive visions of noble sacrifice that subsume earlier questioning but as statements that remain in dialectical tension with prior uncertainty. The expected moment of completion, the satisfaction that committed art provides, never arrives. Instead, Yeats offers a poem that reveals its own inadequacy, exposing art's fundamental inability to satisfy the desire of both poet and audience for meaningful closure. Just as the rose poems mark that which the national artist cannot speak into being, the birth of a new Ireland, "Easter, 1916" marks the essence of the Rising, this event that is part of a history yet to be written, as that which exceeds the bounds of the aesthetic object.

The opening stanza depicts an Ireland awash in materialism and dull modernity, men and women whom the poet has met

> at close of day
> Coming with vivid faces
> From counter or desk among grey
> Eighteenth-century houses.

The adjective "vivid" suggests that there exists something more in these "faces" that pass among the once bright emblems of Yeats's ideal Ascendancy past, aristocratic homes become "grey" offices and shops. Yet that "something more" is not made clear. Instead, Yeats turns upon himself, confessing that the "polite meaningless words" that he had exchanged with these people merely concealed his own disdain, "a mocking tale or a gibe" that he would soon relate "To please a companion / Around the fire at the club." This vision of life filled with "meaningless" language—likely a reference to the rhetoric of newspapers and political speeches that Yeats so despised—again hints at the possibility of something else, the possibility of "meaningful" words that might now be spoken by the national artist. Once "certain that they and I / But lived where motley is worn," the poet, having recognized his own folly, is prepared to reveal the true heroism momentarily glimpsed in these "vivid faces," to articulate, in a language other than the superficial speech of modernity, the full significance of their sacrifice: "All changed, changed utterly: / A terrible beauty is born."

The two lines are called upon to bear considerable rhetorical weight, and that is exactly the point. The word "changed," emphasized by repetition and the adverb "utterly," begs the question: Changed to *what?*[33] The colon at the close of the first line portends an answer, but what follows is equally cryptic. The indefinite article, though referring broadly to the rebellion, is vague, while the word "terrible" suggests at once tragedy (noble sacrifice?) and horror (meaningless death?). The noun "beauty" seems to put us on firmer ground, though the predicate "is born" calls attention to the abstract nature of the preceding word, forcing us to ask a question that the poem again does not answer: Exactly what is this beauty that is born out of a failed rebellion and fifteen executions? The lines, of course, work well as poetry, neatly evoking the full range of emotions that Yeats and others likely experienced when contemplating the revolution. And they work well as poetry precisely because they do not work well as rhetoric. The poem plays upon the audience's desire for closure, hinting that the true nature of the rebel's "vivid faces" will be revealed in meaningful language, but then frustrates that desire by offering two lines that ask more than they answer. There is beauty, but the poet does not render that beauty, in the manner of committed art and in the mode of rational thought/language, as something immediately knowable.

To appreciate the full impact of Yeats's strategy on an Irish audience, we need only to recall the poetry of the rebels themselves, widely circulated before and shortly after the Rising. For Patrick Pearse, Thomas MacDonagh, and Joseph Plunkett, the beauty of martyrdom is quite clear: the ultimate expression of loyalty and devotion to the cause, the heroic embracing of a death that will lead to communal rebirth. Thus, in "The Mother," Pearse offers a speaker who understands the full significance of her sons' martyrdom:

I do not grudge them: Lord, I do not grudge
My two strong sons that I have seen go out
To break their strength and die, they and a few,
In bloody protest for a glorious thing,
They shall be spoken of among their people,
The generations shall remember them,
And call them blessed.[34]

The poem counterbalances the grief of a mother with a clear affirmation of noble death, providing a form of committed art that prompts men to action and confers in advance meaning upon the Rising. Yeats, in contrast, rejects not simply this message but also all such messages, recognizing that the act of giving meaning to the actions of the rebels would simply return his own art to everyday meaninglessness, to the realm of practical art, nationalist idealism, and Enlightenment rationalism where the chaos of the world can be reduced, classified, and served up as an object of knowledge—the "truth" of the Rising.

The second stanza of "Easter, 1916" works again to subvert audience desires, as Yeats describes (but does not name) four participants: Constance Markievicz, Pearse, MacDonagh, and Maud Gonne's husband, John MacBride. Each portrait emphasizes what these people were: a woman devoted to nationalist idealism "Until her voice grew shrill," a schoolmaster and artist, and a poet who "Was coming into his force." MacBride, who "had done most bitter wrong / To some who are near my heart," is recalled as "A drunken, vainglorious lout."[35] In calling attention to what these individuals were, particularly given that the word "dreamed" is used to describe the final figure, the stanza works rhetorically to create anticipation. We expect the national artist to reveal what the rebels have now become, to express the reality behind the poet's earlier, artificial dream. What Yeats provides, however, is more artifice, words that can only express the moment of transformation, the instant of change, and not the full meaning of that transformation. Yeats writes of MacBride:

He, too, has resigned his part
In the casual comedy;
He, too, has been changed in his turn,
Transformed utterly:
A terrible beauty is born.

The verb "resigned" and the passive construction "has been"[36] draw attention to the fact that some transformation has occurred, but the force of the lines and of the entire stanza is to emphasize only the negative, what these figures had been in a world where all had seemed to play the role of the jester, blindly donning the fool's motley. Again, the final two lines are called to serve a rhetorical function that they simply cannot: to provide the audience with the true meaning of what these individuals have become. The art object thus stands in dialectical tension with modernity, evoking a change that it refuses to package, classify, and make meaningful.

The third stanza presents a fragment of the natural world, as if the true significance of the rebellion might be discovered not in the ordinary realm of urban modernity but in the realm of the pastoral, the romantic. Here, the poet seeks for a metaphor that will "speak"—make comprehensible—the transformation that he has only alluded to as "terrible beauty." Poet and audience, however, merely discover a metaphor for what the rebellion is not: "Hearts with one purpose alone" that "seem / Enchanted to a stone / To trouble the living stream." The stone is not what the rebels have become but what they were, devoted to a single cause, unyielding and cold. Juxtaposed with natural images of things that "Minute by minute . . . change"—"birds that range / From cloud to tumbling cloud," the diving of "long-legged moor-hens" for food, and the mating cries of "hens to moor-cocks"—the stone seems lifeless "in the midst of all." Something has changed in the hearts of the rebels, something has been born, paradoxically, out of their refusal to change, yet the poem can only hold that paradox open, naming what the rebels had been but not what they have become, the truth of the Rising that is never articulated.

"Too long a sacrifice / Can make a stone of the heart," begins the final stanza, as Yeats returns to the position of the critical nationalist who recognizes, in the death of the rebels themselves, the "terrible" nature of patriotic idealism. Yet, like all positions embraced by the poem in this closing section, all modes of comprehending what has occurred, disdain gives way to further questioning: "O when may it suffice?" The question immediately leads Yeats to adopt a contrary pose. Tapping into conventional nationalist rhetoric, he briefly wears the mask of the pious mother, the woman who, like the speaker in Pearse's poem, recognizes that martyrdom is merely a brief sleep preceding a greater good comprehensible only to God:

> That is Heaven's part, our part
> To murmur name upon name,
> As a mother names her child
> When sleep at last has come
> On limbs that had run wild.

The rational man, however, rejects even this comfort, recognizing that the martyrs are not sleeping children but dead men. Indeed, Yeats now puts on the mask of the practical statesman, pondering the question that haunts his own letters:

"Was it needless death after all? / For England may keep faith / For all that is done and said." Britain may in fact honor its prior commitment to Home Rule. Yet this is cold comfort, for Home Rule renders the rebel deaths as "needless," while the alternative, a meaningful sacrifice, merely opens the door to further violence. Yeats thus falls back on the tenuous affirmation, "dream thou," sounded in "The Song of the Happy Shepherd": "We know their dream; enough / To know they dreamed and are dead."

For the poet, however, it is not "enough." The paradox of the third stanza—change born of that which is changeless—returns and again remains unresolved: "And what if excess of love / Bewildered them till they died?" The question neatly captures the sense of uncertainty that pervades the poem. If we stress the first three words, "And what if," the question is defiantly rhetorical, suggesting that the rebels, though driven by blind idealism, are heroic precisely because they remained true to that idealism. Yet, if we stress the phrase "excess of love" and the verb "Bewildered," we are back with the unchanging stone, the brutal heart of the insurgent who, deluded in his cause, fails to recognize that his actions may have defeated the dream of Home Rule. The strength of the poem is that neither answer is satisfactory, for the truth of Easter 1916 defies immediate understanding, always exceeding the poet's words. Thus, Yeats ends the only way he can:

> I write it out in a verse—
> MacDonagh and MacBride
> And Connolly and Pearse
> Now and in time to be,
> Wherever green is worn,
> Are changed, changed utterly;
> A terrible beauty is born.

Yeats simply offers names, that basic linguistic sign so inadequate for communicating the full complexity of the person it signifies. For the reader who yearns for something more, for a national audience expecting a form of practical art that might give the meaning behind the names, frustration is bound to occur. Yet that is the deeply rooted power of "Easter, 1916," the autonomous art object that refuses to be what the audience desire, that evokes the transformation and rebirth of Ireland, while resisting the temptation to articulate, classify, or prescribe this fundamental change, this "terrible beauty."

EPILOGUE

I am no Nationalist, except in Ireland for passing reasons; State and Nation are the work of intellect, and when you consider what comes before and after them they are . . . not worth the blade of grass God gives for the nest of the linnet.

—W. B. Yeats, "A General Introduction for My Work"

Like so many of his categorical pronouncements from the late 1930s, Yeats's concluding remarks from this 1937 essay, published after his death under the title "A General Introduction for My Work," are intended to convey finality. Explicitly dismissing his commitment to Irish nationalism as a "passing" phase and implicitly offering one last dig at the Auden generation, those young writers who "have thought out opinions that join them to this or that political party" (*LE*, 215), the great poet declares his faith in an aesthetics that transcends "State and Nation." The true aim of the poet is to bring "phantasmagoria" (*LE*, 204) into his works by tapping into the collective memory of all humanity, those mythic and folk traditions that extend back through Shakespeare, Dante, and Homer. As Yeats had written in *The Trembling of the Veil*, "revelation is from the self, but from that age-long memoried self . . . that teaches the birds to make their nest"—an aphorism that helps to explain why a "blade of grass" in a "linnet's nest" is more valuable than all creations of the rational mind or "intellect" (*Au*, 216). If Yeats's goal is thus to renounce the nationalist significance of his art, this final choice of metaphors would seem more than fitting; that is, until we recall his fondness for comparing the process of nest building to the process of creating the organically unified nation.[1] Just as the bird, though working alone, builds the nest according to instinct, the individual, by striving to fulfill his or her own creative vision, will rediscover the collective, "age-long" racial memory of the community, thereby helping to construct a nation that emerges according to a common design. Considered from this vantage, the rhetorical certainties conveyed in Yeats's words are belied by the figurative language, as if the poet, though he would reject the political dimensions of his art, cannot help but return to an issue that had played such a key role in his artistic development: the fascinating and difficult labor of nation-building. The figure that emerges at the close of this seminal essay is thus not the aloof poet who is content with his life's work, not the great artist who has triumphed over the mundane world of politics, but the sleepless figure of "Man and Echo" who "lie[s] awake night after night," his thoughts continually circling back upon the question, "Did that play of mine send out / Certain men the English shot?"

He never did get the answers right to that question, nor did he ever settle on one final response to the larger questions of (gendered) identity, history, epistemology, and modernity that I have explored throughout this book. But rather than attack Yeats for failing to articulate the contours of a truly postcolonial Ireland, whatever that might ultimately mean, or defend the nativist, neocolonial, and authoritarian views that he sometimes adopts, I have endeavored to demonstrate how Yeatsian nationalism operates not as one position but as a series of fluid stances that manifest themselves throughout his life as he negotiates the turning gyres of Irish history. Although phrases such as "national consciousness" or "liberationist poetics" make for convenient labels, they fail to encompass the complexity of Yeats's political thought. More important, though, they tend to encourage readings of the poetry and drama that would sort his works into ready-made political compartments. While my own readings expressly focus on one discrete aspect of Yeats—the multiple ways in which his writings respond to the ambiguities, paradoxes, and contradictions of Irish (post)coloniality—my intention throughout has been to privilege the artist himself. The circular movements of the chapters in this book are designed to mirror the circular movements of Yeats's mind, as the conflicted nationalist and nationalist critic struggles to imagine a new Ireland that is diverse and unified, culturally unique and part of the global community, modern but not Western, rooted in the traditions of the past but not paralyzed by a single-minded attachment to the past.

Yeats's slide into authoritarian politics during the 1930s is, in some respects, the product of his frustration with an Ireland that had failed to transform itself by addressing these issues, an Ireland dominated by a form of Western consciousness that, for Yeats, is characterized by an atavistic nationalist program bent on enforcing political "opinions" and by a middle-class culture driven by consumerism. Like the dramatist who took refuge in the drawing room of the Big House hoping to discover an audience more amenable to his political and aesthetic ideals, the Yeats of the 1930s takes refuge in myth and the cycles of his visionary system. Struggling to fuse a Protestant tradition of modern, creative, forward-thinking leaders with a Catholic peasant tradition rooted in the fecund soil of primitive folk imagination, Yeats, in poems such as "Under Ben Bulben," seeks to perpetuate a neocolonial vision of an Ireland guided by a benevolent aristocracy, famously enjoining "Irish poets" to "Sing the peasantry, and then / Hard-riding country gentlemen." Gazing with bitterness on an Ireland in which mass consciousness has supplanted heroic individuality, he returns, in "Parnell's Funeral," to the solitary figure of the individualistic hero who has been betrayed by the people: "Had Cosgrave eaten Parnell's heart, the land's / Imagination had been satisfied." Wound in the mummy cloth of *A Vision*, he follows the course of civilizations "dying each other's life, living each other's death" (*V2*, 271), and, though "Aeroplane and Zeppelin will come out," as he writes in "Lapis Lazuli," the poet achieves a sense of tragic joy, imagining an Eastern world in which "Two Chinamen," nonplussed by the chaos of modernity, watch "all the tragic scene" with "gay" and "ancient, glittering eyes."

Yet if the poems from the 1930s frequently signal a retreat from history, the disillusioned artist's attempts to reconcile the contradictions of Irish post-coloniality on a mythic level, they also display an antithetical impulse, as the sleepless poet, plagued by questions he can never fully answer, continually returns to the place, as he memorably puts it in "The Circus Animals' Desertion," "where all the ladders start," the littered ground of an Ireland in transition. In this space of the unfolding present, authoritarian pronouncements give way to further meditations. While the ghostly poet of "Under Ben Bulben" would, in the manner of Hamlet's father, have his readers "swear" allegiance to a mythic vision of the nation rooted in the peasantry and guided by the aristocracy, the terminally ill poet who wrote "The Black Tower" highlights the tragic end of those legendary figures from Ireland's past who have remained "oath-bound." Based upon Standish O'Grady's play *The Masque of Finn*,[2] in which members of the Fianna brotherhood await the return of a messianic leader, the poem depicts a group of aged warriors who, though besieged and facing starvation, continue to be true to their king. The poem concludes, not with tragic heroism, but with a vision of the tower become a tomb:

> There in the tomb the dark grows blacker
> But wind comes up from the shore
> They shake when the winds roar
> Old bones upon the mountain shake.

The poem's image of "hale men . . . stretched in slumber" awaiting a king who may never return serves as a cautionary reminder, not only to those who would bind themselves to the vision of a new Ireland celebrated in "Under Ben Bulben" but also to those who would remain myopically fixated on Ireland's legendary past at the expense of confronting the present and imagining the future. As is the case with the first of Yeats's "Three Marching Songs"—a poem that begins with the nationalist cry to "Remember all those renowned generations," those men who "have died on the scaffold," only to conclude with the words, "All this is finished, let it fade"—"The Black Tower," Yeats's final poem, offers a voice exiled to the grave that would call upon the Irish to see present and past anew, to "Cast a cold eye" on the blind idealism of the living and on the sacrifices of the dead.

Yeats, however, is not content simply to "enumerate old themes," for we find in "Cuchulain Comforted" an alternative vision of nationhood that exceeds the neocolonial certainty of "Under Ben Bulben" and the bitterly antinationalist position of "The Black Tower." Having received "six mortal wounds," Cuchulain enters a phase between death and rebirth that Yeats, in *A Vision*, terms "the Shiftings" when the individual's "nature is reversed" and he relives his existence in the exact opposite manner (*V*2, 231).[3] For the heroic, passionate, and individualistic Irish hero, this means, in "Cuchulain Comforted," losing his identity among an anonymous group of "Convicted cowards" who sew burial shrouds instead of engaging in battle. The individual is thus subsumed by the group, but the poem, rather than voicing Cuchulain's agony, concludes with a peaceful image of collective song: "They sang, but had nor human notes nor words, / Though all was done in common as before; // They had changed their throats and had the throats of birds." In a prose draft of the poem, Yeats writes that the shades "began to sing and they did not sing like men and women but like linnets that had been stood on a perch and taught by a good singing master" (*LDW*, 212). We are again back to the linnet and to the authoritarian mode of "Under Ben Bulben," as the birds, placed "on a perch," follow the lead of "a good singing master," who represents a form of racial memory that Yeats, no longer himself "a golden bird set upon a golden bough," has discovered and would pass on to future generations.

In the poem, however, perch and singing master disappear, and in their place we have a vision of transformation. The throat of Cuchulain, Yeats's mythic double, and the throats of the shades, the community, are all changed into "the throats of birds." What remains is not song but the possibility of song, not directed thought or language but that which exceeds thought and language. The dying poet remains trapped in words and in the grim reality of the present, but in this moment of passive acceptance we have the potential for something more: a different song, an alternative vantage, a new vision of an inchoate community emerging according to a pattern that has yet to be conceived. What remains, in other words, is not an end but a new beginning. "Content to live it all again," as he wrote in "A Dialogue of Self and Soul," Yeats is prepared "to follow to its source" the tangle of roots that run deeply into the wet soil of his homeland, another first step on his journey to discover in art an Irish nation that has never been imagined.

NOTES

Introduction

1. Howes, *Yeats's Nations*, 1.

2. Ramazani, *The Hybrid Muse*, 21–48. Most of the readings in Fleming, *W. B. Yeats and Postcolonialism*, respond to and build upon previous debates concerning Yeats's politics. For an early indictment of Yeats's fascist leanings, see O'Brien, "Passion and Cunning," 207–278. For a detailed and persuasive response to O'Brien, see Cullingford, *Yeats, Ireland, and Fascism*. For an account of and partial response to those political attacks that center on Yeats as a modernist, see Bush, "The Modernist under Siege," 325–333. For a thorough overview of Yeats and politics, see Allison, "The Attack on Yeats," 61–73. Excerpts from these authors and others are included in Allison's indispensable collection, *Yeats's Political Identities*.

3. Fanon, *Wretched of the Earth*, 203.

4. Said, *Culture and Imperialism*, 229–230.

5. Ibid., 220–238; Kearney, *Postnationalist Ireland*, 113–115; Deane, *Celtic Revivals*, 28–50; Eagleton, *Heathcliff and the Great Hunger*, 301–310. Edward Said views Yeats as a nationalist who wrestles with and highlights the dangers of Fanon's first stage in decolonization yet "stopped short of imagining full political liberation" (238). Richard Kearney argues that in works such as *Cathleen ni Houlihan* and "Easter, 1916," Yeats "offered the myth of Mother Ireland as symbolic compensation for the colonial calamities of history." This "mythological motherland served as a goddess of sovereignty who, at least at the imaginary level, might restore a lost national identity by summoning her sons to the sacred rite of renewal through sacrifice" (113)—the very bedrock of a militant Republican tradition in force to this day. For Seamus Deane, whose position accords broadly with those of Terry Eagleton, John Wilson Foster, the early criticism of Declan Kiberd, W. J. McCormack, and others, Yeats's "so-called fascism is, in fact, an almost pure specimen of the colonialist mentality" (49). Although Deane sympathizes with Yeats's willingness to reject modern rationalism, he perceives in Yeats a deluded attempt to transform history into myth, to discover in an imagined Anglo-Irish past the Ireland he could not discover in a present dominated by the largely Catholic middle class.

The collection *W. B. Yeats and Postcolonialism* marks what can be termed the second wave of postcolonial Yeats criticism. Broadly speaking, the articles follow two basic patterns. The regressive features of Yeatsian nationalism are mentioned and rejected, as the critic, building upon and extending Said, presents a liberationist Yeats who shares affinities with Salman Rushdie, Christopher Okigbo, Derek Walcott, Evan Boland, or Seamus Heaney, embraces hybridity and "double consciousness" (xxvi), and "set[s] up dialectical oscillations which complicate the epistemology of postcolonialism" (xix). Or, the reverse occurs: the liberationist elements are mentioned and dismissed, as the critic, building upon Deane, presents a nationalist Yeats who, trapped in imperialism's binary logic, ultimately fails to become a truly "postcolonial" writer.

6. See the recently published collections, Booth and Rigby, *Modernism and Empire*, and Bartolovich and Lazarus, *Marxism, Modernity, and Postcolonial Studies*.

7. Chatterjee, *The Nation and Its Fragments*, 6.

8. Renan, "What Is a Nation?" 83.

9. Nandy, *The Intimate Enemy*, xi.

10. As Marjorie Howes notes in *Yeats's Nations*, Yeats posited for his model of national unity "a group mind that was comprised of many minds but looked and functioned like a single consciousness" (69).

11. *Freeman's Journal*, January 29, 1907.

12. See, for example, Kline, *The Last Courtly Lover*, 124–164.

13. See, for example, Foster, *Modern Ireland*, 431–460.

14. Young, *Troubled Mirror*, 4.

15. See, for example, Eagleton, *Heathcliff and the Great Hunger*, 301–302.

16. If, as Leonard Orr writes in his introduction to *Yeats and Postmodernism*, "Yeats has been left as a modernist because he has been studied almost exclusively from within a modernist framework, using critical techniques developed under modernist and premodernist aesthetics" (3), the essays in this collection "begin the process of postmodernizing Yeats" (10). If, as Deborah Fleming notes in *W. B. Yeats and Postcolonialism*, critics have failed to recognize "that Yeats articulates much more fully than most postcolonial writers the artist's dilemma in an emerging nation" (xvii), the readings that appear in this collection treat Yeats the modernist as a construct that requires not so much reexamination as replacement. The opening essay, one of two specifically devoted to Yeatsian modernism, illustrates this drive, as Cristina J. Thaut posits an early Yeats who "is colonial/nationalist/modern" but later "becomes postcolonial/liberationist/postmodern" (6).

17. See Bush, "The Modernist under Siege," 326–327.

18. Auden, *Selected Poems*, 81.

19. All quotations of Yeats's poetry are taken from *The Variorum Edition of the Poems of W. B. Yeats*. An isolated quotation is followed by an in-text reference to the poem's title. When a poem is discussed at length, the first quotation is followed by an in-text reference to the page number from *The Variorum Edition*.

CHAPTER ONE.   Mixing Everything Up at the Beginning

1. Heaney, *Opened Ground*, 41.

2. In his essay, "Passion and Cunning," Conor Cruise O'Brien summarizes the prevailing understanding of Yeats's relationship with Irish politics: "The long phase of nationalist commitment (1887–1903) was followed by a long phase (1903–1916) of de-

tachment from almost all practical politics (except those to which the theater exposed him), by a critique of Irish nationalist politics, and by the formation of an aristocratic attitude which did not find practical political expression until after 1916 when—after a new flare-up of nationalist feeling—he re-entered Irish politics on the right, in the Free State Senate" (264). It should be noted that Yeats's engagement with the theater from 1903 to 1916 is perhaps not quite the retreat O'Brien suggests, as the Irish National Theatre was for Yeats the very foundation of his cultural nationalist project.

3. Harris, "Blow the Witches Out," 475.

4. See, for example, O'Brien, "Passion and Cunning," 221–228; and Kearney, *Post-nationalist Ireland*, 114.

5. Innes, "Forging the Conscience," 137–138.

6. Smyth, *Decolonization and Criticism*, 18.

7. Said, *Culture and Imperialism*, 224.

8. Foster, *W. B. Yeats: A Life*, 1:329.

9. Said, *Culture and Imperialism*, 230.

10. Harris, "Blow the Witches Out," 480.

11. Maxwell, *Critical History*, 39.

12. Arnold, "Study of Celtic Literature," 295, 346.

13. Arnold, "The Nadir of Liberalism," 67.

14. Renan, "Poetry of the Celtic Races," 6, 8; Arnold, "Study of Celtic Literature," 344, 346.

15. Arnold, "Study of Celtic Literature," 297.

16. Ibid., 296–297.

17. Young, *Colonial Desire*, 71–72.

18. Kiberd, *Inventing Ireland*, 32.

19. Ibid.

20. Dowden, *Shakspere*, 66.

21. Arnold, "Study of Celtic Literature," 344, 347–348.

22. Young, *Colonial Desire*, 63.

23. Dowden, *Shakspere*, 66.

24. Ibid., 32.

25. Ibid. For a detailed discussion of the various appropriations of Shakespeare by Dowden and other Victorians, see Taylor, *Reinventing Shakespeare*, 162–230.

26. Edwards, *Threshold of a Nation*, 207.

27. Soyinka, *Art, Dialogue and Outrage*, 220.

28. Said makes this point in *Culture and Imperialism*: "When most European [Enlightenment and post-Enlightenment] thinkers celebrated humanity or culture they were principally celebrating ideas and values they ascribed to their own national culture, or to Europe as distinct from the Orient, Africa, and even the Americas" (44).

29. Desai, *Yeats's Shakespeare*, 28.

30. Lee, *Life of William Shakespeare*, n.p., quoted in Desai, *Yeats's Shakespeare*, 28.

31. Kiberd, *Inventing Ireland*, 269.

32. Arnold's juxtaposition of the "hard" and "soft" (re)inscribes prevailing British notions concerning the essential potency of Saxon society versus the essential impotency of Celtic society. Yeats was certainly not immune to these assumptions, and his writings,

beginning in the early 1900s, frequently reveal (phallic) anxiety over his *Celtic Twilight* poetry and drama. "My work has got far more masculine" (*L*, 397), he triumphantly explains to Augusta Gregory in 1903, and in a 1904 letter to George Russell he notes that Celtic poetry now "speaks to me with the sweet insinuating feminine voice of the dwellers in that country of shadows and hollow images. I have dwelt there too long not to dread all that comes out of it" (*L*, 434). For an excellent discussion of Yeats, Arnold, and gender-encoded constructions of the Celt, see Howes, *Yeats's Nations*, 16–43.

33. Arnold, "Study of Celtic Literature," 291.

34. Ibid.

35. *Variorum Plays*, 459. All drama quotations are taken from *The Variorum Edition of the Plays of W. B. Yeats*, hereafter cited in-text.

36. Arnold, "Study of Celtic Literature," 341, 346.

37. Ibid., 347.

38. For a detailed treatment of British stereotypes concerning the "wild," "bestial," and "effeminate" Celt, see Curtis, *Apes and Angels*.

39. Arnold, "Study of Celtic Literature," 344, 346.

40. Bhabha, *The Location of Culture*, 145. Bhabha distinguishes two types of "narratives" that emerge in the discourses of nationhood: the "pedagogical" and the "performative." Within the former, "the people" are constituted as "historical 'objects,'" a homogeneous entity that "give[s] the discourse an authority that is based on the pre-given or constituted historical origin *in the past*" (145). Within the latter, "the people" are constituted as "the 'subjects' of a process of signification that must erase any prior or originary presence of the nation-people to demonstrate the prodigious, living principles of the people as contemporary" (145). The key point for Bhabha is that, during "the production of the nation as narration there is a split between the continuist, accumulative temporality of the pedagogical, and the repetitious, recursive strategy of the performative" (145). By attending to this process of repetition, Bhabha highlights the inability of the performative to achieve "closure," to reach that point when a heterogeneous people are identical with the nation's construction of the people. At this point in *On Baile's Strand*, Yeats exposes an instant of epistemological and ontological rupture by emphasizing the disjunction between the individual desiring subject, the Celtic Fool, and a larger imperial narrative that would incorporate him as docile citizen, the subject whose desires are identical with imperial notions of progress.

41. Conchubar's use of the word "stranger" is consistent with the binary logic of imperial discourse, as such discourse continually defines the nation in opposition to a threatening, external Other.

42. Kiberd, *Inventing Ireland*, 25.

43. Arnold, "Study of Celtic Literature," 346, 345, 346.

44. Ibid., 346.

45. Ibid., 347. Indeed, fact, or reason, certainly is a form of "despotism" in Arnold's formulation.

46. Chatterjee, *Nationalist Thought*, 17.

47. Ibid.

48. Arnold, "Study of Celtic Literature," 344.

49. Desai, *Yeats's Shakespeare,* 163.

50. See Fanon, *Black Skin, White Masks;* Memmi, *The Colonizer and the Colonized;* and JanMohamed, *Manichean Aesthetics.*

51. Memmi, *The Colonizer and the Colonized,* ix.

52. In "The Hosting of the Sidhe," the Sidhe are female spirits who move upon the wind and lure mortal men with their beauty, yet they fade before they can be embraced:

> Away, come away:
> Empty your heart of its mortal dream.
> The winds awaken, the leaves whirl round,
> Our cheeks are pale, our hair is unbound,
> Our breasts are heaving, our eyes are agleam,
> Our arms are waving, our lips are apart;
> And if any gaze on our rushing band,
> We come between him and the deed of his hand,
> We come between him and the hope of his heart. (*VP,* 140–141)

53. Césaire, like a number of postcolonial dramatists, uses masks in *A Tempest.*

54. Césaire, *A Tempest,* 11–12.

55. Arnold, "Study of Celtic Literature," 346.

56. Skene, *Cuchulain Plays,* 154.

57. That is, in the manner of Césaire's Ariel and Caliban.

58. In "Blow the Witches Out," Susan C. Harris argues that "witchcraft" represents a fundamental threat to Conchubar's patriarchal kingdom, for he embraces conventional nationalist notions of public and private, masculine and feminine, the woman as beautiful nation for whom men, as *Cathleen ni Houlihan* dramatizes, give their lives. "Witchcraft," writes Harris, "makes it possible for men to resemble women, for women to leave the hearth, for mortals to encounter the occult without being violently ripped from the human world, for the occult to enter the mortal world with results other than the immediate destruction of the hero" (485).

59. Innes, "Forging the Conscience," 125.

60. The phrase "stolen spoon" recalls the Fool's "stolen fowl."

61. Holloway, *Joseph Holloway's Abbey Theatre,* 58.

62. Varadharajan, *Exotic Parodies,* 95.

63. Ibid., xi.

64. Ibid., 94; Spivak, "Can the Subaltern Speak?" 306.

65. Césaire, *A Tempest,* 15.

66. Adorno, *Minima Moralia,* 25.

CHAPTER TWO. Setting Ireland's House in Order

1. The traditional Celtic aisling or vision poem represents Ireland as a beautiful woman. For a discussion of this tradition as it relates to Yeats's love poetry, see Cullingford, *Gender and History,* 58–59.

2. For broader discussions of the relationship between gender and nationalism, see, among others, Mayer, *Gender Ironies of Nationalism*; McClintock, *Imperial Leather*; Spivak, *In Other Worlds*; and Yuval-Davis, *Gender and Nation*.

3. Synon, "Poet and Prophet," 3, quoted in Strand, "American Lecture Tours," 140.

4. For a discussion of this trope within the Indian context, see Chatterjee, *The Nation and Its Fragments*, 116–157. According to Chatterjee, nationalist discourse attempts to preserve a fundamental division "between the outer and the inner," the "material" and the "spiritual" (120), or, considered as a discourse derived from patriarchal imperialism, between the public and the private. Devoted to acknowledging the material impact of colonization and, simultaneously, to asserting the existence of an indigenous, unified community untarnished by imperialism, nationalist discourse charges the male to interact with and actively combat the outer, public world of imperialism, while the female, particularly the domestic female, is valorized as a symbol of an ordered private sphere and the spiritual guardian of the true nation.

5. Synon, "Poet and Prophet," 3, quoted in Strand, "American Lecture Tours," 141.

6. Extensive scholarship exists on constructions of female identity within the discourses of Irish nationalism. See, among others, Kearney, *Postnationalist Ireland*, 108–142; Herr, "The Erotics of Irishness," 1–34; Innes, *Woman and Nation*, 9–25; and Martin, "Death of a Nation," 65–86.

7. Butler, *Bodies that Matter*, 10, 2.

8. Ibid., 10.

9. Bhabha, *The Location of Culture*, 147.

10. See, for example, Laity, "Yeats and Florence Farr," 620–637; Parkin, "Women in the Plays," 38–57; and Harris, "Blow the Witches Out," 475–489.

11. Butler, *Bodies that Matter*, 10. Howes's *Yeats's Nations* is perhaps the single most important and insightful treatment of these topics to have emerged since Elizabeth Butler Cullingford's invaluable *Gender and History in Yeats's Love Poetry*. My own approach is similar to that of Howes, particularly in terms of my emphasis on the gender-based anxieties and contradictions embedded in the plays, though I depart from her by drawing attention to the works as performances and by focusing on the relationship between audience and representation.

12. Phelan, *Unmarked*, 3.

13. Diamond, "Mimesis, Mimicry," 366.

14. Diamond, *Unmaking Mimesis*, viii; Phelan, "Reciting the Citation of Others," 15–16.

15. Phelan, *Unmarked*, 3.

16. Fay, *Towards a National Theatre*, 53.

17. O'Hegarty, "Revolutionary Ireland," n.p., quoted in O'Brien, "Passion and Cunning," 221; Innes, *Woman and Nation*, 45.

18. For an extended treatment of the conventions of Irish nationalist melodrama, see Herr, *For the Land They Loved*.

19. Valente, "The Myth of Sovereignty," 198.

20. Butler, *Irishwomen and the Home Language*, n.p., quoted in Quinn, "Cathleen ni Houlihan Writes Back," 41; *Sinn Féin*, May 19, 1906.

21. Pethica, "Patronage and Creative Exchange," 210–211. Using the Berg Collection notebooks, Pethica writes: "The most immediately revealing features in the draft are Lady Gregory's two pencil annotations: 'All this mine alone,' at the end of the first section . . . and 'This with W. B. Y.' at the head of the second section" (210–211).

22. McClintock, *Imperial Leather*, 52–53.

23. *Sinn Féin*, May 19, 1906.

24. Martin, "Death of a Nation," 67. See also Lloyd, "Counterparts," 128–149. According to Lloyd, cultural nationalism also responded by promoting images of men rescuing, protecting, and dying for fair Erin, a project that he describes as the "remasculinization of the Irish public sphere" (135).

25. Hywel, "Great Queens of Ireland," 28–29.

26. *Sinn Féin*, July 21, 1906.

27. Holloway, *Joseph Holloway's Abbey Theatre*, 94, 28.

28. Butler, "The Force of Fantasy," 106.

29. For analysis of the commodification of the woman in rural Ireland and Synge's dramatic response, see Doggett, "*Shadow of the Glen*," 985–1008.

30. *Sinn Féin*, May 19, 1906.

31. Butler, *Irishwomen and the Home Language*, n.p., quoted in Quinn, "Cathleen ni Houlihan Writes Back," 41.

32. *The United Irishman*, April 19, 1902.

33. See Foster, *W. B. Yeats: A Life*, 1:165–166.

34. *The United Irishman*, April 19, 1902.

35. Phelan, *Unmarked*, 3.

36. Flannery, *Idea of a Theatre*, 84.

37. For a discussion of Maud Gonne as Cathleen, see Quinn, "Cathleen ni Houlihan Writes Back," 39–59. In *Splendid Years*, the actress Maire Nic Shiubhlaigh notes that "Maud Gonne arrived late the first night and caused a minor sensation by sweeping through the auditorium in the ghostly robes of the Old Woman . . . ten minutes before we were due to begin" (17).

38. *All Ireland Review*, quoted in Quinn, "Cathleen ni Houlihan Writes Back," 46. The Beresford Place reference recalls Gonne's prominent role in a mass meeting, held on December 18, 1899, protesting the Boer War. See Foster, *W. B. Yeats: A Life*, 1:223.

39. Quinn, "Cathleen ni Houlihan Writes Back," 45.

40. Fay, *Fays of the Abbey Theatre*, 119.

41. *Sinn Féin*, May 19, 1906.

42. Memmi, *The Colonizer and the Colonized*, 99.

43. Holloway, *Joseph Holloway's Abbey Theatre*, 27 (emphasis added).

44. Phelan, *Unmarked*, 2.

45. This accords too with Yeats's own rejection of materialism. See Foster, *W. B. Yeats: A Life*, 1:249. Writes Foster: "In 1901 the 'message' of Cathleen was compatible with his preoccupations: the peasant family is preoccupied by material gain, until the spirit of Ireland redeems their son by promising him a glorious death. A critique of money-grubbing and utilitarianism is thus combined with the Fenian ethic" (249).

46. *Sinn Féin*, May 5, 1906.

47. McClintock, *Imperial Leather*, 72.

48. Innes, *Woman and Nation*, 56.

49. Parkin, "Women in the Plays," 48.

50. Cullingford, *Gender and History*, 77. As Cullingford notes, Yeats consistently supported Ireland's suffrage movement (76–77).

51. Laity, "Yeats and Florence Farr," 620–637. In a letter from 1907, Yeats explained to Farr: "The first musician was written for you—I always saw your face as I wrote, very curiously your face even more than your voice, and built the character out of that" (*L*, 482). Yeats's emphasis on Farr's face and not her voice is perhaps symptomatic, as I suggest at the close of this chapter, of the Musician's final role in the performance, when she sings in celebration of Yeats's nationalist performance of domesticity.

52. Phelan, *Unmarked*, 3.

53. As Howes notes in *Yeats's Nations*, the type of "organic national unity" that Yeats sought "must arise not out of homogeneity or conformity, but out of a paradoxical combination of deep, non-rational, mystical community and flourishing individual creativity and will" (69).

54. Synge and A. E. (George Russell), among others, wrote plays based on the Deirdre legend.

55. Another point of departure is that Yeats condenses the action to focus only on the final moments of Deirdre's life and uses the chorus to fill in background for the audience.

56. Fanon, *Wretched of the Earth*, 153.

57. For an extensive analysis of Yeats's representations of the East, see Rickard, "Studying a New Science," 94–112; and Weaver, "Yeats's Imagined East," 301–329.

58. The use of "Eastern merchants" in this manner has precedent in *The Countess Cathleen* (1892). In *Yeats's Nations*, Howes writes of that play: "Though Yeats specifies that the devils [who come to steal peasant souls] are dressed as 'eastern merchants,' no one reading or watching the play could have failed to make the equation between England and materialism that was prevalent in Ireland at the time" (51). In *Deirdre*, however, the merchants cannot be read as transparent signifiers of British colonizers, for their purpose is clearly something "other" than material gain.

59. *Irish Daily Independent*, March 14, 1898, quoted in Toomey, "Who Fears to Speak," 241.

60. Lefort, *Political Forms*, 212–214.

61. North, *Political Aesthetic*, 36.

62. See, for example, Douglas Hyde's versions of the Deirdre legend.

63. Hywel, "Great Queens of Ireland," 32.

64. Benton, "Women Disarmed," 161.

65. *Bean na hEireann*, quoted in Quinn, "Cathleen ni Houlihan Writes Back," 41.

66. The extent to which Irish women should devote their energies to the nationalist cause was a divisive issue for Ireland's two major suffrage movements, the Irish Women's Franchise League and Cumann na mBan. While the former primarily emphasized women's rights, the latter focused on nationalism, asserting that independence from British rule was the necessary first step toward female emancipation. See McKillen, "Irish Feminism and Nationalist Separatism," 72–90.

67. Ward, *Unmanageable Revolutionaries*, 106.

CHAPTER THREE. Rewriting History in a Time of Violence

1. For a detailed account of *The Tower*'s publication history and of the various orderings of the poems, see Finneran, "Construction of Yeats's *The Tower*," 35–55.

2. In addition to the critics mentioned in this chapter, see Kiberd, *Inventing Ireland*, 286–326; Lloyd, *Anomalous States*, 59–87; and Howes, *Yeats's Nations*, 102–130. Kiberd and Lloyd view Yeats as a poet actively engaged in the formation of a new national identity through works that meditate upon moments of violent change in the present and that attempt, though often fail, to incorporate those foundational moments into a new history for and vision of Ireland. Lloyd's central claim that the later Yeats, writing "in the wake of the Irish Free State's foundation, subject[s] all acts of foundation to the most rigorous examination," is closest to my own (60). Marjorie Howes offers a further important complication by introducing gender: "Yeats's Big House poems represent Anglo-Irishness as crisis by embedding it in constructions of gender, sexuality, genealogy and family that were unstable, defamiliarized and denaturalized" (103).

3. For a full discussion of the "post" debate within the broader context of postcolonial studies, see Shohat, "Notes on the 'Post-Colonial,'" 99–113; and McClintock, "The Angel of Progress," 84–96. For an account of this debate in relation to Irish studies, see Howe, *Ireland and Empire*, 146–168.

4. This tendency to respond in kind to imperial discourse, to idealize, for example, empire's "savage" Irish peasant as delightfully primitive, a link to a "pure" Ireland preceding the stain of imperial intervention, was common to most forms of Irish nationalism, particularly the type of cultural nationalism associated with Yeats. For a discussion of cultural nationalism and the (re)writing of history, see Thuente, "Folklore of Irish Nationalism," 42–60. As Thuente notes, imperial histories of failed revolutions, supposed confirmation of Ireland's penchant for anarchy and the need for a firm hand when dealing with the Irish race, were rewritten by Irish nationalists as "part of their attempt to reinterpret Irish history as a source of pride rather than tears or shame" and to celebrate those "daring heroes whose defeat nevertheless represented a moral victory against English treachery, whose courage should be imitated, and whose defeats cried out for revenge" (57).

5. Eagleton, *Heathcliff and the Great Hunger*, 63.

6. Poems that come immediately to mind include "Parnell's Funeral," "Come Gather Round Me, Parnellites," and "Three Marching Songs."

7. Deane, *Celtic Revivals*, 32.

8. Ibid., 33.

9. Ibid., 32.

10. Torchiana, *Yeats and Georgian Ireland*, 312.

11. Bhabha, *The Location of Culture*, 142.

12. See, for example, Tratner, *Modernism and Mass Politics*, 135–165. During his discussion of "Nineteen Hundred and Nineteen," Tratner briefly alludes to the postcolonial when he suggests that Yeats, in directly confronting the horrors of the Anglo-Irish War, "begins to create a terrorist poetry, a poetry that is truly postcolonial because it goes beyond the entire colonial world that formed the mind of Yeats himself" (152). To be sure, Tratner's focus is on class and not empire, but his somewhat offhanded use of the term "postcolonial" is instructive. The creation of "a terrorist poetry"—an unfortunate

metaphor given Yeats's own anxieties about the practical force of his poetry and given too the effects of terrorism in Ireland during the twentieth century—indicates precisely the opposite of a liberating temporal rupture, the opposite of a clean break between the "present" and the vicissitudes of an imperial occupation in the past whose very legacy is terrorism and paramilitary violence.

13. Wilde, *The Critic as Artist*, 50.

14. Deane, *Celtic Revivals*, 49.

15. Boyce, *Nationalism in Ireland*, 295.

16. Davis, *Literary and Historical Essays*, 231–232.

17. Boyce, *Nationalism in Ireland*, 318; Mitchell and O' Snodaigh, *Irish Political Documents*, 48. For additional discussion of Sinn Féin and the 1918 election, see Cronin, *Irish Nationalism*, 117–125; and Lyons, *Ireland Since the Famine*, 380–397. As Cronin notes, although Sinn Féin had no part in the Rising, "British officials and the general public persisted in calling it 'the Sinn Féin Rebellion'" (118).

18. As Boyce notes in *Nationalism in Ireland*, "The casualties among the IRA, the heroic deeds, the fasts, hunger strikes, deaths in prison . . . all created a host of martyrs for the cause, so that the republic attained an almost mystical quality" (325).

19. Ibid., 323.

20. O'Brien, "An Unhealthy Intersection," 5–6, quoted in Cullingford, *Gender and History*, 57.

21. The Conscription Bill was never actually enforced.

22. Yeats to Lord Haldane, October 12, 1918.

23. Duffy, *The Subaltern "Ulysses,"* 10.

24. Cronin, *Irish Nationalism*, 140.

25. Torchiana, *Yeats and Georgian Ireland*, 316.

26. Fanon, *Wretched of the Earth*, 227.

27. Cullingford, *Yeats, Ireland, and Fascism*, 118.

28. Bradford, *Yeats at Work*, 72. In *Ascendancy and Tradition*, W. J. McCormack also notes this change, suggesting, in a reading not incompatible with my own, that "Public Opinion gradually emerges to crystallize a consensus of long-ripening habit, faith in the future, and 'knowledge' of the past which is evoked mockingly in the first two stanzas" (314–315).

29. Bradford, *Yeats at Work*, 78.

30. Lyons, "The War of Independence," 245. Writing five decades later and hardly from an aggressively nationalistic perspective, Lyons with his employment of the same term testifies to the indelible mark left by the British occupational forces upon the popular imagination: "the Auxiliaries made their own comment [on the infamous burning of Cork] when they *swaggered* about the streets of Dublin with burnt corks in their caps" (418, emphasis added).

31. In *Yeats, Ireland, and Fascism*, Cullingford cites as evidence a cancelled draft from Yeats's 1924 Tailteann Games speech: "A fortnight before the great war a friend of mine was standing beside an English member of Parliament watching a Review in one of the London Parks. My friend said as the troops marched past 'It is a fine sight.' And the Member of Parliament answered 'It is a fine sight, but it is nothing else, there will never be another war.' There will never be another war, that was our opium dream" (118). It is also

of some significance that in the drafts, Yeats repeatedly toyed with the phrase "women love shows" in this section (Bradford, *Yeats at Work*, 75). As I note later in this chapter, women were increasingly associated by Yeats with extreme, blind nationalism. The inclusion of that phrase in so many of the drafts suggests that the poet, in castigating imperial certainties, may also have had in mind imperialism's binary counterpart, militant nationalism.

32. Cullingford, *Yeats, Ireland, and Fascism*, 106.

33. Robinson, *Lady Gregory's Journals*, 137.

34. Jeffares, *Man and Poet*, 304; and Foster, *W. B. Yeats: A Life*, 2:183.

35. Indeed, in this poem, much more so than in "Nineteen Hundred and Nineteen," we see an implicit lamentation for an ideal colonial past in which tenant and Ascendancy landlord existed in harmony.

36. The description of Black and Tan violence here may also be contrasted with Yeats's description of another well-known atrocity in an October 1922 letter to J. C. Grierson: "We have had years now of murder and arson in which both nations have shared impartially. In my own neighbourhood the Black and Tans dragged two young men tied alive to a lorry by their heels, till their bodies were rent in pieces. 'There was nothing for the mother but the head' said a countryman and the head he spoke of was found on the road side" (*L*, 690–691).

37. In *The Irish Story*, R. F. Foster also calls attention to the local Irish context evoked by the phrase "seven years ago": "When [Yeats] wrote [that phrase] in 1921 . . . he was obviously thinking of 1914: that recurring memory of being assured by a friend watching a military display in the park that this was all part of the past, and modern civilization had done away with war. But when we read 'seven years ago' in a poem titled 'Nineteen Hundred and Nineteen,' we obviously think of 1912 — the introduction of the Home Rule Bill, with all its brave hopes. And by the time this title was attached to the poem, readers would also know that 1919 was the date when the Anglo-Irish War began. Thus Yeats turned his poem about the dislocations of the world after the Great War into a poem about the Irish war instead" (76–77).

38. Debate in the British Parliament centered upon a number of provisions in the bill — British control over such elements of Irish government as foreign policy, including relations with the Crown, control of the police, and the collection of revenues — and, of course, upon the status of Ulster. See Lyons, "The Developing Crisis," 131–132.

39. *Irish Times*, January 25, 1913, quoted in Torchiana and O'Malley, "Some New Letters," 23.

40. Finneran, *Notes*, 469.

41. Although Yeats composed "Nineteen Hundred and Nineteen" prior to "Meditations in Time of Civil War," he places the latter before the former in *The Tower*. This strategic positioning further disrupts the reader's desire to find order in history.

42. *McGarrity Papers*, quoted in Cronin, *Irish Nationalism*, 154.

43. De Valera, "Proclamation," quoted in Coogan, *De Valera*, 314.

44. Provisional Irish Government, "Proclamation," quoted in Churchill, *Winston S. Churchill*, 3339.

45. Bhabha, *The Location of Culture*, 152.

46. Two months earlier, Yeats had written to T. Sturge Moore: "The National army is in control here and the people are with them but the Irregulars come out at night.

I wonder how the future of European civilisation will be affected by the rejection of majority rule, first in Russia and now in Ireland. It may lead to a Military Government or at any rate to a powerfully armed Civil Government" (*LSM,* 46).

47. Howes, *Yeats's Nations,* 124.

48. The tower was Norman in origin, but for Yeats it symbolized the connection between his own work and Irish culture, an Ireland that had produced individuals, proud and defiant like the tower itself, such as Goldsmith, Swift, Grattan, and Berkeley. As Yeats wrote to T. Sturge Moore regarding the cover design of the volume, "I like to think of that building as a permanent symbol of my work plainly visible to the passer-by. As you know, all my art theories depend upon just this—rooting of mythology in earth" (*LSM,* 114). Yeats had bought it in his early fifties when newly married and proceeded to restore it as his residence, in part because the tower was near Lady Gregory's estate, Coole Park.

49. Ryan, *The 1916 Poets,* 201.

50. In "Symbolism and Obscurity," Michael North writes: "As if to forestall old readers of his poetry from turning back to *The Rose,* or from thumbing through their old Rosicrucian pamphlets, Yeats says this rose has 'old thorns innumerable.' The epithet 'symbolic' therefore seems a little wary" (7).

51. Howes, *Yeats's Nations,* 125.

52. Unterecker, *A Reader's Guide,* 179.

53. Indeed, Yeats, linking Ireland's national history with that of his own family, fears that his descendants too will "lose the flower," becoming like those who "lived where motley is worn" ("Easter, 1916") in prerevolution Ireland, "Through too much business with the passing hour, / Through too much play, or [in an allusion to the ardent nationalist Maud Gonne] marriage with a fool" ("Meditations in Time of Civil War").

54. Pearse, *Plays, Stories, Poems,* 44.

55. Unterecker, *A Reader's Guide,* 180.

56. See note 36.

57. See Cullingford, "Jacques Molay," 763–789.

58. Ibid., 763–764.

59. Ibid., 765.

CHAPTER FOUR.   Discovering a "New Vintage," a New Vantage

1. Having returned to Ireland in 1714 following the collapse of the Tories, Jonathan Swift laments:

Remove me from this land of slaves,
Where all are fools, and all are knaves;
Where every knave and fool is bought
Yet kindly sells himself for nought. (*Complete Poems,* 330)

A young George Bernard Shaw proclaims in 1876, "Every Irishman who felt that his business in life was on the higher planes of the cultural professions felt that he must have a metropolitan domicile and an international culture; that is, he felt that his business was to get out of Ireland" ("Preface," xxxviii). Samuel Beckett opines in 1956, "I didn't like living in Ireland. You know the kind of thing—theocracy, censorship of books, that kind of thing. I preferred to live abroad" (*New York Times,* May 6, 1956).

2. That is, with the exception of "cynical commentators" who, as Declan Kiberd notes in "Yeats, Childhood and Exile," "have marvelled at just how many years Ireland's national poet managed to spend outside his native land" (134). In *A Colder Eye,* Hugh Kenner muses: "How many of [Yeats's] 26,891 days on earth Ireland's foremost man of letters spent in Ireland would be laborious to estimate: perhaps, counting numerous brief trips, about one-third, and in that case a lesser fraction even than James Joyce, the professional exile, who got out of the country for good in 1904 but spent twenty-two all-but-unbroken years there first" (25).

3. In "Modernism, Ireland and Empire," C. L. Innes notes: "Joyce and Yeats have both been appropriated as stars of the European and English modernist pantheon, and their writing has been acclaimed in proportion to the degree it can be tied and confined to aesthetic concerns, with an emphasis on reflexivity, self-containment and self-consciousness about the form and media of art, to the exclusion of political concerns" (137).

4. A "hopelessly romantic nationalist" is perhaps an accurate summary of Joyce's estimation of Yeats when they met in Dublin in 1902. Of that encounter, Yeats wrote: "I praised his work but he said, 'I really don't care whether you like what I am doing or not. It won't make the least difference to me. Indeed I don't know why I am reading to you.' Then, putting down his book, he began to explain all his objections to everything I had ever done. Why had I concerned myself with politics, with folklore, with the historical setting of events, and so on? Above all why had I written about ideas, why had I condescended to make generalizations? These things were all the sign of the cooling of the iron, of the fading out of inspiration. . . . Presently he got up to go, and, as he was going out, he said, 'I am twenty. How old are you?' I told him, but I am afraid I said I was a year younger than I am. He said with a sigh, 'I thought as much. I have met you too late. You are too old'" (quoted in Ellmann, *James Joyce,* 102–103).

5. Kearney, *Postnationalist Ireland,* 115. Exiled Irish writers themselves, as Barbara Freitag notes in *Exiles and Migrants,* have often "cultivated" stereotypical notions of physical exile as the only means to artistic freedom: "In an attempt to justify their leaving, Irish writers draw on the traditional picture of enforced exile. Enforced in the sense that the writer has no choice but to flee. The anti-individual forces they are up against are intent on pressuring them into complete submission. These forces are poised to trap them, gag them, pinion them down, thwart them mentally and psychologically, or, to apply the most frequently used term to describe this deplorable condition, paralyse them. So in order to preserve their artistic integrity they must flee the country. 'Art and Ireland are simply incompatible' is the message George Moore delivers in all his literary works. Accordingly, in these writers' fiction, the artist invariably goes into exile, as do all gifted and talented people, leaving behind an Ireland which is pronounced dead, and quite beyond redemption—unless of course the writer himself is accepted as the Saviour of the nation and allowed to rescue her from her deathbed through his writing" (74).

6. Lamberti, "*The Third Policeman,*" 64–65. The ghost of Fanon is also evident in Kiberd's essay, "Yeats, Childhood and Exile," the only work to focus exclusively on the question of Yeats and exile. Emphasizing the poet's early nostalgia for the Sligo of his

youth, "a dream landscape, a never-never-land to which it was hopeless to expect to return," Kiberd argues that Yeats, "more than any other writer, gave credence to the cult of [western Ireland] among revivalist artists, seeing [this realm] as an organic community, a microcosm of what Ireland once was and might again become." Kiberd then turns to the pitfalls of national consciousness. By linking the west with childhood, Yeats unintentionally reaffirms British stereotypes that characterized the Irish "as hopelessly childlike, broths of boys, veering between a tear and a smile, quick to anger and quick to forget" (128–131).

7. Gurr, *Writers in Exile*, 23–24. Gurr's model assumes a clear division between a provincial homeland and a larger, cosmopolitan world that fosters artistic creations. As such, his model is useful but schematic. How do we account for writers, such as Yeats, who inhabit spaces between the two?

8. "It is," notes Christine Brooke-Rose in "Exsul," "also possible to feel an exile in one's own country" (300). This is not, however, to suggest that exile—whether physical or imagined—should necessarily be read as an abstract move devoid of human cost for the individual. Edward Said, for example, notes the tendency of Western critics to fetishize exile as an ideal form of "placelessness" while ignoring the exile's painful sense of detachment from his or her homeland. See Said, *Reflections on Exile*, for a full analysis of the potentialities and pitfalls of exile as a political and aesthetic stance.

9. Kanaganayakam, "Exiles and Expatriates," 204; Said, *Representations of the Intellectual*, 52.

10. Heaney, *Opened Ground*, 136.

11. Kanaganayakam, "Exiles and Expatriates," 206.

12. Said, *Representations of the Intellectual*, 53.

13. Fanon, *Wretched of the Earth*, 148.

14. Anticipating my broader argument, Richard Kearney notes in *Postnationalist Ireland* that "it is unwise . . . to ignore how certain forms of nationalism have served, historically, as legitimate ideologies of resistance and emancipation" (57).

15. Lazarus, "National Consciousness," 198. Abdel-Malek, *Nation and Revolution*, 4.

16. Lazarus, "National Consciousness," 198–199.

17. Cullingford, *Yeats, Ireland, and Fascism*, 182–184.

18. Fanon, *Wretched of the Earth*, 169.

19. Cullingford, *Yeats, Ireland, and Fascism*, 175.

20. Fanon, *Wretched of the Earth*, 197.

21. Yeats further argues, "This country has passed through one of those crises which all countries have made the occasion of a new act of creative energy for the creation of tradition. No country that I know, after a revolution such as we have gone through, has been content to take without examination the traditions of the past, and I cannot imagine any place where innovation is more necessary than in the outward image of the law" (*SS*, 116).

22. Fanon, *Wretched of the Earth*, 200.

23. Kiberd, *Inventing Ireland*, 292.

24. In *New Commentary*, Jeffares notes that one manuscript version begins: "This is no country for old men" (213). The shift to "That" is significant, for it emphasizes the speaker's detachment, his position as one who has departed.

25. Finneran, "Construction of Yeats's *The Tower*," 55.

26. Kiberd, *Inventing Ireland*, 441.

27. The most famous example is Mangan's "Dark Rosaleen."

28. McCormack, *Ascendancy and Tradition*, 58.

29. Ray, *En-Gendering India*, 98.

30. Foster, *Modern Ireland*, 516.

31. Ray's comments on the Indian writer Rabindranath Tagore, whom Yeats befriended and whose work he admired, are applicable to this more conservative Yeats. Having rejected the pitfalls of Indian nationalism, Tagore "retreated to the peripheral safety of a pastoral Bengal where his status as an intellectual and financial magus allowed him to continue his own small experiments in education and village work in a tradition that resembled a benevolent feudalism" (*En-Gendering India*, 99).

32. Chatterjee, *Nationalist Thought*, 11.

33. Ibid.

34. Ibid., 42.

35. In later editions of *The Tower*, Yeats includes two "Fragments" that voice a more general attack on Enlightenment thought. The first offers an ironic commentary on the "birth" of a modern, mechanized society created, Eve-like, from John Locke:

Locke sank into a swoon;
The Garden died;
God took the spinning-jenny
Out of his side.

36. Bradford, "Yeats's Byzantium Poems," 113.

37. While recuperating in Switzerland from an illness, Yeats, upon learning that *The Tower* had garnered favorable reviews in the Irish press, remarked: "Perhaps the reviewers know that [I] am ill, and think that I am so ill that I can be commended without future inconvenience" (*L*, 740).

38. Kiberd, *Inventing Ireland*, 315.

39. See, for example, discussions of Maud Gonne's play, *Dawn*, in Cairns and Richards, "Tropes and Traps," 128–137.

40. *Irish Catholic Register*, Dublin, 1925, quoted in Cullingford, *Gender and History*, 141.

41. Cullingford, *Gender and History*, 150. Cullingford goes on to examine what other feminist critics have correctly noted, the degree to which the poem, in its attempts to "capture" the mindset of Leda, invites a problematic identification between reader and rape victim in which the reader is called to experience the rape as a decidedly erotic act: "Yeats uses his description of rape to flout Irish taboos against the verbal expression of sexuality. In its repetition of male cultural assumptions about women's bodies, however, his poem paradoxically contributes to the disempowerment of the rape victim" (159).

42. Gikandi, *Ngugi wa Thiong'o*, 120.

43. Chatterjee, *Nationalist Thought*, 11.

44. Ibid.

45. Achebe, "Interview," 343.

46. Finneran, *Notes*, 497.

47. Young, *Troubled Mirror*, 82. If there was a painting that "inspired" the poem, it likely was a watercolor by Cecil Salkeld. After discussing the "Ephesian topers" with Yeats during an afternoon of walking, Salkeld, in his own words, "sat up late . . . and finished a water-colour picture of a weird centaur at the edge of a dark wood: in the foreground, in the shade of the wood, lay the seven Ephesian 'topers' in a drunken stupor, while far behind on a sunny distant desert plain elephants and the glory of a great army passed away into the distance. Next day I showed the picture to Yeats. . . . Later that night, W. B. came down to supper with a perfectly clear countenance; it was plain the poem was finished . . . . When the ladies had withdrawn, he produced a pigskin-covered brandy flask and a small beautifully written manuscript: 'Your picture made the thing clear,' he said. 'I am going to dedicate the poem to you'" (quoted in Jeffares, *New Commentary*, 249–250).

48. Coote, *W. B. Yeats: A Life*, 485–486.

49. In *Gender and History*, Cullingford notes that Yeats "became obsessed by cleanliness: George [Georgie] Yeats describes his interrogating the nuns at Waterford about how often the floors were washed" (188).

50. The dash appears in each of the drafts. My thanks to Richard Finneran for providing copies of the drafts.

51. Unpublished Journal Entry, quoted in Torchiana, *Yeats and Georgian Ireland*, 82.

52. Kermode, *Romantic Image*, 68.

CHAPTER FIVE. Learning "to chaunt a tongue men do not know"

1. Marjorie Howes made this point during a 2003 lecture in Sligo on "Last Poems."

2. For recent discussions of Ireland's ambiguous position with respect to the British empire, see Attridge and Howes, *Semicolonial Joyce*, 1–20; and Cleary, "Misplaced Ideas?" 101–124.

3. Larsen, *Modernism and Hegemony*, xxiv.

4. Eagleton, *Criticism and Ideology*, 153; idem, *Heathcliff and the Great Hunger*, 299.

5. Said, *Culture and Imperialism*, 238.

6. Rajan, "Yeats and the Fragment," 72–89. Rajan notes, "The countertruth to the assertion that Yeats ignores the fragment may be that Yeats writes only in fragments. Pound and Eliot seek the whole in the parts. Yeats dissolves the whole in cycles of recurrence that at any given point can be manifested only partially" (77).

7. Jameson, "Modernism and Imperialism," 59; Rajan, "Yeats and the Fragment," 83.

8. My decision to focus on the revised versions of the early poems is motivated by a desire to show how the early verse both anticipates and, more important, is shaped by the type of fluid and sophisticated Yeatsian nationalism that I have outlined in the previous chapters.

9. For a groundbreaking analysis of Yeats's poetry in light of Adorno, see Ramazani, *Yeats and the Poetry of Death*, 52–67.

10. Adorno, *Minima Moralia*, 15.

11. Adorno, *The Adorno Reader*, 242.

12. Ibid.; Schulte-Sasse, *Theory of the Avant-Garde*, xix.

13. Lazarus, "Modernism and Modernity," 139.

14. Adorno, *The Adorno Reader*, 338.

15. Ibid., 260.

16. Joyce, *Portrait of the Artist*, 205.

17. Ngugi, *Decolonising the Mind*, 16.

18. Late in life, Yeats returns to this point when addressing a group of Indian artists and intellectuals: "I denounced the oppression of the people of India; being a man of letters, not a politician, I told how they had been forced to learn everything, even their own Sanskrit, through the vehicle of English till the first discoverer of wisdom had become bywords for vague abstract facility" (*EI*, 520). Yeats can be accused here of assuming the pose of the Western, enlightened subject who must guide the Eastern, deluded subject down the path toward freedom.

19. Kiberd, *Inventing Ireland*, 165.

20. In 1908, Yeats rejects the notion of returning to a "pure" Irish literature: "It is impossible to divide what is new and, therefore, Irish, what is very old and, therefore, Irish, from all that is foreign, from all that is an accident of imperfect culture, before we have had some revelation of Irish character, pure enough and varied enough to create a standard of comparison" (*IDM*, 117–118).

21. Theodor Adorno, in discussing *Endgame*, uses the tape recorder as an example of how, in Beckett, language returns to the audience in its true form, meaninglessness that produces, in the hearer, a beneficial sense of uneasiness. Referring to *Krapp's Last Tape*, he writes: "Whereas a later work by him is organized around the image of the tape recorder, the language of *Endgame* resembles another language familiar from the loathsome party game, where someone records the nonsense spoken at a party and then plays it back for the guests' humiliation. The shock, overcome on such an occasion only by stupid tittering, is here carefully composed. Just as alert experience seems to notice everywhere situations from Kafka's novels after reading him intensely, so does Beckett's language bring about a healing illness of those already ill: whoever listens to himself worries that he also talks like that" (*The Adorno Reader*, 339).

22. See Gayatri Spivak's essay of that title.

23. In *Book of Yeats's Poems*, Hazard Adams writes: "The poet places his rose on the cross of time, which means that its appearance is a sacrifice to its true being, a tragic denigration of its timeless essence" (47).

24. Adorno, *Negative Dialectics*, 5, quoted in Jarvis, *Adorno*, 165.

25. Eysteinsson, *The Concept of Modernism*, 49; Adorno, *Gesammelte Schriften*, 104–105; Schulte-Sasse, "Foreword," xix.

26. Jeffares, *New Commentary*, 78.

27. Adorno, *The Adorno Reader*, 215.

28. Adams, *Book of Yeats's Poems*, 84.

29. Ibid., 85.

30. Ibid.

31. See Keane, *Terrible Beauty*.

32. Foster, *Modern Ireland*, 481.

33. In "Poetry and Politics," Peter Kuch similarly notes the "semantic instability" of this phrase: "It is the aporia of the text. What is this terrible beauty that is born? Every response to the question seems only to elicit further questions, every reading to suggest other readings" (201).

34. Ryan, *The 1916 Poets*, 24.

35. MacBride was accused by his wife, Maud Gonne, of drunken violence, physical and verbal abuse, and sexual abuse of her eleven-year-old daughter, Iseult, MacBride's step-daughter. Learning of these charges in 1905, Yeats describes them in a letter to Augusta Gregory as "the blackest thing you can imagine." See Foster, *W. B. Yeats: A Life*, 1:330–331.

36. In "Yeats and the Fragment," Rajan notes of this line that "the agency of change remains unstated, because the verbs—'has been changed' and 'Transformed'—are in the passive voice" (62).

Epilogue

1. For a discussion of the contradictions of Yeatsian cultural nationalism and of Yeats's use of the nest metaphor in his poem, "The Tower," see North, *Political Aesthetic*, 51–52.

2. Foster, *W. B. Yeats: A Life*, 2:648.

3. Vendler, *Yeats's "Vision,"* 249.

BIBLIOGRAPHY

Abdel-Malek, Anouar. *Nation and Revolution*. Translated by Mike Gonzalez. Albany: State University of New York Press, 1981.

Achebe, Chinua. "Interview with Chinua Achebe," by Bill Moyers. In *A World of Ideas*, edited by Betty Sue Flowers. New York: Doubleday, 1989.

Adams, Hazard. *The Book of Yeats's Poems*. Tallahassee: Florida State University Press, 1991.

Adorno, Theodor. *The Adorno Reader*. Edited by Brian O'Connor. Oxford: Blackwell, 2000.

————. *Gesammelte Schriften*. Vol. 11, *On Literature*. Frankfurt: Suhrkamp, 1974.

————. *Minima Moralia: Reflections from a Damaged Life*. Translated by E. F. N. Jephcott. London: Verso, 1974.

————. *Negative Dialectics*. Translated by E. B. Ashton. London: Routledge, 1973.

Allison, Jonathan. "The Attack on Yeats." *South Atlantic Review* 55, no. 4 (November 1990): 61–73.

————, ed. *Yeats's Political Identities: Selected Essays*. Ann Arbor: University of Michigan Press, 1996.

Arnold, Matthew. "The Nadir of Liberalism." In *The Last Word*, edited by R. H. Super, 54–77. Ann Arbor: University of Michigan Press, 1977.

————. "On the Study of Celtic Literature." In *Lectures and Essays in Criticism*, edited by R. H. Super, with the assistance of Sister Thomas Marion Hoctor, 291–395. Ann Arbor: University of Michigan Press, 1962.

Attridge, Derek, and Marjorie Howes, eds. "Introduction." In *Semicolonial Joyce*. Cambridge: Cambridge University Press, 2000.

Auden, W. H. *Selected Poems*. Edited by Edward Mendelson. New York: Vintage Books, 1979.

Bartolovich, Crystal, and Neil Lazarus, eds. *Marxism, Modernity, and Postcolonial Studies*. New York: Cambridge University Press, 2002.

Bean na hEireann, no. 16, 1910.

Beckett, Samuel. "Moody Man of Letters." *New York Times*, May 6, 1956.

Benton, Sarah. "Women Disarmed: The Militarization of Politics in Ireland, 1913–1923." *Feminist Review* 50 (Summer 1995): 148–172.

Bhabha, Homi K. *The Location of Culture*. London: Routledge, 1994.

Booth, Howard J., and Nigel Rigby, eds. *Modernism and Empire*. Manchester: Manchester University Press, 2000.

Boyce, D. George. *Nationalism in Ireland*. London: Routledge, 1995.

Bradford, Curtis B. *Yeats at Work*. Carbondale: Southern Illinois University Press, 1965.

————. "Yeats's Byzantium Poems: A Study of Their Development." *PMLA* 75, no. 1 (March 1960): 110–125.

Brooke-Rose, Christine. "Exsul." *Poetics Today* 17, no. 3 (Fall 1996): 289–303.

Bush, Ronald. "The Modernist under Siege." In *Yeats's Political Identities: Selected Essays*, edited by Jonathan Allison, 325–334. Ann Arbor: University of Michigan Press, 1996.

Butler, Judith. *Bodies that Matter*. New York: Routledge, 1993.

————. "The Force of Fantasy: Feminism, Mapplethorpe and Discursive Excess." *Differences* 2, no. 2 (Summer 1990): 105–125.

Butler, Mary E. *Irishwomen and the Home Language*. Gaelic League Pamphlets, no. 6. Dublin: The Gaelic League, 1901.

Cairns, David, and Shaun Richards. "Tropes and Traps: Aspects of 'Woman' and Nationality in Twentieth-Century Irish Drama." In *Gender in Irish Writing*, edited by Toni O'Brien Johnson and David Cairns, 128–137. Buckingham, UK: Open University Press, 1991.

Césaire, Aimé. *A Tempest*. Translated by Richard Miller. New York: Ubu Repertory Theater, 1992.

Chatterjee, Partha. *The Nation and Its Fragments: Colonial and Postcolonial Histories*. Princeton, NJ: Princeton University Press, 1993.

————. *Nationalist Thought and the Colonial World: A Derivative Discourse?* Minneapolis: University of Minnesota Press, 1986.

Churchill, Winston S. "The Situation in Dublin (Fighting at the Four Courts): June 30, 1922, House of Commons." In *Winston S. Churchill: His Complete Speeches, 1897–1963*, edited by Robert Rhodes James, 4: 3338–3342. New York: Chelsea House, 1974.

Cleary, Joe. "Misplaced Ideas? Locating and Dislocating Ireland in Colonial and Postcolonial Studies." In *Marxism, Modernity, and Postcolonial Studies*, edited by Crystal Bartolovich and Neil Lazarus, 101–124. New York: Cambridge University Press, 2002.

Coogan, Tim Pat. *De Valera: Long Fellow, Long Shadow*. London: Hutchinson, 1993.

Coote, Stephen. *W. B. Yeats: A Life*. London: Hodder and Stoughton, 1997.

Cronin, Sean. *Irish Nationalism: A History of Its Roots and Ideology*. New York: Continuum, 1980.

————. *The McGarrity Papers*. Tralee: Anvil, 1972.

Cullingford, Elizabeth Butler. *Gender and History in Yeats's Love Poetry*. Syracuse: Syracuse University Press, 1996.

————. "How Many Jacques Molay Got Up *The Tower*: Yeats and the Irish Civil War." *ELH* 50, no. 4 (Winter 1983): 763–789.

————. *Yeats, Ireland, and Fascism*. New York: New York University Press, 1981.

Curtis, L. Perry, Jr. *Apes and Angels: The Irishman in Victorian Caricature*. Revised Edition. Washington, D.C.: Smithsonian Institution Press, 1997.

Davis, Thomas. *Literary and Historical Essays, 1846*. Poole, Eng.: Woodstock Books, 1998.

Deane, Seamus. *Celtic Revivals: Essays in Modern Irish Literature, 1880–1980*. Winston-Salem, NC: Wake Forest University Press, 1985.

Desai, Rupin W. *Yeats's Shakespeare.* Evanston, IL: Northwestern University Press, 1971.

De Valera, Eamon. "Proclamation," Easter, 1922, private collection of Tim Pat Coogan.

Diamond, Elin. "Mimesis, Mimicry, and the 'True-Real.'" In *Acting Out: Feminist Performances,* edited by Lynda Hart and Peggy Phelan, 363–382. Ann Arbor: University of Michigan Press, 1993.

———. *Unmaking Mimesis: Essays on Feminism and Theatre.* London: Routledge, 1997.

Doggett, Rob. "*In the Shadow of the Glen*: Gender, Nationalism, and 'A Woman Only.'" *ELH* 67, no. 4 (Winter 2000): 985–1008.

Dowden, Edward. *Shakspere: A Critical Study of His Mind and Art.* New York: Harper and Brothers, 1918.

Duffy, Enda. *The Subaltern "Ulysses."* Minneapolis: University of Minnesota Press, 1994.

Eagleton, Terry. *Criticism and Ideology: A Study in Marxist Literary Theory.* London: NLB, 1976.

———. *Heathcliff and the Great Hunger: Studies in Irish Culture.* London: Verso, 1995.

Edwards, Philip. *Threshold of a Nation: A Study in English and Irish Drama.* Cambridge: Cambridge University Press, 1979.

Ellmann, Richard. *James Joyce.* New York: Oxford University Press, 1982.

Eysteinsson, Astradur. *The Concept of Modernism.* Ithaca: Cornell University Press, 1990.

Fanon, Frantz. *Black Skin, White Masks.* Translated by Charles Lam Markmann. New York: Grove Press, 1967.

———. *The Wretched of the Earth.* New York: Grove Press, 1963.

Fay, Frank J. *Towards a National Theatre: The Dramatic Criticism of Frank J. Fay.* Edited by Robert Hogan. Dublin: Dolmen Press, 1970.

Fay, W. G., and Catherine Carswell. *The Fays of the Abbey Theatre: An Autobiographical Record.* New York: Harcourt, Brace and Company, 1935.

Finneran, Richard. "'From Things Becoming to the Thing Become': The Construction of W. B. Yeats's *The Tower.*" *South Atlantic Review* 63, no. 1 (Winter 1998): 35–55.

———. *Notes to The Collected Poems of W. B. Yeats.* Revised 2d ed. New York: Macmillan, 1989.

Flannery, James W. *W. B. Yeats and the Idea of a Theatre: The Early Abbey Theatre in Theory and Practice.* New Haven: Yale University Press, 1976.

Fleming, Deborah, ed. *W. B. Yeats and Postcolonialism.* West Cornwall, CT: Locust Hill Press, 2001.

Foster, R. F. *The Irish Story: Telling Tales and Making It Up in Ireland.* London: Penguin, 2001.

———. *Modern Ireland, 1600–1972.* New York: Penguin Books, 1989.

———. *W. B. Yeats: A Life.* Vol. 1, *The Apprentice Mage, 1865–1914.* Oxford: Oxford University Press, 1997.

———. *W. B. Yeats: A Life.* Vol. 2, *The Arch-Poet, 1915–1939.* Oxford: Oxford University Press, 2003.

Freeman's Journal, "The People and the Parricide," January 29, 1907.

Freitag, Barbara. "From George Moore to Brian Moore: Irish Writers Making a Fetish of Exile." In *Exiles and Migrants: Crossing Thresholds in European Culture and Society,* edited by Anthony Coulson, 72–82. Portland, OR: Sussex Academic Press, 1997.

Gikandi, Simon. *Ngugi wa Thiong'o*. Cambridge Studies in African and Caribbean Literature. Cambridge: Cambridge University Press, 2000.

Gurr, Andrew. *Writers in Exile: The Identity of Home in Modern Literature*. Atlantic Highlands, NJ: Humanities Press, 1981.

Harris, Susan C. "Blow the Witches Out: Gender Construction and the Subversion of Nationalism in Yeats's *Cathleen ni Houlihan* and *On Baile's Strand*." *Modern Drama* 39 (1996): 475–489.

Heaney, Seamus. *Opened Ground: Selected Poems, 1966–1996*. New York: Farrar, Straus and Giroux, 1998.

Herr, Cheryl. "The Erotics of Irishness." *Critical Inquiry* 17, no. 1 (Autumn 1990): 1–34.

———. *For the Land They Loved*. Syracuse: Syracuse University Press, 1991.

Holloway, Joseph. *Joseph Holloway's Abbey Theatre: A Selection from His Unpublished Journal Impressions of a Dublin Playgoer*. Edited by Robert Hogan and Michael J. O'Neill. Carbondale: Southern Illinois University Press, 1967.

Howe, Stephen. *Ireland and Empire: Colonial Legacies in Irish History and Culture*. Oxford: Oxford University Press, 2000.

Howes, Marjorie. "Last Poems." Lecture presented at Yeats International Summer School, Sligo, Ireland, August 2003.

———. *Yeats's Nations: Gender, Class, and Irishness*. New York: Cambridge University Press, 1996.

Hywel, Elin ap. "Elise and the Great Queens of Ireland: 'Femininity' as Constructed by Sinn Féin and the Abbey Theatre, 1901–1907." In *Gender in Irish Writing*, edited by Toni O'Brien Johnson and David Cairns, 23–39. Buckingham, UK: Open University Press, 1991.

Innes, C. L. " 'Forging the Conscience of Their Race': Nationalist Writers." In *New National and Post-Colonial Literatures*, edited by Bruce King, 120–139. Oxford: Oxford University Press, 1996.

———. "Modernism, Ireland and Empire: Yeats, Joyce and Their Implied Audiences." In *Modernism and Empire*, edited by Howard J. Booth and Nigel Rigby, 137–155. Manchester: Manchester University Press, 2000.

———. *Woman and Nation in Irish Literature and Society, 1880–1935*. Athens: University of Georgia Press, 1993.

Irish Catholic Register, Dublin, 1925.

Irish Daily Independent, March 14, 1898.

Irish Times, January 25, 1913.

Jameson, Fredric. "Modernism and Imperialism." In *Nationalism, Colonialism, and Literature*, 43–66. Minneapolis: University of Minnesota Press, 1990.

JanMohamed, Abdul R. *Manichean Aesthetics: The Politics of Literature in Colonial Africa*. Amherst: University of Massachusetts Press, 1983.

Jarvis, Simon. *Adorno: A Critical Introduction*. New York: Routledge, 1998.

Jeffares, A. Norman *A New Commentary on the Poems of W. B. Yeats*. Stanford: Stanford University Press, 1984.

———. *W. B. Yeats: Man and Poet*. 3d ed. New York: St. Martin's Press, 1996.

Joyce, James. *A Portrait of the Artist as a Young Man*. 1916. Edited with an Introduction and Notes by Seamus Deane. New York: Penguin Books, 1992.

Kanaganayakam, Chelva. "Exiles and Expatriates." In *New National and Post-Colonial Literatures,* edited by Bruce King, 201–213. Oxford: Oxford University Press, 1996.

Keane, Patrick J. *Terrible Beauty: Yeats, Joyce, Ireland, and the Myth of the Devouring Female.* Columbia: University of Missouri Press, 1988.

Kearney, Richard. *Postnationalist Ireland: Politics, Culture, Philosophy.* London: Routledge, 1997.

Kenner, Hugh. *A Colder Eye: The Modern Irish Writers.* New York: Alfred A. Knopf, 1983.

Kermode, Frank. *Romantic Image.* New York: Vintage Books, 1964.

Kiberd, Declan. *Inventing Ireland.* Cambridge: Harvard University Press, 1995.

———. "Yeats, Childhood and Exile." In *Irish Writing: Exile and Subversion,* edited by Paul Hyland and Neil Sammells, 126–158. New York: St. Martin's Press, 1991.

Kilroy, James. *The 'Playboy' Riots.* Dublin: Dolmen Press, 1971.

Kline, Gloria C. *The Last Courtly Lover: Yeats and the Idea of Woman.* Ann Arbor, MI: University Microfilms International Research Press, 1983.

Kuch, Peter. " 'For Poetry Makes Nothing Happen': The Poetry of Yeats and the Politics of Ireland." *Yeats: An Annual of Critical and Textual Studies* 8 (1990): 188–205.

Laity, Cassandra. "W. B. Yeats and Florence Farr: The Influence of the 'New Woman' Actress on Yeats's Changing Images of Women." *Modern Drama* 28, no. 4 (December 1985): 620–637.

Lamberti, Matthew J. "*The Third Policeman* as a Re-Vision of Yeats." In *New Voices in Irish Criticism,* edited by P. J. Mathews, 64–73. Portland, OR: Four Courts Press, 2000.

Lamming, George. *The Pleasures of Exile.* London: Allison and Busby, 1984.

Larsen, Neil. *Modernism and Hegemony: A Materialist Critique of Aesthetic Agencies.* Minneapolis: University of Minnesota Press, 1990.

Lazarus, Neil. "Modernism and Modernity: T. W. Adorno and Contemporary White South African Literature." *Cultural Critique* 5 (1987): 131–155.

———. "National Consciousness and the Specificity of (Post)Colonial Intellectualism." In *Colonial Discourse/Postcolonial Theory,* edited by Francis Barker, Peter Hume, and Margaret Iverson, 197–220. Manchester: Manchester University Press, 1994.

Lee, Sidney. *A Life of William Shakespeare.* London: Macmillan, 1898.

Lefort, Claude. *The Political Forms of Modern Society.* Cambridge: Cambridge University Press, 1986.

Lloyd, David. *Anomalous States: Irish Writing and the Post-Colonial Moment.* Durham, NC: Duke University Press, 1993.

———. "Counterparts: *Dubliners,* Masculinity, and Temperance Nationalism." In *Semicolonial Joyce,* edited by Derek Attridge and Marjorie Howes, 128–149. Cambridge: Cambridge University Press, 2000.

Lyons, F. S. L. "The Developing Crisis, 1907–1914." In *A New History of Ireland.* Vol. 6, *Ireland under the Union, II, 1870–1921,* edited by W. E. Vaughan, 123–144. Oxford: Oxford University Press, 1996.

———. *Ireland Since the Famine.* New York: Scribner's Sons, 1971.

———. "The War of Independence, 1919–21." In *A New History of Ireland.* Vol. 6, *Ireland under the Union, II, 1870–1921,* edited by W. E. Vaughan, 240–259. Oxford: Oxford University Press, 1996.

Martin, Angela K. "Death of a Nation: Transnationalism, Bodies, and Abortion in Late Twentieth-Century Ireland." In *Gender Ironies of Nationalism: Sexing the Nation*, edited by Tamar Mayer, 65–86. London: Routledge, 2000.

Maxwell, D. E. S. *A Critical History of Modern Irish Drama, 1891–1980*. Cambridge: Cambridge University Press, 1984.

Mayer, Tamar, ed. *Gender Ironies of Nationalism: Sexing the Nation*. London: Routledge, 2000.

McClintock, Anne. "The Angel of Progress: Pitfalls of the Term 'Post-Colonialism.'" *Social Text* 10, no. 2–3 (1992): 84–98.

————. *Imperial Leather: Race, Gender and Sexuality in the Colonial Context*. New York: Routledge, 1995.

McCormack, W. J. *Ascendancy and Tradition in Anglo-Irish Literary History from 1789 to 1939*. Oxford: Oxford University Press, 1985.

McKillen, Beth. "Irish Feminism and Nationalist Separatism, 1914–1923." *Eire-Ireland* 17, no. 3 (Fall 1982): 52–90.

Memmi, Albert. *The Colonizer and the Colonized*. Boston: Beacon Press, 1965.

Mitchell, Arthur, and Pádraig Ó Snodaigh, eds. *Irish Political Documents, 1916–1949*. Dublin: Irish Academic Press, 1985.

Nandy, Ashis. *The Intimate Enemy: Loss and Recovery of Self under Colonialism*. Delhi: Oxford University Press, 1983.

Ngugi wa Thiong'o. *Decolonising the Mind: The Politics of Language in African Literature*. London: James Currey, 1994.

North, Michael. *The Political Aesthetic of Yeats, Eliot, and Pound*. Cambridge: Cambridge University Press, 1991.

————. "Symbolism and Obscurity in 'Meditations in Time of Civil War.'" *Critical Quarterly* 19, no. 1 (Spring 1977): 5–18.

O'Brien, Conor Cruise. "Passion and Cunning: An Essay on the Politics of W. B. Yeats." In *In Excited Reverie*, edited by A. Norman Jeffares and K. G. W. Cross, 207–278. New York: Macmillan, 1965.

————. "An Unhealthy Intersection." *New Review* 2, no. 16 (1975): 3–8.

Orr, Leonard, ed. *Yeats and Postmodernism*. Syracuse: Syracuse University Press, 1991.

Parkin, Andrew. "Women in the Plays of W. B. Yeats." In *Woman in Irish Legend, Life, and Literature*, Irish Literary Studies 14, edited by S. F. Gallagher, 38–57. Gerrards Cross, Buckinghamshire, Eng.: Colin Smythe, 1983.

Pearse, Pádraic H. *Plays, Stories, Poems*. Dublin: Talbot Press, 1963.

Pethica, James. "Patronage and Creative Exchange: Yeats, Lady Gregory and the Economy of Indebtedness." In *Yeats and Women*, 2d ed., edited by Deirdre Toomey, 168–204. New York: St. Martin's Press, 1997.

Phelan, Peggy. "Reciting the Citation of Others; or, A Second Introduction." In *Acting Out: Feminist Performances*, edited by Lynda Hart and Peggy Phelan, 13–31. Ann Arbor: University of Michigan Press, 1993.

————. *Unmarked: The Politics of Performance*. London: Routledge, 1993.

Quinn, Antoinette. "Cathleen ni Houlihan Writes Back: Maud Gonne and Irish National Theatre." In *Gender and Sexuality in Modern Ireland*, edited by Anthony Bradley and Maryann Gialanella Valiulis, 39–59. Amherst: University of Massachusetts Press, 1997.

Rajan, Balachandra. "Its Own Executioner: Yeats and the Fragment." *Yeats: An Annual of Critical and Textual Studies* 3 (1985): 72–89.

Ramazani, Jahan. *The Hybrid Muse: Postcolonial Poetry in English*. Chicago: University of Chicago Press, 2001.

——. *Yeats and the Poetry of Death: Elegy, Self-Elegy, and the Sublime*. New Haven: Yale University Press, 1990.

Ray, Sangeeta. *En-Gendering India: Woman and Nation in Colonial and Postcolonial Narratives*. Durham, NC: Duke University Press, 2000.

Renan, Ernest. "The Poetry of the Celtic Races." In *The Poetry of the Celtic Races, and Other Studies*, translated by William G. Hutchison, 1–60. Port Washington, NY: Kennikat Press, 1896.

——. "What Is a Nation?" *The Poetry of the Celtic Races, and Other Studies*, translated by William G. Hutchison, 61–83. Port Washington, NY: Kennikat Press, 1896.

Rickard, John. "Studying a New Science: Yeats, Irishness, and the East." In *Representing Ireland: Gender, Class, Nationality*, edited by Susan Shaw Sailer, 94–112. Gainesville: University Press of Florida, 1997.

Robinson, Lennox, ed. *Lady Gregory's Journals, 1916–1930*. New York: Macmillan Company, 1947.

Ryan, Desmond, ed. *The 1916 Poets*. Dublin: Allen Figgis, 1963.

Said, Edward W. *Culture and Imperialism*. New York: Vintage Books, 1993.

——. *Reflections on Exile and Other Essays*. Cambridge: Harvard University Press, 2000.

——. *Representations of the Intellectual*. New York: Pantheon Books, 1994.

Schulte-Sasse, Jochen. "Foreword." In *The Theory of the Avant-Garde*, by Peter Bürger, vii–xlvii. Translated by Michael Shaw. Minneapolis: University of Minnesota Press, 1984.

Shaw, George Bernard. "Preface." In *Immaturity*. New York: William H. Wise, 1930.

Shiubhlaigh, Maire Nic. *Splendid Years: Recollections of Maire Nic Shiubhlaigh as Told to Edward Kenny*. Dublin: J. Duffy, 1955.

Shohat, Ella. "Notes on the 'Post-Colonial.'" *Social Text* 10, no. 2–3 (1992): 99–113.

Sinn Fein, "The Industrial Movement," July 21, 1906.

——, "Letters to Nora," May 5, May 19, 1906.

Skene, Reg. *The Cuchulain Plays of W. B. Yeats: A Study*. New York: Columbia University Press, 1974.

Smyth, Gerry. *Decolonization and Criticism: The Construction of Irish Literature*. London: Pluto Press, 1998.

Soyinka, Wole. *Art, Dialogue and Outrage: Essays on Literature and Culture*. Ibadan, Nigeria: New Horn Press, 1988.

Spivak, Gayatri Chakravorty. "Can the Subaltern Speak?" In *Marxism and the Interpretation of Culture*, edited by Cary Nelson and Lawrence Grossberg, 271–313. Chicago: University of Illinois Press, 1988.

——. *In Other Worlds: Essays in Cultural Politics*. New York: Methuen, 1987.

Strand, Karin Margaret. "W. B. Yeats's American Lecture Tours." Ph. D. diss., North-western University, 1978.

Swift, Jonathan. *The Complete Poems*. Edited by Pat Rogers. New York: Penguin Books, 1983.

Synon, Mary. "Poet and Prophet of Anglo-Irish Here," *Chicago Journal*, February 25, 1914.

Taylor, Gary. *Reinventing Shakespeare: A Cultural History, From the Restoration to the Present*. New York: Oxford University Press, 1989.

Thaut, Cristina J. "The 'Rough Beast': A Postcolonial and Post-modern Yeats." In *W. B. Yeats and Postcolonialism*, edited by Deborah Fleming, 3–25. West Cornwall, CT: Locust Hill Press, 2001.

Thuente, Mary Helen. "The Folklore of Irish Nationalism." In *Perspectives on Irish Nationalism*, edited by Thomas E. Hachey and Lawrence J. McCaffrey, 42–60. Lexington: University Press of Kentucky, 1989.

Toomey, Deirdre. "Who Fears to Speak of Ninety-eight?" In *Yeats Annual* no. 14, edited by Warwick Gould, 209–261. New York: Palgrave, 2001.

Torchiana, Donald T. *W. B. Yeats and Georgian Ireland*. Evanston, IL: Northwestern University Press, 1966.

Torchiana, Donald T., and Glenn O'Malley, eds. "Some New Letters from W. B. Yeats to Lady Gregory." *Review of English Literature* 4, no. 3 (July 1963): 9–47.

Tratner, Michael. *Modernism and Mass Politics: Joyce, Woolf, Elliot, Yeats*. Stanford: Stanford University Press, 1995.

The United Irishman, "All Ireland," April 19, 1902.

Unterecker, John. *A Reader's Guide to William Butler Yeats*. Syracuse: Syracuse University Press, 1996.

Valente, Joseph. "The Myth of Sovereignty: Gender in the Literature of Irish Nationalism." *ELH* 61, no. 1 (1994): 189–210.

Varadharajan, Asha. *Exotic Parodies: Subjectivity in Adorno, Said, and Spivak*. Minneapolis: University of Minnesota Press, 1995.

Vendler, Helen. *Yeats's "Vision" and the Later Plays*. Cambridge: Harvard University Press, 1963.

Ward, Margaret. *Unmanageable Revolutionaries: Women and Irish Nationalism*. London: Pluto Press, 1983.

Weaver, Rebecca. "W. B. Yeats's Imagined East and Ireland in the Postcolonial Context." In *W. B. Yeats and Postcolonialism*, edited by Deborah Fleming, 301–329. West Cornwall, CT: Locust Hill Press, 2001.

Wilde, Oscar. *The Critic as Artist*. Los Angeles: Sun and Moon Press, 1997.

Yeats, William Butler. *The Collected Letters of W. B. Yeats*. Vol. 3. Edited by John Kelly and Ronald Schuchard. Oxford: Oxford University Press, 1994.

————. *The Collected Works of W. B. Yeats*. Vol. 3, *Autobiographies*. Edited by William H. O'Donnell and Douglas N. Archibald, with the assistance of J. Fraser Cocks III and Gretchen Schwenker. New York: Scribner, 1999.

————. *The Collected Works of W. B. Yeats*. Vol. 5, *Later Essays*. Edited by William H. O'Donnell, with assistance from Elizabeth Bergmann Loizeaux. New York: Charles Scribner's Sons, 1994.

—————. *The Collected Works of W. B. Yeats.* Vol. 8, *The Irish Dramatic Movement.* Edited by Mary FitzGerald and Richard J. Finneran. New York: Scribner, 2003.

—————. *The Collected Works of W. B. Yeats.* Vol. 10, *Later Articles and Reviews: Uncollected Articles, Reviews, and Radio Broadcasts Written after 1900.* Edited by Colton Johnson. New York: Scribner, 2000.

—————. *A Critical Edition of Yeats's A Vision* (1925). Edited by George Mills Harper and Walter Kelly Hood. London: Macmillan, 1978.

—————. *Essays and Introductions.* New York: Macmillan, 1961.

—————. *Explorations.* New York: Macmillan, 1962.

—————. *Letters on Poetry from W. B. Yeats to Dorothy Wellesley.* New York: Oxford University Press, 1940.

—————. *The Letters of W. B. Yeats.* Edited by Allan Wade. New York: Macmillan, 1954.

—————. *Memoirs: Autobiography–First Draft Journal.* Edited by Denis Donoghue. New York: Macmillan, 1972.

—————. *Mythologies.* New York: Macmillan, 1959.

—————. *The Senate Speeches of W. B. Yeats.* Edited by Donald R. Pearce. London: Prendeville, 2001.

—————. *Uncollected Prose by W. B. Yeats.* Vol. 1, *First Reviews and Articles, 1886–1896,* edited by John P. Frayne. New York: Columbia University Press, 1970.

—————. *Uncollected Prose by W. B. Yeats.* Vol. 2, *Reviews, Articles and Other Miscellaneous Prose, 1897–1939,* edited by John P. Frayne and Colton Johnson. London: Macmillan, 1975.

—————. Unpublished Journal. September 6, 1909.

—————. *The Variorum Edition of the Plays of W. B. Yeats.* Edited by Russell K. Alspach and Catherine C. Alspach. New York: Macmillan, 1966.

—————. *The Variorum Edition of the Poems of W. B. Yeats.* Edited by Peter Allt and Russell K. Alspach. New York: Macmillan 1957.

—————. *A Vision* (1937). A reissue with the author's final revisions. New York: Macmillan, 1956.

—————. *W. B. Yeats and T. Sturge Moore: Their Correspondence, 1901–1937.* Edited by Ursula Bridge. New York: Oxford University Press, 1953.

—————. Yeats to Lord Haldane, October 12, 1918. National Library of Scotland, Edinburgh.

Young, David. *Troubled Mirror: A Study of Yeats's "The Tower."* Iowa City: University of Iowa Press, 1987.

Young, Robert J. C. *Colonial Desire: Hybridity in Theory, Culture and Race.* London: Routledge, 1995.

Yuval-Davis, Nira. *Gender and Nation.* London: Sage, 1997.

GENERAL INDEX

INDEX OF WORKS BY YEATS

ROB DOGGETT

is assistant professor of English at SUNY, College at Geneseo.